Comparative Territorial Politics

Series Editors
Michael Keating
University of Aberdeen
Aberdeen, UK

Arjan H. Schakel
Maastricht University
Maastricht, The Netherlands

Michaël Tatham
University of Bergen
Bergen, Norway

Territorial politics is one of the most dynamic areas in contemporary political science. Rescaling, new and re-emergent nationalisms, regional devolution, government, federal reform and urban dynamics have reshaped the architecture of government at sub-state and transnational levels, with profound implications for public policy, political competition, democracy and the nature of political community. Important policy fields such as health, education, agriculture, environment and economic development are managed at new spatial levels. Regions, stateless nations and metropolitan areas have become political arenas, contested by old and new political parties and interest groups. All of this is shaped by transnational integration and the rise of supranational and international bodies like the European Union, the North American Free Trade Area and the World Trade Organization. The Comparative Territorial Politics series brings together monographs, pivot studies, and edited collections that further scholarship in the field of territorial politics and policy, decentralization, federalism and regionalism. Territorial politics is ubiquitous and the series is open towards topics, approaches and methods. The series aims to be an outlet for innovative research grounded in political science, political geography, law, international relations and sociology. Previous publications cover topics such as public opinion, government formation, elections, parties, federalism, and nationalism. Please do not hesitate to contact one of the series editors in case you are interested in publishing your book manuscript in the Comparative Territorial Politics series. Book proposals can be sent to Ambra Finotello (Ambra.Finotello@palgrave.com). We kindly ask you to include sample material with the book proposal, preferably an introduction chapter explaining the rationale and the structure of the book as well as an empirical sample chapter.

More information about this series at
http://www.palgrave.com/gp/series/14910

Linda Basile

The Party Politics of Decentralization

The Territorial Dimension in Italian Party Agendas

Linda Basile
University of Siena
Siena, Italy

Comparative Territorial Politics
ISBN 978-3-319-75852-7   ISBN 978-3-319-75853-4 (eBook)
https://doi.org/10.1007/978-3-319-75853-4

Library of Congress Control Number: 2018935396

© The Editor(s) (if applicable) and The Author(s) 2019
This work is subject to copyright. All rights are solely and exclusively licensed by the Publisher, whether the whole or part of the material is concerned, specifically the rights of translation, reprinting, reuse of illustrations, recitation, broadcasting, reproduction on microfilms or in any other physical way, and transmission or information storage and retrieval, electronic adaptation, computer software, or by similar or dissimilar methodology now known or hereafter developed.
The use of general descriptive names, registered names, trademarks, service marks, etc. in this publication does not imply, even in the absence of a specific statement, that such names are exempt from the relevant protective laws and regulations and therefore free for general use.
The publisher, the authors, and the editors are safe to assume that the advice and information in this book are believed to be true and accurate at the date of publication. Neither the publisher nor the authors or the editors give a warranty, express or implied, with respect to the material contained herein or for any errors or omissions that may have been made. The publisher remains neutral with regard to jurisdictional claims in published maps and institutional affiliations.

Cover illustration: michal812/Alamy Stock Photo

Printed on acid-free paper

This Palgrave Macmillan imprint is published by the registered company Springer International Publishing AG part of Springer Nature.
The registered company address is: Gewerbestrasse 11, 6330 Cham, Switzerland

To my beloved sister Maria. All that I am, I owe to you.

Preface

Why (Another) Book on Italian Decentralization?

On December 4, 2016, Italians were called to vote in a referendum on a constitutional reform proposed by then-Prime Minister Matteo Renzi and his Democratic Party; it had already been approved by both the Senate and the Chamber of Deputies. The reform touched on a variety of state functions and institutions, including a thorough revision of the distribution of competencies across territorial levels. It was ultimately rejected, leaving the existing system in place.

On October 22, 2017, another referendum was held in the regions of Lombardy and Veneto. Citizens were asked whether their regions should undertake the necessary institutional steps to ask the central state for "additional special forms and conditions of autonomy." The two referenda received broad support from the entire political spectrum[1] and were approved with 95.29% of the vote in Lombardy (with 38.26% turnout) and 98.1% of the vote in Veneto (with 57.2% turnout).[2]

The above-cited referenda, though profoundly different in both scope and purpose, represent the two most recent attempts (as of this writing) to change the territorial organization of the state. They are simply the two latest episodes in the never-ending *pursuit of decentralization in Italy*. With its long quest to define its own territorial organization, Italy epitomizes the political tensions surrounding the relationships between the center and the peripheries in contemporary European states. The history of its path to decentralization can therefore be seen as part of a broader narrative of territorial politics in Europe.

Since the 1970s, a renewed interest in territorial issues has flourished in the field of political science—Derek W. Urwin (1983, 221) called this a "political vogue ... in studies of Western industrial societies." Nevertheless, the author believes that "vogues reflect actual phenomena and perceived trends in behavior." More than 30 years later, a growing body of literature is shedding new light on issues related to territorial cleavages and their political translation in European party systems. This considerable collection of research, publications, and standing groups can no longer be dismissed as a "vogue" in the social sciences, a fascinating exercise for an inner circle of academic experts. But if it to be assumed that political science mirrors underlying social developments and related institutional transformations, it is essential to ask: Why do territorial politics matter? Why do the territorial redistributions of resources within states still generate interest, even in an increasingly globalized world? And why might Italy represent an interesting case study?

To answer these questions, this preface provides a few reasons why there is a need for another book on Italian decentralization.

1. *Because recent history and contemporary events suggest that the territorial organization of the state is still a topical issue in many European states.*

As is often the case, history raises the questions that the social sciences are designed to answer. The modern European states formally created over the nineteenth century were generally the results of processes of homogenization and integration of different territorial communities. These so-called nation-states seldom fully acknowledged the rights of minorities, while assimilating the self-determination of the historical entities into new central authorities. In the aftermath of the World War II, however, that scenario changed radically: functional and identity pressures, as well as structures of political opportunity like the European Union (EU), triggered processes of decentralization across Europe (Hooghe et al. 2010). Decentralization became one of the most discussed topics among politicians of several countries, which in turn amended their constitutions to allow for more cultural distinctions and regional autonomies. Inspired by pure federal systems, such as those of the United States and Switzerland, countries like Spain, Italy, the United Kingdom—even traditionally centralized France—have undergone processes of decentralist reform, though these are far from being completed. Western European states have redistributed powers downward in several ways, assembling innovative and often creative institutional architectures. Moreover, events like the Scottish referendum[3] in 2014 and the unrest following the contested referendum in Catalonia[4] in October 2017 confirm that territorial politics are still a relevant issue in Europe.

2. *Because the politics of decentralization provide an interesting example for the study of party competition.*

From a purely normative point of view, the decentralizing processes undertaken across Europe encourage further research on possible alternatives to centralized state organization. However, political science is not interested exclusively in the final outcomes of a policy change or reform process but also in the dynamics that underlie the decision-making processes, the actors that influence its development, and the strategic reasoning behind it as well as the institutional and ideological constraints shaping decisions. In a sense, political science looks at what happens behind the scenes, in the backstage of politics. In particular, this book focuses on the processes of decentralization from the perspective of political parties by investigating how party strategies and the dynamics of party competition influence the territorial structure of the state. They will therefore be the key protagonists of this narrative. Moreover, this book suggests a new way to think about the strategies of party competition: it suggests that parties make three distinct yet interrelated decisions when they elaborate their stance on a particular issue, determining how much attention to pay to the issue (manipulation of salience), which policy option they will endorse (manipulation of position), and which justifications and arguments they will use to support their position (manipulation of frames).

3. *Because the process of decentralization is a specific policy change that can be analyzed to shed light on the dynamics of reform within a political system.*

In addition to decentralization, this book is concerned with the processes behind reforms and policy changes in general. As Green-Pedersen and Walgrave (2014, 9) argue, focusing on a policy issue to investigate the process of agenda setting and policy change is comparable to "injecting a tracer liquid into a living body to measure the circulation of fluids and determine any deficiency therein." In other words, a close inspection of the political dynamics surrounding the territorial organization of the state allows us to examine the actors, processes, and interactions that underlie the agenda-setting process more broadly in a given political system. It is like sending a scout out to explore the "black box" of how policy is made in a specific situation. This scout can provide a detailed report of all the actors and mechanisms observed, which can then be used as a template to explain other processes of policy change.

It is worth pointing out that decentralization is "not just another policy output tailored to win votes" (Sorens 2009, 268); the norms of a state's territorial structure help determine the rules of the game and more precisely the allocation of powers to different layers of authority. Nevertheless, while this policy dimension has its peculiarities, the theoretical models used to explain the party politics of decentralization should be applicable to other policy areas with appropriate adaptations.

4. *Because the Italian case represents an interesting example of the impact of party politics on the processes of policy change and, more specifically, of decentralization.*

Italy represents a good test case for studying the evolution of the territorial dimension over time. First, it is deeply divided into distinct communities, and peripheral demands have often manifested into full-fledged political mobilization. Second, since the Republic's creation it has undergone a number of crucial reforms that have reshaped the territorial organization of the state, transforming it from a central, unitary structure to a decentralized system leaning toward federalism—and the process has by no means concluded. Third, it is a parliamentary, multiparty system with coalition governments, where political parties play a relevant role in policy making.

To better serve all these purposes, this book does two things. First, it provides a detailed account of the Italian process of decentralization, seen from the perspective of political parties. Second, it assesses whether and to what extent the dynamics of party competition are likely to affect policy change.

This book addresses the topic of the *party politics of decentralization in Italy* within several different yet interrelated theoretical frameworks. The underlying purpose is to provide insight and food for thought for different areas of interest, offering essential research and interpretation that should prove useful to a variety of audiences. First, the historical account of Italy's decentralization should be of interest to scholars and commentators of

Italian history as well as those concerned more broadly with the processes of territorial restructuring in contemporary nation-states. Second, the analysis of the dynamics of party competition should suggest some avenues for future studies of party politics. Third, the focus on the processes and mechanisms underlying the main reforms should be helpful to those interested in agenda setting and policy change.

In writing this book, I followed the often-cited advice of Norberto Bobbio, who said that "the duty of learned men, today more than ever, is to sow *doubts*, rather than gather *certainties*" (2005, 3). I therefore attempt to address the research questions and shed some light on the topic, while keeping in mind the limits of my research and the questions I leave unanswered. Far from being a major shortcoming, however, I hope this will be seen as an added value of the book: a serious and rigorous study, as this work hopes to be, should not be conceived to provide the last word on a topic. Rather, it should aim to add new insights to a body of knowledge for future studies as well as raising interest in its topic.

Structure of the Book

The structure of this book has been formulated to accompany the reader through a step-by-step reconstruction of the research process behind it. The reader will therefore be introduced to the research questions at the core of this study in Chap. 1 (i.e., *the what* of the research). They are clearly defined, along with the main concepts involved, and the data, research design, and methodology are described (i.e., *the how*). Chapter 2 will set the scene by providing a thorough account of the process of decentralization in Italy, the path followed, and the policy outcomes achieved over time. This description will serve as the basis for the empirical analysis of the influence of party politics conducted in Chaps. 3, 4, and 5, focusing on the three components of party strategy—namely salience, position, and frames. Each of these empirical chapters will present the specific theoretical models and hypotheses in greater detail than the broader theoretical framework presented in Chap. 1. Chapter 3 discusses how the attention a party pays to an issue triggers related policy changes (manipulation of salience). In Chap. 4, the focus shifts to the concrete positions adopted by parties on decentralization to assess whether the pattern of party competition on this issue has been consensual or adversarial, and how this pattern influenced the process of reform (manipulation of position). Chapter 5 examines the role of frames in party competition.

Finally, the conclusion draws a connection between the empirical analyses presented in this volume and provides answers to the core research questions. It is to be expected, however, that this work will do more to pave the way for future research.

Siena, Italy   Linda Basile

Notes

1. Parties from both left and right expressed their support for the autonomist demands included in the referendum. Some of the opposition parties within the regional governments expressed criticism, such as the *Partito Democratico* (PD) in Lombardy, which disagreed with the choice to call for an unnecessary referendum that served a purely political purpose. Nevertheless, these parties did not waver in their support for the enhanced autonomy of Lombardy and Veneto (see, for example, the PD's declaration regarding Lombardy: www.pdlombardia.it/federalismo-differenziato, accessed October 22, 2017). Other parties declared their open opposition to these referenda, including the *Articolo 1 Movimento Democratico e Progressista* Party (Art.1 MDP, created by a left-wing split from the PD in February 2017) in Veneto and the *Rifondazione Comunista* (RC) party in both Lombardy and Veneto, which accused the regional institutions of promoting a "demagogic referendum" created by the *Lega Nord* (LN) for political purposes (see, for instance, the declaration of RC Lombardy: www.rifondazionelombardia.it/referendum-autonomia-lombardia/mozione-approvata-a-larga-maggioranza-dal-cpr-del-23-luglio-sul-tema-del-referendum-sullautonomia-lombarda, accessed October 22, 2017).
2. Source: Official websites of the regions of Lombardy (www.referendum.regione.lombardia.it/#/home) and Veneto (http://referendum2017.consiglioveneto.it/sites/index.html#!/riepilogo) (accessed October 24, 2017).
3. On September 18, 2014, Scottish citizens were asked to vote in a referendum on Scottish independence. The referendum was defeated, with 55.3% voting no. Following the British referendum to leave the EU on June 23, 2016, Scottish First Minister Nicola Sturgeon of the Scottish National Party announced her party's intention to ask for a second referendum on Scottish independence, since the majority of Scottish citizens voted to remain in the EU.
4. On October 1, 2017, the Generalitat de Catalunya held a referendum on the region's independence from Spain, though it was declared illegal by the central government. Over 2 million Catalans voted, with 92% voting yes. At the time this volume is being drafted, the consequences of this referendum are still uncertain.

REFERENCES

Bobbio, Norberto. 2005. *Politica e cultura*, ed. F. Sbarberi. Torino: Einaudi.
Green-Pedersen, Christoffer, and Stefaan Walgrave. 2014. Political Agenda Setting: An Approach to Studying Political Systems. In *Agenda Setting, Policies, and Political Systems. A Comparative Approach*, ed. Christoffer Green-Pedersen and Stefaan Walgrave, 1–16. Chicago: University of Chicago Press.
Hooghe, Liesbet, Gary Marks, and Arjan H. Schakel. 2010. *The Rise of Regional Authority: A Comparative Study of 42 Democracies*. Abingdon: Routledge.
Sorens, Jason. 2009. The Partisan Logic of Decentralization in Europe. *Regional & Federal Studies* 19 (2): 255–272.
Urwin, Derek W. 1983. Harbinger, Fossil or Fleabite? 'Regionalism' and the West European Party Mosaic. In *Western European Party Systems: Continuity & Change*, ed. Hans Daalder and Peter Mair, 221–256. Beverly Hills/London: SAGE Publications.

Acknowledgments

When I started to work on this book, I was told it would be a long and difficult process. Moreover, it would require time, and life would inevitably get in the way. The fact I was able to finish it at all is not due to my own efforts alone: along the way, I was lucky enough to meet people who have encouraged, supported, and helped me in my efforts. In fact, I have a rather long list of people to whom I am thankful.

First of all, my biggest thanks go to the Center for the Study of Political Change (CIRCaP) at the University of Siena, where I got my PhD and where I have had the privilege to work since 2014. I am proud to be part of an exceptional team, from which I learned how to do (good) scientific research. And besides being excellent scholars, my colleagues and professors are wonderful people; I am indebted to each of them for their support, for their patience when I felt discouraged by the development of this book, and for the warm and friendly environment they are able to create every day.

In developing and enriching my research, I benefited greatly from discussions I had with several scholars who provided me with valuable insights. The list of all these people would be too long, but I have to mention at least a few of them: Christina Isabel Zuber, who encouraged me to submit my book proposal and who has always believed in the potential of my work, sometimes more than I have myself; Emanuele Massetti, who has often spent time reading my work and providing me valuable suggestions; and Marcello Carammia, who helped me discover agenda-setting literature. I would also like to thank the Observatoire de la Vie Politique Régionale (OVPR) at the University of Lausanne, which invited me to hold a seminar on December 15, 2016, when this book was still in its infancy.

If the language used in this book is pleasant and relatively free of mistakes, it is thanks to my excellent proofreader and friend Josh Raisher, who has patiently corrected my English since I first met him years ago.

I am also grateful to the editors of "Comparative Territorial Politics," Michael Keating, Arjan H. Schakel, and Michaël Tatham, for their trust in my work. I would also like to thank the Palgrave editorial team for its guidance and support in the preparation of this manuscript, and in particular Imogen Gordon Clark and Ambra Finotello.

All these people and institutions have been decisive in shaping and developing my research. Nonetheless, the usual disclaimer applies: I take full responsibility for the content of this book.

A special thanks goes to Angelo, my boyfriend and life partner and a wonderful man. He has always been at my side, and always supported me. I am lucky to share my life, as well as my goals, small and large, with him. I took a lot of time from us to write this book, and I promise we will make it up afterward.

I also want to thank my family: my parents, Alfio and Giuseppina; my niece Vittoria Maria; my brother Angelo; and my sister-in-law Floriana and her daughter Bianca, who have always supported me along the way. I was able to finish this book "with a little help from my friends": Fabiana, Giusy, Irene, Liana, Liliana (and newborn Claudio Mario), Laura, Ornella, and Rosamaria.

This book is dedicated in loving memory to my sister Maria. She will always live in the people she loved, helped, and cheered up, myself included. She is always present in my thoughts and my resilience, in my eagerness to study and my desire for knowledge, in my choice of words—because "words do have a meaning, hence they are important"—and in my curiosity. Her unconditional faith helped me grow up and face life's challenges. If I have been able to complete this work and write this book, I owe it to my sister. I hope you are proud of me, wherever you are.

Contents

1 The Party Politics of Decentralization: Theory, Definitions, Research Design, and Methods   1

2 Setting the Scene: The Direction and Pattern of Decentralization in Italy   27

3 Salience: Putting Decentralization on the Agenda: The Role of Political Parties   67

4 Position: Sharp Conflict or Shared Consensus?   109

5 Frames: The Art of Justifying Preferences   185

Concluding Remarks   217

Appendix   225

Index   247

List of Figures

Fig. 2.1	Frequency distribution of annual policy change on decentralization	56
Fig. 3.1	Box and whiskers plot of the median value of salience of decentralization in Italian party manifestos for each election (1948–2013) (%)	78
Fig. 3.2	Median salience for each election (left axis, %) and percentage change on the Decentralization Index for each electoral year (right axis, %)	88
Fig. 3.3	Median salience in the PSA and salience in LN's manifestos for each election (left axis, %); vote share LN (right axis, %) (Note 1: Median salience was calculated by excluding the values for LN's documents. Note 2: For the 2006 and 2013 elections the salience values for LN are those of the CdL and the PdL coalition manifestos, respectively, because the LN formally joined these documents.)	92
Fig. 3.4	Median salience and salience in PCI/PDS/Ulivo/PD's manifestos for each election (left axis, %); vote share PCI/PDS/Ulivo/PD (right axis, %) (Note: Median salience was calculated by excluding the values for PCI/PDS/Ulivo/PD's documents.)	95
Fig. 3.5	Median salience and salience in PSI's manifestos for each election (left axis, %); vote share PSI (right axis, %) (Note: Median salience was calculated by excluding the values for PSI's documents.)	96
Fig. 3.6	Directional intensity on decentralization of PCI/PDS/PD, DC, and PSI (left axis, %); median salience at PSA level (right axis, %)	102
Fig. 4.1	Party electoral strategies on decentralization and determinants	116
Fig. 4.2	Party voting behavior on decentralization and determinants	122

xx LIST OF FIGURES

Fig. 4.3	Directional intensity of party manifestos (salience per directional certainty): 1948–1992	131
Fig. 4.4	Directional intensity of party manifestos (salience per directional certainty): 1994–2013 (values for LN 2008 omitted.)	132
Fig. 4.5	Number of subtopics in the political discourse (left axis) and entropy score (right axis)	144
Fig. 4.6	Directional certainty on decentralization concerning specific policy areas (entire corpus of document; $n = 120$)	147
Fig. 4.7	Likelihood of voting for reforms compared to role in government: First and Second Republic	172
Fig. 4.8	Likelihood of voting for reforms and directional intensity on decentralization: First and Second Republic	173
Fig. 5.1	Mean salience of frames related to functional pressures for each electoral year (1948–2013)	192
Fig. 5.2	Position and salience of the efficiency frame, before and after the emergence of LN (1992): parties are classified according to their overall attitude toward decentralization (i.e. centralist, ambiguous, or decentralist)	193
Fig. 5.3	Position and salience of the democracy frame, before and after the emergence of LN (1992): parties classified according to their overall attitude towards decentralization (Note: To improve the readability, party manifestos showing a salience on the democracy frame higher than 2 were excluded. They were PRI 1963 [decentralist], PDS 1996 [decentralist], and RI 1996 [decentralist].)	197
Fig. 5.4	Position and salience of the territorial solidarity frame, before and after the emergence of LN (1992): parties classified according to their overall attitude toward decentralization	200
Fig. 5.5	Mean salience of frames related to identity pressures for each electoral year (1948–2013)	202
Fig. 5.6	Position and salience of the national unity frame, before and after the emergence of LN (1992): parties classified according to their overall attitude toward decentralization	204
Fig. 5.7	Mean salience of frames related to political opportunity structures for each electoral year (1948–2013)	207
Fig. 5.8	Position and salience of the foe frame, before and after the emergence of LN (1992): parties classified according to their overall attitude toward decentralization	208
Fig. 5.9	Position and salience of the autonomist frame, after the emergence of LN (1992): parties classified according to their overall attitude toward decentralization	209

List of Tables

Table 1.1	Coded policy areas	14
Table 1.2	List of coded frames	16
Table 2.1	Typology of forms of territorial organization of the state	28
Table 2.2	Italy's forms of territorial structure (1948–2017)	52
Table 4.1	Typology of documents according to the salience and directional certainty on decentralization (cell percentages: number of documents in brackets.)	124
Table 4.2	Documents with value 0 on directional certainty (ambiguous strategies: blurring and contradictory strategies.)	128
Table 4.3	Number of documents, and related positions, dealing with each policy subtopic, classified according to the party's overall strategy on decentralization (accommodative, ambiguous, adversarial)/consistency of party position on subtopics with overall strategy on decentralization (%)	148
Table 4.4	Parties' voting behavior cross tabulated with electoral position on decentralization, role in government, and left-right ideological positioning (%)	167
Table 4.5	Logistic regression of party voting behavior on decentralist reforms	170
Table A.1	List of parties, number of seats in Parliament, elected deputies of the parties whose manifestos have been coded (%), salience, directional certainty, directional intensity, and party typology on decentralization (Chap. 4)	226
Table A.2	List of parties and acronyms	245

CHAPTER 1

The Party Politics of Decentralization: Theory, Definitions, Research Design, and Methods

A Study on the Party Politics of Decentralization

The need to estimate party attitudes on policy dimensions has long been a compelling research topic. This burgeoning branch of political science aims to unravel the ideological profiles of the actors who compete in the electoral arena and take part in the process of policy making. The underlying assumption is that understanding what parties think (or claim to think) will shed light on both electoral dynamics (i.e., how people vote) and legislative choices (i.e., how parties govern once they are elected) (Benoit and Laver 2006).

The multilevel organization of contemporary political systems also deserves special attention. Most western European countries are characterized today by the overlap of multiple tiers of authority, ranging from the local level to the European level (Marks et al. 2008a). Within this framework, political parties are expected to express their positions on the redistribution of competences and resources across different layers of authority, hence *the territorial dimension is relevant for party competition*, which is likely to significantly affect the territorial structure of the state (Hopkin and van Houten 2009; Toubeau and Wagner 2015).

At the intersection of these research agendas, there is *the estimation and analysis of party strategies concerning the territorial dimension*, which is the core topic of this book.

This chapter includes an introduction to the primary research questions addressed in this study, a short literature review, and a summary of terminological choices, providing the reader a sense of the background of the topic and how this research was carried out (section "Setting Up the Study"). It then describes the research design, the methodology, and the data used for the empirical analyses (section "From Concepts to Measurements: Operationalization, Data, and Research Design"). The last section of this chapter outlines the integrated theoretical model adopted in this study to analyze party strategies on decentralization (section "An Integrated Model of the Party Politics of Decentralization").

Setting Up the Study

The Puzzle of Research

There are two arguments at the core of this study: first, that territorial issues matter in contemporary politics, and second, that they are a matter of party competition. Let's see what these two statements actually mean.

Over the second half of the twentieth century, several centralized nation-states in Europe gradually transferred powers and competencies to subnational levels (Marks et al. 2008b). Territorial reforms are still on the top of many countries' political agendas, concerning areas from Catalonia to Scotland through Italy's northern regions. These processes of territorial restructuring were triggered by social, economic, and historical factors (Duchacek 1970; Schakel 2009; Hooghe et al. 2010), which were ultimately translated into concrete reforms by decision makers. Because political parties are, at least in parliamentary systems, the central political actors in policy- and decision-making processes (Green-Pedersen 2007, 274), the analysis of party strategies on territorial issues represents a valid and useful way for understanding the design and implementation of territorial reforms (Verge 2013).

It has become common to understand decentralist reforms—that is, reforms pushing the territorial organization of the state in a decentralizing direction—as a democratic way to resolve center–periphery conflicts, providing the institutional means to accommodate autonomist demands arising from the peripheries of the state. Yet this is only part of the story. Decentralist reforms are not only a matter of accommodation of peripheral claims but have to do with politically "setting the rules of the game" (Sorens 2009, 268); they entail redistributions of competencies across different layers of authority and open government opportunities at the subnational level, thus setting up new arenas of political contest and centers of political power. In other words, changing the territorial structure of the state introduces political dynamics beyond the territorial demands of ethnic minorities and autonomist movements. The main implication of this argument is that *decentralist reforms are a crucial issue of political debate and party competition* in any political system. Hence, at least in parliamentary systems like the Italian one, the pattern of territorial reforms and the resulting policy outputs are deeply influenced by the dynamics of party competition, not only between statewide and autonomist parties but also among parties at the state level (Hopkin and van Houten 2009; Verge 2013).

Against this backdrop, this book contributes to the research on party politics and territorial issues by providing a systematic analysis at both the *system* and *individual* party levels. What role do parties—both statewide and autonomist—play in processes of decentralization? Do they influence the timing of reforms? Is decentralization a contested or consensual issue? Does the pattern of party competition affect the policy output? What is the rationale behind party preferences on decentralization? How do parties frame their political discourse on it?

This book then addresses all of these questions through a theoretical framework that integrates insights from the existing literature on agenda setting, party politics, mandate theory, and issue framing, which is outlined in the last section of this chapter. Before going ahead with the core themes of this book, however, it is worthwhile to take a step back to see what has already been said on the topic and how this work can contribute to the existing literature.

What Has Been Said and Remains Unanswered

Despite the political relevance of the territorial dimension, the literature has long neglected the relationship between party politics and territorial reforms (Hopkin and van Houten 2009). The dominant accounts of political and party systems, in fact, have often been based on utter adherence to the paradigm of national integration (Keating 2008). Territorial cleavages have been treated as anachronistic "legacies of the past" (Caramani 2004, 292), relics standing in contrast to the modernity epitomized by the development of nation states and the related processes of territorial homogenization. Indeed, this bias has not completely disappeared.

Nevertheless, some scholars, inspired by Lipset and Rokkan's pivotal 1967 essay, have managed to maintain and even grow interest in territory in political science, even when it has seemed old-fashioned and inconsistent with the contemporary world. These efforts have borne fruit in recent decades: phenomena like the surge of peripheral mobilization movements and protests and the ongoing decentralization of state structures in western Europe have increased awareness of the enduring strength and importance of territory in contemporary political systems. Within this framework, a branch of research has developed focusing on the role played by political parties in territorial politics.

One strand of the most recent literature on the topic focuses on peripheral mobilization and the growth of ethno-regionalist parties (as in Urwin 1983; De Winter and Türsan 1998; Tronconi 2009). Other areas of study concern the territorial organization of political parties and the empowerment of regional branches (Hopkin 2003, 2009; Laffin et al. 2007; Van Houten 2009; Thorlakson 2009), the patterns of voting behavior in subnational electoral arenas (Jeffery and Hough 2009), and the evolution of regional party systems (Tronconi and Roux 2009). Finally, in the 2000s scholars began to analyze the attitudes of statewide parties toward the territorial dimension, which this work focuses on as well (see, for instance, Maddens and Libbrecht 2009; Mazzoleni 2009a, b; Sorens 2009; Libbrecht et al. 2013; Alonso 2012; Verge 2013; Toubeau and Massetti 2013; Toubeau and Wagner 2015).

The research carried out so far in this last area can be divided into at least two main groups. The first group includes those works in which party preferences on territorial issues are considered the main independent variable explaining the dynamics of territorial reforms (Sorens 2009; Meguid 2009; Hopkin 2009; Mazzoleni 2009b, Toubeau and Massetti 2013). One of the earliest contributions to this topic actually dates back to Rokkan and Urwin (1983, 167), who examined the role political parties play as intermediaries of the central government's response to territorial questions, while addressing the "effect that political parties have upon unity or division in the condition of territorial diversity." Similarly, Rhodes and Wright (1987, 13–14) explicitly dealt with the function of political parties as a "vehicle for the articulation of both ideologies and alternative courses of action," which should be taken into account in the examination of the "factors influencing the accommodation of territorial interests." Some of these works have focused on the partisan dynamics of territorial reforms within single decentralizing countries, like Italy (Leonardi et al. 1987;

Mazzoleni 2009b; Massetti and Toubeau 2013), while others have focused mostly on governing parties (Sorens 2009) in an attempt to explain why institutions at the central level of authority initiate decentralist reforms.

In the second body of research, party attitudes on the territorial dimension actually constitute the main dependent variable. Several works deal with what Meguid (2009, 7) defines as the "puzzle of decentralization"—namely, whether, to what extent, and why parties, especially statewide ones, might voluntarily reduce state competencies by transferring power and resources to the subnational levels. These works have focused predominantly on party position, salience, and determinants of party preferences in relation to territorial questions. Within this body, there are works dealing with both relevant case studies (Maddens and Libbrecht 2009; Verge 2013) and individual party families (Huysseune 2002).

These contributions have provided essential directions for further research on this topic. This book contributes to this literature by integrating all the different perspectives that have been used thus far, while suggesting further theoretical approaches. In particular, three core arguments of this study provide new insights to the literature of territorial party politics.

First, through the lens of the policy agenda approach, this work points out the need to distinguish between the system and individual levels of analysis. This book argues that it is only when an issue becomes relevant at the party system level (i.e., among the major parties that compete in the electoral arena) that it has a significant chance to appear on the policy agenda (Chap. 3).

Second, by examining the entire range of possible party positions, this book also sheds light on a political communication strategy often neglected in the literature: the ambiguous strategy. Moreover, it examines the dynamics of party competition in two different arenas—namely, the electoral and the legislative ones—to assess empirically whether parties actually implement their electoral pledges once in parliament (Chap. 4).

Third, this work introduces frames in the discussions of party strategies, pointing out the importance of how parties choose to justify and connect their positions to their broader sets of values (Chap. 5).

"Words Are Important"

There is a memorable quote from the 1987 Bernardo Bertolucci movie *The Last Emperor*: "If you cannot say what you mean, you will never mean what you say." It is a warning about the importance of clarity in terminology.

Giovanni Sartori (1970, 1038) pointed out how using appropriate and meaningful definitions has a profound impact on empirical analysis in the social sciences: "We cannot measure unless we know first what it is that we are measuring."

Accordingly, before proceeding with the theoretical model and the empirical analysis, it is necessary to clarify the exact meanings attributed to the words used in this book in order to define and narrow the object of study. This will provide definitions of the main concepts, which will later be operationalized and measured.

Territorial Dimension, Decentralization, and Territorial Party Politics

This section begins by defining the group of concepts concerning the territorial dimension, territorial politics, and decentralization.

Lipset and Rokkan (1967, 10) used the notion of the *territorial dimension* to define the portion of political space characterized by polarization between the central elite and local opposition. This dimension encompasses what the authors define as the center–periphery cleavage—namely, the relationship between a dominant geographic-political entity (the center) and a set of distant, dependent, and divided subcentral entities (the peripheries). Such center–periphery relationships involve decisions concerning the *territorial distribution of authority* within a state, defined by Duchacek (1970, 12) as the "recognition or creation of geographically limited authority to deal with matters of local import." In turn, such a distribution of powers hinges on a decision-making process that is usually defined as *territorial politics*—that is, "the arena of political activity concerned with the relations between central political institutions in the capital city and those sub-central political organization and governmental bodies within the accepted boundaries of a state" (Rhodes and Wright 1987, 2).

This work will first define *territorial authorities* as those geographical spaces delimited by boundaries, while the *territorial dimension* constitutes the political space featuring issues related to the organization of such authorities and the relationships between them. Such territorial political space should be understood as a directional one, in that political actors may lean toward one of the two poles on a continuum but cannot choose among a set of alternative options; on the one pole there is greater autonomy for the peripheries, while on the opposite pole there is a stronger central authority.

The "territorial" label, however, introduces a plethora of other issues. For clarity's sake, they can be classified around two basic dichotomies. The first centers around the question of *decentralization versus centralization* and includes all those issues concerning the territorial architecture of the state—namely, the redistribution of powers, competencies, and resources across territorial authorities. It should be pointed out that the concept of decentralization features a dynamic component, because it implies a top-down process, triggered by the central government toward the subnational levels and, at least in theory, is a reversible process, although entrenched by constitutional guarantees (see also Chap. 2). The second cluster, expressed by the dichotomy *cultural differentiation versus homogenization*, is made up of those matters dealing with the acknowledgment and protection of the identity, culture, and ethnic distinctiveness of territorial authorities. As the title reveals, this book mostly focuses on the set of issues related to the institutional aspects of the territorial dimension—namely, the processes of decentralization. Indeed, although the cultural aspect of the territorial dimension is by no means a secondary one, the reforms and processes of policy change analyzed in this study concern mostly the redistribution of powers and resources, rather than identity matters. This is actually a feature of the Italian political debate on territorial issues, which has predominantly dealt with such institutional aspects throughout the process of reform.

Drawing on this concept of the territorial dimension, the related concept of territorial politics refers to those political activities, relationships, and interactions among political actors revolving around the territorial dimension. When such interactions take place among political parties, they can be referred to as *territorial party politics*, which specifically denotes party activities concerning the territorial dimension.[1]

A Working Definition of Party Strategies

As argued earlier, a discussion of *party politics* could include a wide range of party activities, from a party's formation to its internal organization through its *competition* with other parties. To stay within a manageable scope, this study concentrates exclusively on this last activity.

Parties compete among themselves to secure political power, expressed in terms of electoral gains (parties as vote seekers), governing positions (parties as office seekers), and opportunities to shape policy in areas of particular interest (parties as policy seekers), with these three goals often being interrelated (Strøm 1990, 570). To achieve their goals, parties have to develop appropriate and effective *strategies*, which can include the choice to ally with some parties and compete with others as well as the choice to *make decisions on policy issues* (Elias et al. 2015). It is this latter aspect that this book explores in the most depth.

This book conceives of *party strategies (on issues)* as the result of the manipulation of three tools: salience, position, and frames. To develop a full-fledged strategy to compete on a specific policy dimension, parties are required to decide whether and to what extent they will pay attention to this policy dimension (i.e., the manipulation of salience), the direction to pursue (i.e., the manipulation of position), and the way in which their positions will be justified (i.e., the manipulation of frames).

It should be specified that this behavior is not limited to election campaigns. Rather, parties keep competing during interelectoral periods (between elections), with the context of their competition shifting from the electoral to the legislative arena (ibid.). Accordingly, though this study focuses mostly on parties' electoral strategies, some attention will be also paid to party strategies in the institutional arena, where electoral rhetoric needs to be translated into concrete voting and legislative behavior (Chap. 4).

To sum up, this book uses concepts of party competition in different policy dimensions to thoroughly analyze the strategies parties adopt to compete over the territorial dimension. As discussed earlier, conceptualization—and the subsequent operationalization of concepts—is an essential precondition for measurement. To this end, the next section introduces an original coding scheme designed to operationalize three normally abstract elements of party strategy (salience, position, and frame) and turn them into concrete variables.

From Concepts to Measurements: Operationalization, Data, and Research Design

Measuring Party Strategies on the Territorial Dimension: A Method Based on Content Analysis[2]

Over time, scholars have created different measurement instruments to "map" party competition over policy dimensions. Among them, the content analysis of political texts, such as electoral manifestos,[3] has evolved into a useful "research technique for making replicable and valid inferences from texts … to the context of their use" (Krippendorff 2004, 18).

It is defined as an unobtrusive and nonreactive method (ibid., 40), in that a systematized and rule-based coding procedure should allow the investigator a very limited scope for subjective interpretation (though admittedly any nonautomated content analysis process, including the one proposed in this study, will contain some amount of subjective evaluation). Content analysis could thus be defined as a way to quantify information that is intrinsically qualitative.

This study introduces an original coding scheme for the content analysis of party manifestos, one that is designed to estimate party strategies on the territorial dimension and is based on a solid theoretical framework. The coding categories, in fact, were deductively generated from the model outlined in the previous section describing party strategies on territorial issues, breaking them down into three steps that describe the manipulation of salience, position, and framing.

The reader could at this point wonder about the rationale behind developing a new coding scheme rather than relying on existing datasets—and, in fact, there are valid data sources already available that would allow the measurement of party strategies on the territorial dimension. For instance, there are large datasets covering several policy dimensions based on content analysis of party manifestos, surveys of party voters and elites, analysis of roll-call votes made by party legislators, and expert surveys of country specialists (Benoit and Laver 2006), and they all contain at least one variable measuring the territorial dimension.

The problem, however, is that these multidimensional datasets rely on broad definitions of the territorial dimension, the price of working with large numbers of variables to make comparisons across different policy dimensions (Protsyk and Garaz 2013). This means that important information on the topic at the center of this study could be lost, or vague to the point that it is no longer useful. Several recent works have proposed applying new coding schemes specifically designed to measure party preferences toward a single policy dimension, like the territorial one, to the content analysis of party manifestos. However, even existing single-issue approaches fail to provide full accounts of party strategies on the territorial dimension that encompass the elements of salience, position, and framing within a single theoretical model. They often focus exclusively on salience and position (e.g., Maddens and Libbrecht 2009; Libbrecht et al. 2013), while the study of framing is generally still in its infancy (Sinardet and Morsink 2011; Chaney 2013). Moreover, existing datasets have thus far paid scant attention to ambiguous strategies. The content analysis framework suggested in this study attempts to fill these gaps by proposing a new instrument that is more precise while still grounded in existing scholarly efforts.

This coding scheme has been designed to be carried out by hand rather than with the help of computer-assisted content analysis. Though computerized techniques have the unequivocal advantage of reducing the chances of coding errors and make it possible to analyze a large amount of text easily, manual coding is nevertheless preferable for both theoretical and methodological reasons. First and foremost, the study of a single issue presupposes a deep knowledge of it, and a coder who has a certain level of experience with territorial politics might observe some "subtle" references to the issue that a computer might miss. Second, but no less important, coding software uses a set of keywords that it will search for within a document, and words like *region, governance, subsidiary principle,* and *autonomy* might be used in contexts other than discussions of territorial politics. The term *region* might identify either the "European" region or the main subnational territorial authority under the Italian constitution, for example, while a concept as central to this study as *decentralization* could also refer to something other than the redistribution of resources to subnational levels, such as the privatization of previously public owned functions and businesses.

As it is essential for the purposes of this study to reduce the misinterpretation of words as much as possible, manual coding procedures have been used and are recommended for any application of these tools to other cases. The price, of course, is reduced reliability and an increase to the amount of human labor the work requires, which might restrict the use of this sort of analysis to fewer test cases. As always, this is a choice future researchers will have to make for themselves, balancing what their research goals require with what is practically possible.

Translating Words to Numbers: The Coding Scheme

This coding scheme builds on the conceptualization of party strategies as competitive tools that can be separated into a three-step decision process involving the manipulation of salience, position, and frame. The following subsections describe these strategies in detail as well as how they can be measured through the content analysis of party manifestos.

Salience
The first choice a party makes when communicating its position on territorial issues is whether to ignore the issues entirely (a neglecting strategy) or recognize and emphasize them in its own agenda; in other words, to give this policy dimension salience or not. Thus when measuring salience the main questions are whether the territorial dimension has actually entered the party agenda and how much political parties deal with it.

The measurement of salience follows the approach described in literature on the content analysis of party documents, such as the Comparative Manifesto Project (CMP). Documents are read and divided into quasi-sentences (hereafter: QSs).[4] All the QSs related to territorial issues are coded under the *territorial dimension* category, using the definition of the territorial dimension provided earlier. They are then summed up, divided by the total number of QSs in the entire document, and multiplied by 100, which results in a percentage. The formula is as follows:

$$\text{Salience of territorial dimension} = \frac{\sum_{i=0}^{n} \text{territorial issues QS}}{\sum_{i=1}^{n} \text{QS total}} \times 100$$

Position
Once a party decides to address territorial issues, it must choose which direction on the political continuum to support. This generally means choosing one side or the other—namely centralization or decentralization of competencies. However, parties will sometimes take positions closer to the middle and pursue a strategy of careful ambiguity. This can manifest as either a "blurring" strategy (Rovny 2013) or a "broad appeal" (Somer-Topcu 2015) or "contradictory" strategy, for instance, supporting decentralization in some policy areas (such as healthcare) while opposing territorial redistribution of competencies in others (such as education) (Chap. 4).

The proposed coding scheme seeks to measure the entire range of decentralist and centralist positions, including the blurred and contradictory ones, by using a two-step procedure. First, the QSs coded under the territorial dimension category are distinguished into three main subcategories and assigned different codes. The decentralist code (code 101) applies to statements expressing a preference for a redistribution of competencies to subnational levels as well as those supporting the promotion and protection of local and regional identity, culture, and symbols; those QSs that express opposing positions are coded as centralist (code 102). A neutral code (code 100) is applied when a QS refers to territorial issues but does not express any clearly supportive or opposing stance on them. For instance, a sentence like "Regions are increasingly assuming a public role, carrying out competencies of great political significance that were transferred from the State and once areas of exclusive national competence" (*Rifondazione Comunista* 2001) describes the state of the art of the process of decentralization in Italy but does not provide any information whatsoever on whether the party is favorable or not to such an increase of regional powers.

Once codes are applied to each manifesto, directional certainty is calculated following a common academic approach (Maddens and Libbrecht 2009; Libbrecht et al. 2013; Alonso 2012, 69), as the sum of QSs coded as decentralist minus the sum of those coded as centralist, divided by the total number of QSs dealing with territorial issues. As for the neutral sentences—that is, those coded as 100—they are not included in the numerator because they do not express any direction on the policy dimension. Values of directional certainty range from −1 to +1, including zero.

The formula is thus:

$$\text{directional certainty} = \frac{\sum_{i=0}^{n}\left[\text{decentralist}(\text{code }101) - \text{centralist}(\text{code }102)\right]}{\sum_{i=1}^{n}\text{territorial issues }(\text{codes }100+101+102)}$$

Assume, for instance, that a document contains 18 decentralist sentences (code 101), 5 centralist sentences (code 102), and 9 neutral sentences (code 100), for a total of 32 statements on territorial issues. Using the formula above, the value of directional certainty is (18 − 5) / 32 = 0.4. The positive sign indicates an overall decentralist direction, although the proximity to zero suggests there is a certain ambiguity due to the 5 centralist statements and 9 neutral ones. If all the statements had been decentralist, rendering the formula (32 − 0) / 32 = 1, the direction would have been decidedly decentralist; if they had all been centralist, rendering the formula (0 − 32) / 32 = −1, the negative sign would have indicated straightforward opposition to decentralization; finally, if they had all been neutral, rendering the formula (0 − 0) / 32 = 0, or evenly divided between decentralist and centralist statements, rendering the formula (16 − 16) / 32 = 0, it would indicate a blurred position (in the first case) or a contradictory position (in the second).

Coding Decentralization in Specific Policy Areas
To achieve more granular analysis of party positioning, the coding scheme also allows the researcher to assign a further code to those QSs that deal with territorial issues but expressly refer to a specific policy area in which the decentralization of competencies should occur, like health, education, or fiscal policy. Such information also allows the analysis of those cases in which parties have taken contradictory stances, favoring decentralization in certain policy areas while opposing it in others (Chap. 4).

To analyze support for decentralization on concrete policy subfields, 25 policy areas (Table 1.1) have been identified, each of them associated with a code. Then, a 0, 1, or 2 is added, according to whether the QS is neutral, decentralist, or centralist. A statement expressing support for fiscal federalism would be coded as 221, for example: 2 for policy field, 2 referring to fiscal federalism, and 1 because the QS expresses a decentralist orientation.

For each policy area, salience and directional certainty are calculated according to the same formulas used for the territorial dimension in general. The directional certainty of each subpolicy field is calculated by subtracting the negative stances adopted in that area from the positive ones, then dividing this value by the overall number of QSs coded under that policy area.

Frames
Classic models of party competition limit the strategic tools available to parties for manipulation of salience and positioning (Meguid 2009). However, parties have a further tool at their disposal—namely, the definition and justification of the policy problem, or *issue framing*.

The list of frames given in Table 1.2 was developed deductively by drawing from the literature on territorial politics to define categories applicable to the largest possible number of countries. Specifically, it was generated by looking at the main pressures shared by decentralizing countries across western Europe that scholars have identified as primary triggers of territorial restructuring, thus providing the main reasons and rationales behind decentralization processes. They can be grouped into three main clusters: *functional pressures, identity pressures* (Schakel 2009), and *structures of political opportunity*. Their meaning and rationale will be thoroughly explained in Chaps. 2 and 5.

Table 1.1 Coded policy areas

Code	Policy areas (add digits 0, 1, or 2 to the policy area codes)
21-	**Constitutional reform:** Statements concerning constitutional reforms dealing with the redistribution of competencies to subnational levels (e.g., concerning Title V of the Italian Constitution).
22-	**Fiscal policy:** Statements concerning the allocation of revenue powers and spending responsibilities across different territorial layers.
23-	**Education:** Statements concerning the transfer of competencies and powers from central ministries of education to the subnational levels.
24-	**Health:** Statements concerning the transfer of competencies and powers from central ministries of health to the subnational levels.
25-	**Identity and cultural policies:** Statements concerning the promotion and protection of linguistic and cultural identities vs. the defense of national identity and symbols.
26-	**Agriculture:** Statements concerning the transfer of competencies and powers in the field of agriculture from the central government to the subnational levels.
27-	**Labor and employment:** Statements concerning the transfer of competencies and powers in the fields of labor and employment from the central government to the subnational levels.
28-	**Social welfare:** Statements concerning the transfer of competencies and powers in the fields of child care, pensions, social services, voluntary services, youth aids, and so on from the central government to the subnational levels.
29-	**Cultural policy:** Statements concerning the transfer of competencies and powers from central ministries of culture and art to the subnational levels.
210-	**Law and order:** Statements concerning the transfer of competencies and powers in the field of security, including police and justice, from the central government to the subnational levels.
211-	**Foreign policy and defense:** Statements concerning the transfer of competencies and powers in the fields of foreign policy, defense, and military intervention from the central government to the subnational levels.
212-	**Domestic macroeconomic issues:** Statements concerning the transfer of competencies and powers in the fields of budgetary policy and economics from the central government to the subnational levels.
213-	**Reforms:** Statements containing a generic reference to a territorial reorganization of the competencies across different administrative layers (used only to count generic references, when other codes were not applicable).
214-	**Legislative power:** Statements concerning the regions' legislative autonomy.
215-	**Administrative power:** Statements concerning the competencies of regional and local public administration.
216-	**City planning, housing, community development:** Statements concerning the transfer of competencies and powers in the fields of housing policy and city planning from the central government to the subnational levels.

(*continued*)

Table 1.1 (continued)

Code	Policy areas (add digits 0, 1, or 2 to the policy area codes)
217-	**Environment:** Statements concerning the transfer of competencies and powers in the fields of the environment and conservation from the central government to the subnational levels.
218-	**Tourism:** Statements concerning the transfer of competencies and powers in the field of tourism from the central government to the subnational levels.
219-	**Energy policy:** Statements concerning the transfer of competencies and powers in the field of energy policy from the central government to the subnational levels.
220-	**Transports and infrastructures:** Statements concerning the transfer of competencies and powers in the field of transportation and infrastructure from the central government to the subnational levels.
221-	**Immigration policy:** Statements concerning the transfer of competencies and powers in the fields of immigration policy and border control from the central government to the subnational levels.
222-	**Business, trade, and consumer rights:** Statements concerning the transfer of competencies and powers in the fields of business, trade, and consumer rights from the central government to the subnational levels.
223-	**Sports:** Statements concerning the transfer of competencies and powers in the field of sports from the central government to the subnational levels.
224-	**Communication:** Statements concerning the transfer of competencies and powers in the field of communications (e.g., media and broadcasting) from the central government to the subnational levels.
225-	**Craftsmanship:** Statements concerning the transfer of competencies and powers in the field of craftsmanship from the central government to the subnational levels.
226-	**Civil protection:** Statements concerning the transfer of competencies and powers in the field of civil protection from the central government to the subnational levels.

When the QSs coded as territorial also contain a reference to one of these frames, the associated code is applied. Each frame has an initial two- or three-digit code, ranging from 10 to 100. A second digit is added to that: 0 if neutral, 1 if decentralist, 2 if centralist. The same procedures used to measure the salience and the directional certainty of policy areas are also applied to the measurement of frames.

The TERRISS Dataset
The coding scheme described in the previous sections has been applied to 120 Italian party manifestos, along with other programmatic documents when manifestos were not available. These documents cover all the elections held in Italy from 1948 to 2013.[5] The coding process resulted in the *TERRISS Dataset*,[6] which includes all the data derived from the coded

Table 1.2 List of coded frames

Pressures	Code	Frames (add digits 0, 1, or 2 to the frame codes)
Functional pressures	10-	**Efficiency:** References to territorial restructuring as a way to ensure (or hinder) the flexibility and efficiency of public administration and government machinery.
	20-	**Territorial solidarity:** References to the redistribution of economic resources between richer and poorer regions to bridge socioeconomic gaps.
	30-	**Democracy:** References to territorial restructuring as a way to ensure (or hinder) the accountability of political actors and increase (or decrease) citizens' participation in political processes.
	40-	**Liberalism:** References to territorial restructuring as a way to develop (or jeopardize) a liberal state, with limited authority for the government.
Identity pressures	50-	**Identity:** References to attachment to local or regional values, culture, and symbols.
	60-	**National unity:** References to national unity as a value to protect vs. references to national unity as an obsolete principle.
Political opportunity structures	70-	**European Union:** References to the European Union as a political framework in which subnational levels might pursue greater autonomy within the framework of a "Europe of the regions".
	80-	**Subsidiary principle:** References to the principle of subsidiarity as defined in Article 5 of the Treaty on European Union, according to which decisions should be made as closely as possible to the citizen and constant checks should be made to verify that action at the EU level is justified in light of the possibilities available at national, regional, and local levels.
	90-	**Autonomist movements and parties:** References to movements and parties aiming at the mobilization of peripheral unrest.
	100-	**Political foes:** References to political actors that endorse opposing views on territorial reforms and are thus seen as an obstacle to a party's views on the redistribution of power across different layers.

manifestos. The units of analysis of the TERRISS Dataset are parties or coalitions[7] for each electoral year. The dataset includes variables measuring salience and position on issues within the territorial dimension as well as subpolicy areas and frames and variables summarizing the profile of each party or coalition, such as vote share obtained in the most recent election, left-right ideology, number of seats obtained, participation or nonparticipation in government, and votes for or against territorial reform in the following legislative period.

Reliability and Validity of the Measurement Instrument

To assess the consistency and accuracy of the measurements obtained, reliability and validity tests have been performed.

The reliability of the data obtained has been assessed by comparing an early round of coding completed by the author with a later round of coding completed by the author after gaining further practical experience and improved coding abilities (Krippendorff 2004, 215). This "intraobserver reliability" test is weaker than the "intercoder reliability" one; nevertheless, in light of practical constraints, it represents an acceptable second-best solution. The test confirmed a high level of consistency between the early and later coding rounds.

A correlative test of validity (ibid., 333), which evaluates new measurement instruments using existing tools, has been applied to these data. As already explained, the TERRISS Dataset builds on previous works on the content analysis of party manifestos, such as the CMP, which also includes categories measuring party attitudes on the territorial dimension.[8] The CMP has coded Italian manifestos over the same time span as that used to create the TERRISS Dataset; however, because not all the documents coded by the TERRISS Dataset coincide with those used by the CMP,[9] the correlation tests include only those cases from this study that perfectly match the documents coded by the CMP.

The first validity test compares the quasi-sentence divisions used in the TERRISS Dataset with those used by the CMP dataset. This comparison is important, as it rules out the possibility that differences in the measurement of salience could be due to differences in the procedure used to split sentences. However, there is a strong, positive correlation between the two datasets on the number of QSs that have been identified within the text: (Pearson pairwise correlation coefficient, $r = .91$, $p < 0.001$, $n = 96$).

For a more substantial validity test, measures of salience and directional certainty obtained from the TERRISS Dataset have been correlated with analogous measures drawn from the CMP dataset. Before showing these correlations, two points require explanation. First, the CMP does not contain a variable for directional certainty; it can be calculated, however, by using codes Per301 (percentage of decentralist statements) and Per302 (percentage of centralist statements).[10] Second, the CMP does not feature a neutral code. However, when these differences are accounted for, there is a satisfactory degree of common variance across the different measures. Indeed, there is a significant, positive, and strong correlation between the measures of overall salience of territorial issues in the CMP and the TERRISS Dataset ($r = .79$, $p < 0.001$, $n = 96$), and a strong, positive, and significant correlation between a calculation of position on territorial issues derived from the CMP data and the directional certainty in the TERRISS Dataset ($r = .72$, $p < 0.001$, $n = 73$).[11]

The weaker coefficient and the fewer parties expressing a direction on territorial issues can be explained by the fact that the TERRISS Dataset, with its issue-specific nature, tends to slightly overestimate the number of QSs coded within this category. To cite one example, a multidimensional dataset like the CMP would probably code statements concerning the decentralization of the health or education system under the category of health or education. Nonetheless, the results of the validity tests seem to confirm that, despite its unique nature, the TERRISS Dataset measures the concepts at stake effectively, while adopting a more fine-grained approach.

The Research Design: Choosing a Case Study

As already noted, the TERRISS Dataset collected data from Italian parties contesting elections in the post–World War II period until 2013. Italy represents a good case for the study of processes of decentralization.

In choosing the most appropriate research design, it should be kept in mind that the "goal of scientific research is inference" (King et al. 1994, 34), meaning using the collected data and empirical analysis to make valid generalizations about unobserved facts. The research design describes the approach chosen to use empirical data in a meaningful and effective manner. To be valid, the generalizations achieved should meet two requirements: first, the relationship between independent and dependent variables should not be "spurious"—that is, the impact of other intervening variables on the dependent variable (i.e., threats to internal validity) should be excluded; second, the causal relationship should not be biased by the selection of the specific cases (i.e., threats to external validity). The choice of the research design should therefore take into account the need to control all the relevant variables through the thoughtful selection of test cases and variables.

This study proposes a comprehensive account of territorial party politics, which should exclude the possibility of interference by incorporating all of the data that could be related to the subject; in terms of the classic dilemma between "few variables, many cases" and "many variables, few cases" (Collier 1993), this work opts for the latter. Among nonexperimental research designs, a statistical method would have allowed greater generalization by examining a wider number of cases. However, it would also imply adopting a narrower set of independent variables, thus imposing severe constraints on the potential explanatory significance of the theoretical framework. The adoption of a comparative method or case study, on the other hand, limits the analysis to a small number of selected cases, and has a "weak capacity to sort out rival explanation," as argued by Lijphart (ibid., 107). At the same time, these latter options have the clear advantage of providing a dense, fine-grained description of the topic under scrutiny, while controlling for other potential variables through the process of case selection.

The usefulness of these two approaches to scientific political inquiry can be enhanced by applying "these methods in such a way as to minimize their weaknesses and to capitalize on their inherent strengths" (Lijphart 1971, 693). While both the comparative method and the case study could represent strong options assuming a robust explanatory model, the case study allows the development of intensive and methodologically rigorous analysis, even with limited resources (ibid., 691); furthermore, a case study can include a large amount of data over a long time span.

Concerning the problem of producing valid generalizations with only a single case study, this work uses Lijphart's arguments (ibid., 691–692), which point out that a case study may, at least indirectly, "make an important contribution to the establishment of general propositions and thus to theory-building in political science."

It should also be noted that there are in fact six distinct "ideal" types of case study, not one; this work aims to fulfill the characteristics of the *hypothesis-generating* and *theory-confirming/infirming* case study types. The "hypothesis-generating case studies start out with a more or less vague notion of possible hypotheses, and attempt to formulate definite hypotheses to be tested subsequently among a larger number of cases. Their objective is to develop theoretical generalizations in areas where no theory exists yet" (ibid., 692). The "theory confirming or infirming case stud[ies]" are developed "within the framework of established generalizations" (ibid., 692), which are then tested in the case under scrutiny.

The present study introduces several tentative, preliminary hypotheses to explain the dynamics of party competition in the territorial dimension, relying on different yet interrelated strands of literature. Its analysis also makes use of several existing theoretical propositions. In both cases, these hypotheses are empirically tested using the Italian case study that, as already explained, boasts a number of features that make it a "crucial experiment."

The empirical analyses developed in this book have the potential to contribute to the development of a comprehensive theoretical framework. The latter, in its turn, will eventually generate more specific hypotheses to be tested with other relevant cases in future iterations of the research.

An Integrated Model of the Party Politics of Decentralization

This study is designed to be both descriptive and explanatory. On the one hand, it will guide the reader through the development of the territorial structure of Italy, seen from the perspective of political parties. On the other hand, it will explain whether, to what extent, and how the patterns of party competition have affected these processes by using empirical analysis grounded on a solid theoretical foundation.

To achieve this, the explanatory model presented here draws on contributions from different strands of literature—namely, those focusing on agenda setting, issue framing, and party politics, which together have been integrated into a comprehensive framework. Indeed, communication between these only nominally separate areas of literature might help address this work's research questions from several distinct yet interrelated perspectives.

The model takes as a starting point the process of decentralization in Italy. Two features of that process should be noted at the outset: first, the process of decentralization has been characterized by short periods of intense policy change followed by long periods of stability; second, it began well before the emergence of electorally relevant autonomist movements pursuing decentralist demands (Chap. 2).

Accordingly, the first step of this analysis is to understand when, why, and how decentralist issues enter the policy agenda to be translated into concrete reforms. The agenda-setting literature suggests the uneven timing of these reforms results from the limited attention paid to the issue by political actors, who can only focus on a few policy issues at a time. The issue of decentralization rises to the top of the political agenda only when a majority of the parties pay more attention to the issue; but this means that once it has claimed a place on the political agenda, concrete policy change is likely. One of the many factors that might induce parties to pay attention to a given policy dimension is the activity of a "proponent party," because party competition on issues is largely shaped by a given party's ability to focus attention on its favored issues. However, it is not only "autonomist" parties that play this role. Contrary to most existing literature on territorial party politics (Meguid 2008), this work will go beyond the explanation of decentralization as the result of dialectic confrontation between central actors and peripheral mobilization; it will also look at the dynamics of party competition among statewide parties to explain the "politics of attention" in the area of decentralization. Dealing with party attention in this manner requires looking at the relevance of a specific policy dimension in party agendas, meaning their manipulation of its salience. This will be addressed in Chap. 3.

Attention to a policy dimension is a necessary but not sufficient condition to achieve concrete policy change. Once a set of issues enters the policy agenda, it is still necessary to persuade the majority of policy makers to opt for a specific policy option. To this end, parties use three strategies, assuming that they have not decided to ignore a policy dimension: they can accommodate the position of the proponent party, oppose it, or adopt an ambiguous position. In an electoral campaign, the adoption of one of these strategies will hinge on both strategic and ideological considerations. Once in power, however, other variables are likely to influence party decisions to support or oppose a particular policy reform, which can coincide with the position taken during the electoral campaign or represent a shift in direction. An analysis of the patterns of consensus and conflict concerning policy solutions in the territorial dimension requires a discussion on the manipulation of position in party strategies, which will be the focus of Chap. 4.

Parties, however, do not compete by merely making a decision about the amount of attention to pay to an issue and the direction to adopt; they must also justify their decisions and explain the rationales behind their strategic choices, linking their stance to their broader worldview, ideas, and values. In other words, they have to *frame* the policy dimension. Hence the analysis of frames, which will be the focus of Chap. 5, will complete the picture of party strategies.

Notes

1. Similarly, Toubeau and Massetti (2013, 301) argue that "the party politics of territorial reforms refers to the way in which statewide parties and regionalist parties position themselves and strategize on the territorial

dimension during their competitive interactions, and to the way in which this process of interaction affects the substance of territorial reforms."
2. An earlier version of this section, based on manifesto data from 1963 to 2013, appeared in Basile (2016).
3. The electoral manifestos of political parties have been established as useful instruments for providing information concerning party stances on specific issues. Among the advantages they offer: they are all delivered in the same period, ensuring consistency of data for all the parties included in the analysis; they represent a somewhat official source; and they are present in all democratic countries, thus paving the way for future cross-national comparisons. Of course, manifestos show the "official" positions adopted by parties for general elections, while they fail to capture the intraparty divisions. For a good synthesis of the debate on the use of manifestos, including their advantages and shortcomings, see Ruedin and Morales (2017, 2).
4. This coding scheme follows the general rules for the division of documents into quasi-sentences laid out by the CMP group (Volkens 2001). The QS should be a unit of significance by itself: once a statement has been split, it should still be understandable and express a meaningful concept.
5. For a complete list of the coded documents, see the appendix to this volume.
6. Short for Territorial Issues Dataset.
7. The coded documents usually refer to party manifestos. In some cases, however, parties did not issue manifestos on their own; in these cases, the coalition manifesto has been coded. In other cases, both the single party and the coalition manifestos were coded. However, in those cases, at least for some analyses, only one document (usually the coalition manifesto) was considered. Information about the use of party vs. coalition manifestos is included in the appendix, and they are specified, when relevant, in the analyses.
8. The CMP categories measuring the territorial dimension are Per301 and Per302. For their definitions, consult Codebook version 2017a, available at https://manifestoproject.wzb.eu/datasets (last accessed on October 17, 2017).
9. In some cases, the TERRISS Dataset used original manifestos that were retrieved directly by the author from the archives of political parties or libraries and were thus coded for the first time.
10. The number of statements dealing with territorial issues has been derived by comparing the percentages provided by variables Per301 and Per302 with the variable accounting for the total number of QSs coded in the entire document. The numbers thus obtained have been used according to the same formula to calculate directional certainty.
11. The lower n for this correlation is due to the higher number of documents with no statements coded as territorial in the CMP compared to the TERRISS Dataset.

REFERENCES

Alonso, Sonia. 2012. *Challenging the State: Devolution and the Battle for Partisan Credibility: A Comparison of Belgium, Italy, Spain, and the United Kingdom*. Oxford: Oxford University Press.

Basile, Linda. 2016. Measuring Party Strategies on the Territorial Dimension: A Method Based on Content Analysis. *Regional & Federal Studies* 26 (1): 1–23.

Benoit, Kenneth, and Michael Laver. 2006. *Party Policy in Modern Democracies*. 1st ed. London: Routledge.

Caramani, Daniele. 2004. *The Nationalization of Politics: The Formation of National Electorates and Party Systems in Western Europe*. Cambridge: Cambridge University Press.

Chaney, Paul. 2013. An Electoral Discourse Approach to State Decentralisation: State-Wide Parties' Manifesto Proposals on Scottish and Welsh Devolution, 1945–2010. *British Politics* 8 (3): 333–356.

Collier, David. 1993. The Comparative Method. In *Political Science: The State of Discipline II*, ed. Ada W. Finifter. Rochester: Social Science Research Network.

De Winter, Lieven, and Huri Türsan. 1998. *Regionalist Parties in Western Europe*. London: Routledge.

Duchacek, Ivo D. 1970. *Comparative Federalism: The Territorial Dimension of Politics*. New York: Holt, Rinehart and Winston.

Elias, Anwen, Edina Szöcsik, and Christina Isabel Zuber. 2015. Position, Selective Emphasis and Framing: How Parties Deal with a Second Dimension in Competition. *Party Politics* 21 (6): 839–850.

Green-Pedersen, Christoffer. 2007. The Conflict of Conflicts in Comparative Perspective: Euthanasia as a Political Issue in Denmark, Belgium, and the Netherlands. *Comparative Politics* 39 (3): 273–291.

Hooghe, Liesbet, Gary Marks, and Arjan H. Schakel. 2010. *The Rise of Regional Authority: A Comparative Study of 42 Democracies*. Abingdon: Routledge.

Hopkin, Jonathan. 2003. Political Decentralization, Electoral Change and Party Organizational Adaptation: A Framework for Analysis. *European Urban and Regional Studies* 10 (3): 227–237.

———. 2009. Party Matters: Devolution and Party Politics in Britain and Spain. *Party Politics* 15 (2): 179–198.

Hopkin, Jonathan, and Pieter van Houten. 2009. Decentralization and State-Wide Parties: Introduction. *Party Politics* 15 (2): 131–135.

Huysseune, Michel. 2002. Federalism and the Extreme Right in Italy. *Fédéralisme Régionalisme* 2, January.

Jeffery, Charlie, and Dan Hough. 2009. Understanding Post-Devolution Elections in Scotland and Wales in Comparative Perspective. *Party Politics* 15 (2): 219–240.

Keating, Michael. 2008. Thirty Years of Territorial Politics. *West European Politics* 31 (1–2): 60–81.

King, Gary, Robert O. Keohane, and Sidney Verba. 1994. *Designing Social Inquiry: Scientific Inference in Qualitative Research*. STU—Student ed. Princeton: Princeton University Press.

Krippendorff, Klaus. 2004. *Content Analysis: An Introduction to Its Methodology*. Thousand Oaks: Sage.

Laffin, Martin, Eric Shaw, and Gerald Taylor. 2007. The New Sub-National Politics of the British Labour Party. *Party Politics* 13 (1): 88–108.

Leonardi, Robert, Raffaella Y. Nanetti, and Robert D. Putnam. 1987. Italy—Territorial Politics in the Post-War Years: The Case of Regional Reform. *West European Politics* 10 (4): 88–107.

Libbrecht, Liselotte, Bart Maddens, and Wilfried Swenden. 2013. Party Competition in Regional Elections: The Strategies of State-Wide Parties in Spain and the United Kingdom. *Party Politics* 19 (4): 624–640.

Lijphart, Arend. 1971. Comparative Politics and the Comparative Method. *The American Political Science Review* 65 (3): 682–693.

Lipset, Seymour Martin, and Stein Rokkan. 1967. *Party Systems and Voter Alignments: Cross-National Perspectives*. New York: Free Press.

Maddens, Bart, and Liselotte Libbrecht. 2009. How Statewide Parties Cope with the Regionalist Issue: The Case of Spain; A Directional Approach. In *Territorial Party Politics in Western Europe*, 204–228. London: Palgrave Macmillan.

Marks, Gary, Liesbet Hooghe, and Arjan H. Schakel. 2008a. Measuring Regional Authority. *Regional & Federal Studies* 18 (2–3): 111–121.

———. 2008b. Patterns of Regional Authority. *Regional & Federal Studies* 18 (2–3): 167–181.

Massetti, Emanuele, and Simon Toubeau. 2013. Sailing with Northern Winds: Party Politics and Federal Reforms in Italy. *West European Politics* 36 (2): 359–381.

Mazzoleni, Martino. 2009a. The Saliency of Regionalization in Party Systems: A Comparative Analysis of Regional Decentralization in Party Manifestos. *Party Politics* 15 (2): 199–218.

———. 2009b. The Italian Regionalisation: A Story of Partisan Logics. *Modern Italy* 14 (2): 135–150.

Meguid, Bonnie M. 2008. *Party Competition Between Unequals: Strategies and Electoral Fortunes in Western Europe*. Cambridge: Cambridge University Press.

———. 2009. *Institutional Change as Strategy: The Role of Decentralization in Party Competition*. Toronto: Social Science Research Network.

Protsyk, Oleh, and Stela Garaz. 2013. Politicization of Ethnicity in Party Manifestos. *Party Politics* 19 (2): 296–318.

Rhodes, R.A.W., and Vincent Wright. 1987. Introduction. *West European Politics* 10 (4): 1–20.

Rifondazione Comunista. 2001. *Un voto utile per il paese per costruire una sinistra di alternativa e una sinistra plurale*. Roma: Rifondazione Comunista.

Rokkan, Stein, and Derek W. Urwin. 1983. *Economy, Territory, Identity: Politics of West European Peripheries*. London/Beverly Hills: Sage.

Rovny, Jan. 2013. Where Do Radical Right Parties Stand? Position Blurring in Multidimensional Competition. *European Political Science Review* 5 (1): 1–26.

Ruedin, Didier, and Laura Morales. 2017. Estimating Party Positions on Immigration: Assessing the Reliability and Validity of Different Methods. *Party Politics*, First published online June 16, 2017.

Sartori, Giovanni. 1970. Concept Misinformation in Comparative Politics. *The American Political Science Review* 64 (4): 1033–1053.

Schakel, Arjan H. 2009. Explaining Policy Allocation over Governmental Tiers by Identity and Functionality. *Acta Politica* 44 (4): 385–409.

Sinardet, Dave, and Niels Morsink. 2011. *Contamination or Containment? Sub-State Nationalism in Belgian Political Parties' Electoral Manifestos* (not published). Paper Presented at the ECPR General Conference Reykjavik, August 25–27.

Somer-Topcu, Zeynep. 2015. Everything to Everyone: The Electoral Consequences of the Broad-Appeal Strategy in Europe. *American Journal of Political Science* 59 (4): 841–854.

Sorens, Jason. 2009. The Partisan Logic of Decentralization in Europe. *Regional & Federal Studies* 19 (2): 255–272.

Strøm, Kaare. 1990. A Behavioral Theory of Competitive Political Parties. *American Journal of Political Science* 34 (2): 565–598.

Thorlakson, Lori. 2009. Patterns of Party Integration, Influence and Autonomy in Seven Federations. *Party Politics* 15 (2): 157–177.

Toubeau, Simon, and Emanuele Massetti. 2013. The Party Politics of Territorial Reforms in Europe. *West European Politics* 36 (2): 297–316.

Toubeau, Simon, and Markus Wagner. 2015. Explaining Party Positions on Decentralization. *British Journal of Political Science* 45 (1): 97–119.

Tronconi, Filippo. 2009. *I partiti etnoregionalisti. La politica dell'identità territoriale in Europa occidentale*. Bologna: Il Mulino.

Tronconi, Filippo, and Christophe Roux. 2009. The Political Systems of Italian Regions Between State-Wide Logics and Increasing Differentiation. *Modern Italy* 14 (2): 151–166.

Urwin, Derek W. 1983. Harbinger, Fossil or Fleabite? 'Regionalism' and the West European Party Mosaic. In *Western European Party Systems: Continuity and Change*, ed. Hans Daalder and Peter Mair, 221–256. Beverly Hills/London: SAGE Publications.

Van Houten, Pieter. 2009. Multi-Level Relations in Political Parties: A Delegation Approach. *Party Politics* 15 (2): 137–156.

Verge, Tània. 2013. Party Strategies on Territorial Reform: State-Wide Parties and the State of Autonomies in Spain. *West European Politics* 36 (2): 317–337.

Volkens, Andrea. 2001. *Manifesto Coding Instructions*, 1st ed. Berlin: Wissenschaftszentrum Berlin fur Sozialforschung. https://manifesto-project.wzb.eu/down/papers/handbook_2001_version_1.pdf

CHAPTER 2

Setting the Scene: The Direction and Pattern of Decentralization in Italy

The (Never-Ending) Pursuit of Decentralization

Italy represents an interesting case in the study of territorial politics. It is a culturally heterogeneous country with deep economic and social divisions across its territory; as such, throughout its history it has been torn between localism and unity. The country has had to work hard to define relations between the center and the periphery in a way that grants the necessary autonomy to subnational levels while protecting the state from being torn apart by centrifugal forces.

Since Italy's unification, it has experimented with several different forms of territorial organization. It was created as a strongly centralized and unitary state in 1861, then evolved into a regional state after World War II, one that promotes the autonomy of local authorities below the regions, including provinces and municipalities. The reforms of the early 2000s have been referred to as federalist, but with the process unfinished, it is impossible to say with any certainty which direction the country will take in the future.

This chapter illustrates the evolution of the territorial structure of the Republic of Italy by tracing the normative path of its institutional development. This proceeds in two steps: first, this chapter traces the territorial organization of Italy over time and describes its main features in order to assess whether it is moving toward a more federal structure. Second, it analyzes the pattern of policy changes related to territorial reforms over

© The Author(s) 2019
L. Basile, *The Party Politics of Decentralization*, Comparative Territorial Politics, https://doi.org/10.1007/978-3-319-75853-4_2

time to evaluate whether the state has experienced an incremental, gradual decentralist evolution or followed an uneven, intermittent path. The goal is to create a framework for subsequent empirical analysis, which thoroughly examines the role of political parties in the Italian process of decentralization.

Is It Decentralization or Federalism?

Before diving into the official details of the complex evolution of decentralization in Italy, it is useful to introduce some key definitions and features of the prevailing models of territorial organization and the pressures that triggered these processes. This will help not only for using the most appropriate terminology to define the different phases of territorial restructuring in Italy but also for ascertaining the direction in which Italy is currently evolving in this never-ending process.

There is little consensus in the literature about the specific definitions of *federations* and *decentralized states* (Duchacek 1970, 189–191); however, because it is not the purpose of this book to provide a complete review of the scholarly use of these terms, they will be briefly explained and then used pragmatically to provide a meaningful typology of the different forms of state territorial organization. This typology can be built on two dimensions (Table 2.1): first, the direction of the transfer of powers,

Table 2.1 Typology of forms of territorial organization of the state

		Direction of the transfer of powers		
		None	*Top-down*	*Bottom-up*
Dispersion of powers	None	Unitary states		
	Low: administrative functions to subnational levels		Deconcentration	
	Medium: statutory, financial, administrative, legislative competences to subnational levels		Decentralized states	
	High: exclusive legislative competences on some matters to subnational levels		Devolution/ hold-together federations	Coming-together federations

which can be either top-down (from the central government to the subnational levels) or bottom-up (when territorial authorities voluntarily decide to surrender some key functions upward to a central body); and second, the degree of dispersion of powers (ibid.)—namely, the amount and the type of competencies (legislative, administrative, financial, and statutory) granted to the territorial public authorities[1] that are below the central government of the state.

Unitary and Decentralized Systems

In a unitary system, powers and competencies are not shared across territorial authorities; all authority is concentrated at the central, national level. Most of the modern European states created throughout the nineteenth century were unitary, structured without regard for the boundaries of the older national minorities (Bartolini 2005), and reinforced through a constant process of assimilation, homogenization, and integration of the peripheries. These centralizing trends were due in part to the need to ensure generalized economic progress and eliminate socioeconomic inequalities (Duchacek 1970); conventional war also played a part, as states with stronger central authorities were less vulnerable than those in which powers were dispersed regionally (Hooghe et al. 2010).

Following Italy's unification in 1861, large segments of the ruling Piedmontese political elite pursued policies of political centralization, assimilation, and homogenization to better cope with the social, cultural, and economic differences that existed within the new country (Putnam et al. 1993). They prevailed over the federalists, such as Carlo Cattaneo, who imagined the peninsula as a federation of states in the Swiss or American model (Berneri 1970). The ideal of a federal or regionalized Italy was eventually abandoned, paving the way for the creation of a strongly centralized, unitary state under the rule of the Savoy dynasty. This state structure survived two world wars as well as almost 20 years of fascist dictatorship.

"Decentralist," on the other hand, refers to those political systems resulting from top-down, reversible processes of decentralization in which the central government has transferred powers and resources to subnational levels. These systems can be classified further according to the amount and significance of the powers and competencies that have been surrendered downward (Baldi 2006, 16–17). In its weakest form, this process manifests as *deconcentration*: the central state merely assigns administrative functions and responsibilities to peripheral offices across the territory (e.g., prefectures and local agencies of central authority), which nevertheless remain under the supervision of the central authority. States can be called *decentralized* when they transfer increasing amounts of statutory, financial, administrative, and legislative competency to subnational territorial authorities (such as municipalities, provinces, and regions). The literature also refers to *devolution*, an advanced form of decentralization in which subnational levels, such as regions, are endowed with exclusive legislative competencies in specific policy areas and these prerogatives are enshrined in the constitution. The term has become popular since 1997, when the United Kingdom established the Scottish Parliament and the National Assembly for Wales, which have exclusive authority on a number of devolved matters.

Throughout its Republican history, Italy has moved toward a more decentralized structure, surrendering an increasing amount of statutory, administrative, financial, and legislative autonomy to the regions (i.e., the regional state) and granting local authorities like provinces and municipalities increasing administrative and financial responsibility. In the late 1990s, the British experience with devolution began to influence the political debate in Italy: the *Lega Nord* (LN) started promoting enhanced forms of decentralization—for example, a proposed "Parliament of the Padania"[2] that would be similar to the Scottish Parliament and would transfer exclusive legislative authority to the regions in a number of areas (Vandelli 2002). This political debate resulted in a spate of decentralist reforms, though LN's initial reference to devolution now appears to have been more of a simplification than a deliberate attempt to imitate the British form of territorial government (Keating 2009).

Federal Systems

There are two systems of state organization that can broadly be considered federal, though they differ in the purpose and process of their formation.

On the one hand, there are federal systems whose main purpose is to "hold together" communities (Stepan 1998, 6–7). This group includes the Indian constitution of 1950, the Spanish constitution of 1978, and the Belgian constitution of 1993. It can be difficult to clearly distinguish decentralized systems from hold-together federations: as in decentralized systems, hold-together federations originate from a top-down transfer of competencies toward subnational territorial units. This system is typical of those multicultural and deeply divided societies in which unity is easiest to preserve by accommodating some of the autonomy demands of the peripheries and delegating them more power. The main difference lies in the amount of autonomy granted to subnational levels. As Duchacek (1970, 236) observes, quoting Maurice Duverger, "there is no difference in kind, only in degree: decentralization is mitigated federalism; and federalism is a very emphasized decentralization."

On the other hand, there are the "coming-together" federations (Stepan 1998, 6–7). These have emerged from autonomous territorial authorities' voluntary decision to join forces through a bottom-up process to strengthen their security and economic systems without renouncing their sovereignty entirely. These systems are based on an agreement to surrender some key functions upward, such as foreign policy and defense, while retaining the rest. Using a literal interpretation of the term, only these latter forms of territorial government can be correctly called federations; indeed, the word is derived from the Latin word *foedus*, which refers to a pact or alliance among equals (Riker 1975, 99). The most common examples of this kind of federation are the Swiss and American systems; however, even international pacts and regional associations of states, such as the European Union, feature some elements of a federal structure.

Putting aside the differences in their purposes and formation processes, federal systems all share a few defining characteristics (Duchacek 1970; Riker 1975; Stepan 1998; Swenden 2006; Baldi 2006). While this list is far from exhaustive, it serves as a practical guideline for evaluating shifts toward federalism in countries like Italy:

- *The territorial redistribution of powers is constitutionally granted.* Federations, by definition, originate from a formal pact in which the sovereignty of the component units is guaranteed. This formal pact also protects the federation as a whole from dissolution or the unilateral secession of any of its units.
- *Subnational levels are assigned the residual legislative competences, and they are exercised exclusively.* Federal constitutions usually list the matters assigned to the federal government, leaving residual ones to the member states.

- *Subnational units participate in the process of constitutional reform.* The constitution may be amended only with the direct or indirect participation of its constituent units. This point needs to be qualified: Some countries, such as Switzerland, actually require the direct participation of the constituent units (e.g., cantons) in constitutional change.[3] Others, like the German federation, rely on the mediation of a second chamber.
- *At least two orders of government act directly on their citizens and independently of each other.* This can be defined more accurately as self-rule. In other words, there is no interference between the central (federal) and subnational spheres of influence. In a federation, the central government cannot veto the decisions of the other levels, and vice versa.
- *Financial autonomy.* Each tier of authority enjoys full autonomy to directly levy taxes (i.e., taxation power) to finance the policies under its own authority (i.e., spending powers).
- *There is a second chamber that grants equal representation to unequal territorial units.* In the US and Swiss federations, the American Senate and the Swiss Council of State, respectively, grant each state in the United States and canton in Switzerland two members, regardless of their population (with the exception of the half cantons, which have only one deputy each). Such federal chambers directly participate in law making at the central level.
- *There is an independent judicial court (or the provision for a referendum) to rule on the constitutionality of laws made at both central and subcentral levels as well as on disputes concerning the division of powers between tiers of authority.* This last point further underlines the requirement under any federal system that the veto of a decision made on one level of authority can originate only from an independent body not aligned with either level.

This proposed typology outlines a framework that can be used to describe the evolution of territorial administration in Italy. The country moved from a strongly unitary, centralized state toward forms of increasingly decentralized government, culminating in the recent shift toward a federalist structure. As the next sections illustrate in greater detail, this was unequivocally the result of a top-down transfer of powers, and resulted in a profound decentralization that some would classify as a hold-together federation.

Why Do Central Governments Surrender Their Powers?

As discussed in the previous section, except for coming-together federations, most noncentralized territorial structures are born from top-down processes. This begs the question: why would a central government in a unitary state want to waive powers? The thought of surrendering authority downward to peripheries that modern nation states once sought to integrate might seem a little strange. However, at least three main pressures can be identified as the primary triggers of decentralization processes (Schakel 2009a, b).[4]

First, there are *functional pressures*, such as the desire for greater efficiency, a more responsive democracy (Groppi 2007), and greater solidarity between territories. Postwar political systems have expanded the range of services they deliver to citizens in the course of creating the modern welfare state (Hooghe et al. 2010); in the course of this expansion, it has become apparent that the state cannot "do without the division of tasks that is bound to be accompanied by some dispersion of the decision-making authority. ... The reason is simple enough: political rulers can focus on some problems some of the time but cannot focus on all the problems all of the time and in all localities" (Duchacek 1970, 4). Policy making in fields such as education, health, and transportation requires intimate knowledge of the specific needs of each area. Moreover, by distributing competencies across several levels, state structures can share the costs of the administrative and political machinery, enhancing efficiency and ensuring greater flexibility in decision making.

Moving on to the alleged democratizing effects of decentralization, it is argued that the creation of new levels of authority that are closer to citizens opens further spaces for political participation and increases politicians' accountability; furthermore, local pride should theoretically foster more responsible governance (ibid., 14).

The final functional pressure is the desire to develop solidarity among a state's regions. Decentralized policy making can be the best option for dealing with the socioeconomic peculiarities of each area, especially when these areas are characterized by different levels of socioeconomic development. This can allow each region to create policies that better address its own economic needs, while preserving the central government's redistributive role to bridge gaps between poorer and richer regions.

If functional pressures seem to operate "from above," a second decentralizing force is likely to emerge "from below": *identity pressures* (Schakel 2009b). Local traditions and customs have often developed into demands for greater autonomy for ethno-territorial minorities, which have in turn mobilized autonomist movements and parties. These have exerted a considerable influence on central states, and the latter have often sought to accommodate these territorial claims by granting greater autonomy to subnational communities.

Structures of opportunity (Schakel 2009a), which often support processes of territorial dispersion of power, are a third decentralizing force. The creation of the European Union, for example, has created new economic, institutional, and political opportunities for territorial demands (Keating 2008), ranging from the European Regional Development Fund to the empowerment of the Committee of the Regions. Each of these pressures has played a role in the Italian process of decentralization.

This book argues further that political parties have used all of these arguments to justify and frame their stances toward the processes of decentralization and proposals for reform (Chap. 5).

Whither Decentralization? Patterns and Outcomes of the Process of Decentralization in Italy (1948–2017)

Italy's current form of territorial government is dramatically different from what was envisaged in the constitutional charter that went into effect in 1948. The country has undergone an intense process of policy change concerning the distribution of powers, one that is still not finished. This process has mainly concerned the regions, which have been endowed with legislative autonomy, while other territorial authorities (such as the provinces and the municipalities) have been granted only statutory and regulatory powers.[5] Accordingly, the process of decentralization in Italy has been largely a process of regionalization, in which reforms have predominantly concerned this meso-level of authority. The following sections discuss the decentralizing reforms in the Italian Republic's history by examining the gradual shift of autonomy from the central government to the subnational levels, predominantly the regions, over time; when relevant, this includes the reforms that have increased the autonomy of local levels of government. These sections also assess whether this process has been gradual or uneven and examine the direction of this decentralizing process to evaluate whether it is moving toward a federalist or centralized system.

1948–1967: "Frozen" Regionalism

The Constituent Assembly, elected on June 2, 1946, was faced with the task of reordering Italy's government in the aftermath of the Mussolini dictatorship in a way that would both respect the territorial heterogeneity of the country and set up stable and democratic institutions for its rapid recovery. The committee for autonomies, chaired by Christian Democrat Gaspare Ambrosini, drafted provisions on local autonomies and presented them to the second subcommission of the Constitutional Committee on November 13, 1946,[6] chaired by Umberto Terracini (*Partito Comunista Italiano* [PCI]), which was in charge of those articles concerning the organization of the state.

It was clear even then that a decentralized state that granted autonomy to local authorities would be more efficient as well as closer to the differing social and economic realities of the country. The committee for the autonomies therefore proposed the creation of the regions to provide a meso-level structure between the nation and the municipalities.[7] This solution was strongly favored by the Christian Democrats, in part because of a tradition of Catholic regionalism and in part for purely strategic reasons: the *Democrazia Cristiana* (DC) worried that the left would dominate elections at the national level and saw regional autonomy as a sort of bulwark against communist control (Mazzoleni 2009).

When this project was discussed by the second subcommission, however, doubt and dissent emerged. The proposal to create the regions was approved unanimously, with the exception of Umberto Nobile (PCI),[8] but committee members from almost the entire political spectrum expressed concerns about threats this autonomy could pose to national unity, particularly given the separatist tendencies of some autonomist movements (D'Atena 2016, 52).[9] Such fears led to amendments to the original proposal—namely, Article 5 of the Fundamental Principles of the Constitution (see also below). When the discussion of this crucial article moved to the Constituent Assembly, the leaders of the main leftist parties, including Renzo Laconi[10] and Palmiro Togliatti (PCI) and Pietro Nenni (*Partito Socialista Italiano* [PSI]),[11] expressed further concerns about the creation of the regions and the difficulty of reconciling the need for local autonomy with the unity and integrity of the state. Some members of the assembly even proposed an amendment[12] referring to the unity of the state in Article 1 of the Constitution, enshrining this principle alongside the declaration of the Republic as "democratic."

The amendment was withdrawn and replaced by a proposal from republican Tomaso Perassi to insert an article recognizing local autonomies and decentralization in the section on the state's Fundamental Principles, but as a distinct article,[13] which eventually became Article 5:

> *The Republic is one and indivisible. It recognizes and promotes local autonomies, and implements the fullest measure of administrative decentralization in those services which depend on the State. The Republic adapts the principles and methods of its legislation to the requirements of autonomy and decentralization.*[14]

As D'Atena (2016, 51–52) observes, rather than expressing contradictory principles, this article finds an effective equilibrium between national unity and local autonomy and even inspired the Portuguese (1976) and Spanish (1978) constitutions.

In addition to Article 5, the territorial organization of the state was outlined in Articles 114–133, which form Title V of the second part of the Constitution, "Regions, Provinces, and Municipalities." The first issue addressed was the specification of the local autonomies of the state: alongside the municipalities (the main, core units of the country) and the regions (intermediate level between the state and the municipalities) the Constitution created provinces, which were meant to reduce the concentration of authority at the regional level. The final formulation of Article 114 described three equal layers of authority—"The Republic is divided into Regions, Provinces and Municipalities"[15]—though regions were endowed with a qualitatively different kind of autonomy than the other two levels (VV.AA. 2016, 26). This solution was the result of a compromise between the supporters of strong regionalism and those who preferred to limit the powers of the regions to purely administrative ones. This regionalist structure was enshrined in Article 115 of the Constitution: "Regions are constituted as autonomous bodies having their own powers and functions according to the principles established in the Constitution."[16] The article referred to the 15 ordinary regions envisaged by Article 131 of the Constitution and 5 regions endowed with special autonomy (Special Statute Regions) because of their unique social, economic, or cultural conditions (which resulted in a so-called asymmetrical regionalism).

According to Article 116 of the Constitution: "To Sicily, Sardinia, Trentino-Alto Adige, Friuli-Venezia Giulia and Valle d'Aosta are attributed forms and particular conditions of autonomy in accordance with the special statutes adopted through constitutional laws."[17]

The regions' autonomy consisted primarily in the fact that only regions were endowed with legislative autonomy, though within the limits set out in Article 117: "Regions may legislate within the limits of the fundamental principles established by the laws of the State in the following matters, always providing that this legislation does not conflict with the national interest or that of the other Regions."[18] The Constituent Assembly, however, conferred exclusive legislative autonomy only to the *special regions*. The other regions (*ordinary regions*) were endowed only with concurrent legislative autonomy—that is, the power to make laws within the central government's legislative framework—and the power to implement laws, restricted to the matters listed in Article 117, which generally related to issues of local interest. Further limits to the legislative autonomy of the regions were imposed by Article 127 of the Constitution,[19] according to which "every law approved by the regional council should have been communicated to the Commissioner"; the Commissioner was required to sign a new law within 30 days, "except in cases of opposition by the Government of the Republic"; furthermore, the central government could return a law to the regional council if it held that the law exceeded the jurisdiction of the region or conflicted with national interests or those of the other regions. The central government could also request that the Constitutional Court review a law's legitimacy.

Along with their legislative autonomy, regions were granted administrative autonomy by Article 118 of the Constitution[20] in the same areas listed in Article 117 (principle of parallelism), "except in those exclusively of local interest," which could be allocated to the provinces, municipalities, or other bodies; moreover, the state could delegate further administrative functions to the regions.

Article 119 laid out the basis for the financial autonomy of the regions,[21] though it mentioned the need to "coordinate this autonomy with the finances of the state, the provinces and the municipalities." Scholars argue that it was essentially the autonomy to spend and budget state funding; regions could not raise resources or levy taxes themselves.

Finally, the ordinary regions were granted a final element of territorial autonomy—namely statutory autonomy, pursuant to Article 123: "Every region shall have a statute which, in harmony with the Constitution and the laws of the Republic, shall lay down the rules for the internal organization of the Region."[22]

As this account shows, Italy's postwar process of decentralization was largely top-down and centrally guided, with limited scope for the regions to shape the process. And even this attempt at decentralization was further constrained by the fact that, despite the 15 ordinary regions' formal foundation in the Constitution, their actual implementation was delayed for decades, while the special regions and their assemblies were set up immediately. The problem was that, to render the regions operational, the regional councils had to be elected because they were entitled to "exercise the legislative and statutory power attributed to the Regions" (Article 121).[23] According to Article 122 of the Constitution,[24] "the electoral systems, the number and cases of ineligibility and incompatibility or regional councilors," had to be established "by a law of the Republic"; however, the state passed no such law until 1968.

The only law on local autonomy adopted during those 20 years was the so-called Legge Scelba in 1953,[25] concerning (limited) statutory autonomy for the regions and the functions of the regional bodies. The parliamentary debates on the Legge Scelba reveal the underlying tensions among the political forces on the regionalist issue (Chap. 4). The country's main party, the DC, had been strongly regionalist during the Constituent Assembly but became considerably more ambivalent when it became clear that enhanced regional autonomy would have favored the communist and socialist parties, which had strong popular support in the regions of the so-called red belt—Tuscany, Emilia-Romagna, and Umbria. The leftist parties, on the other hand, were initially less enthusiastic about decentralization but gradually became strong supporters.[26] Beyond ideology, there was a political reason for this shift: throughout the First Republic, although the PCI was the second largest party in the country, it was excluded from the government (the so-called *conventio ad excludendum*). The creation of the regions would have allowed the PCI to obtain power, at least in its regional strongholds (see also Chaps. 3 and 4).

Aside from this initial attempt at regionalism and the limited provisions of the Legge Scelba, the regionalist issue played a minor role in the 1950s, eclipsed by the greater urgencies of the postwar recovery and the cold war (Putnam et al. 1985 and Chap. 3). This stalemate, the result of a combination of party politics dynamics and agenda-setting priorities, lasted 20 years. Between 1948 and 1968, Italy remained a unitary, centralized state, with the exception of the five special autonomies.

1968–1977: The Dawn of a Decentralist Era

The situation changed dramatically during Legislature IV (1963–1968), when functional and identity pressures combined with structures of opportunity to create a favorable political scenario for decentralist processes. Following the impressive economic growth of the 1950s and the 1960s, decentralization supporters increasingly advocated for a redistribution of competencies to subnational levels to overcome the inefficiencies of the Italian central bureaucracy. At the same time, the electorate was gradually shifting to the left, where the PCI and PSI were championing the regionalist issue (Putnam et al. 1993).

Neither the DC nor the competing parties could ignore the pressure from the left for decentralization. At the same time, Christian Democrat leader Aldo Moro was paving a way to an "opening to the left" by offering the PSI a place in the government. Moro took advantage of the fact that relations between the PCI and the PSI had grown cooler after the socialists condemned the Soviet invasion of Hungary in 1956, and that under Pietro Nenni the PSI had shown signals of a willingness to collaborate with the DC.[27]

When newly appointed Prime Minister Aldo Moro invited the socialists to join the government in 1963, one of the central points of the coalition agreement struck by the PSI and the DC, as well as with the *Partito Socialista Democratico Italiano* (PSDI), and the *Partito Repubblicano Italiano* (PRI), was the creation of the ordinary regions (Mazzoleni 2009, 137). Although the first Moro government declared its wish to enact "among its first bills, the laws for the institution of the ordinary regions,"[28] it was only in 1968, at the end of the legislative period, that the Parliament approved *legge* (L.) 108/1968;[29] it was only opposed by the rightist *Movimento Sociale Italiano* (MSI), the *Partito Liberale Italiano* (PLI), and the Monarchists (Chap. 4). The first regional elections were finally held on June 7 and 8, 1970, using a proportional voting system. To implement the decentralization of administrative functions, L. 249/1968 was also passed.[30]

However, the drive to reform was not yet spent. L. 281/1970, adopted in the subsequent Legislature V (1968–1972),[31] laid out financial provisions for the implementation of the ordinary regions to ensure they would have the financial resources necessary to function[32]; the law also enabled the government to issue decrees granting the regions the legislative powers (Article 17) provided by Article 117 of the Constitution. These implementing decrees were finally adopted in 1972,[33] signifying a stark policy change in a decentralist direction. In the same year, L. 775/1970 was also approved,[34] enabling the government to issue decrees concerning the reform of state administration, basically amending the above-mentioned L. 249/1968.

Putnam et al. (1985, 51–56) describe this first phase of regionalism as a "minimalist approach." The financial autonomy envisaged by L. 281/1970 set up a system of limited state transfers with no revenue autonomy within the regions, which were given severely limited decisional powers; moreover, the central state further reaffirmed its control over the regions' activity with the creation of the Regional office of the Presidency of the Council and the Government Commissaries (Putnam et al. 1985, 1993; Baldi 2006; Mazzoleni 2009, 138). Neither the regions nor the supporters of regionalization in the central government were satisfied. Nonetheless, these steps toward regionalism, though modest, sowed the seeds for future decentralizing achievements. Once implemented, these "new" institutional authorities began claiming more powers and questioning the constitutionality of state provisions that limited their competencies (Putnam et al. 1985, 68). The central government had taken its first step on the slippery slope of decentralization and could no longer stop what it had begun.

When Legislature VI (1972–1976) took place, there was both political and popular support for the enhanced autonomy of the regions. According to Putnam et al. (1985, 73–74), the DC's poor showing in 1975 regional elections and the extraordinary electoral breakthrough of the left could be interpreted as a demand from Italian citizens to complete the process of decentralization. On July 22, 1975, Parliament passed L. 382/1975.[35] The law directed the government to approve decrees that would completely transfer competencies and administrative functions to the regions in compliance with constitutional provisions. The law also introduced a mechanism for consultation with the regions before the approval of these decrees (Article 8), representing a first step toward intergovernmental cooperation. Presidential decrees no. 616, 617, and 618 (D.P.R.) were finally approved in 1977 and accepted considerable input on the development of the regional functions from the regions themselves (Baldi 2006), especially where it concerned their administrative autonomy.

1978–1995: The Precarious Equilibrium of Italian Regionalism

When the reformist euphoria had passed, the realities of these regionalist reforms largely lagged behind expectations (Bull and Pasquino 2007): the central state kept legislating on issues of regional competence, with the support of the Constitutional Court, and the regions' financial autonomy remained severely constrained, with regional finances still largely dependent on state transfers (Mazzoleni 2009). Overall, the 1980s were a stalemate on territorial reforms, and political parties paid less attention to the issue (Chap. 3).

The only two important advances in this period were the setup of the State-Regions Conference and the passage of a law on the regulation of local autonomies. The State-Regions Conference[36] was created in 1983 and was initially intended as a body to be convened on an ad hoc basis to coordinate the relationship between the central government and the regions and allow the regions to participate in the development of regional policy. It gradually became a permanent institution with a consultative role,[37] though until 1997 its opinion was compulsory only for budget laws and the Economic and Financial Planning Document. This body represented a further element in Italy's "cooperative regionalism," its structure dependent on loyal cooperation between the different layers of authority.

The second advance was the introduction of L. 142/1990,[38] which renewed and strengthened the autonomy of the other subnational levels—namely, provinces and municipalities—by strengthening their statutory and regulatory autonomy.

The precarious equilibrium attained by the process of decentralization in the 1980s, however, would be undone by new political unrest in the early 1990s.[39]

The political system built after 1948, the so-called First Republic, collapsed under a series of corruption scandals that emerged following judicial inquiries, better known as the *Tangentopoli* (Bribesville) scandals. This political turmoil fueled existing popular dissatisfaction with the inefficiencies and clientelism of the state's structures, which were suffering a severe crisis of legitimacy. At the same time, the process of European integration was going further and faster with the Treaty of Maastricht (1992), opening new windows of opportunity to the demands of regionalist actors (Keating 2001; Baldini and Baldi 2014).

Against this backdrop, an autonomist party, claiming the interests of the richer regions of northern Italy, emerged with surprising electoral strength, forcing the entire political system to grapple serious new problems, including the "northern question" (Bulli and Tronconi 2011) and anger with the central government in Rome over state inefficiency. The LN attracted votes from both the left and the right in the northern regions, building a broad electoral constituency. To manage this changing political scenario, the proportional electoral system was replaced with a plurality system in 1994, with 75% of the seats assigned according to a "first past the post" mechanism. The electoral law was dubbed the "Mattarellum" from its rapporteur, Parliament Member Sergio Mattarella.

Along with the crises under way among the old parties, this law marked the beginning of a new phase of Republican history, the "Second Republic." The party system changed profoundly: it moved toward a two-coalition party system, clustered around a center-right pole—led by the newly founded, neo-liberal, conservative party *Forza Italia* (FI)—and a center-left one—led by the heirs of the communist party, the *Partito Democratico della Sinistra* (PDS), then renamed *Democratici di Sinistra* (DS) and, since 2007, the *Partito Democratico* (PD).[40] In this party system, the LN was alternately a partner of center-right coalitions and a third-party outside the coalition game, for example in 1996. Apart from that year, LN's populist rhetoric was close enough to rightist ideology on issues outside decentralization that it was able to form alliances with the center-right *Polo delle Libertà* (PdL) and *Casa delle Libertà* (CdL) as well as with the party *Popolo delle Libertà* (PDL) from 1994 to 2013. Meanwhile, FI, the leading party of the center-right coalition, was a totally new political creation: it was directed entirely by its founder, billionaire tycoon Silvio Berlusconi, and endowed with a flexible programmatic profile without any underlying ideology. This latter quality allowed FI to hold together a coalition that included both the autonomist LN and the rightist nationalist *Alleanza Nazionale* (AN), the heir of the MSI.

In the electoral campaign of 1994, the first held under the new electoral system, the electoral threat posed by the LN, as well as its freedom to work with or sabotage any governing coalition (Massetti and Toubeau 2013, 361), forced the other parties to bring the decentralist issue back into the political discourse; the statewide parties could no longer ignore the autonomist challenge (ibid.; Bull and Pasquino 2007; Mazzoleni 2009; see also Chap. 3). In the end, the center-right coalition, allied with LN, won a majority of seats, but Legislature XII (1994–1996) was too short to carry out any decentralist reforms. The government fell in 1995 when the autonomist coalition partner withdrew its support from Berlusconi's first government and became more radical in its secessionist rhetoric. As a result of what has been called Bossi's *ribaltone* (turnabout or turnover of alliance), the FI and AN did not propose another coalition with the LN in the next election in 1996.

1996–2001: The Decentralist Makeover

In the 1996 elections, which were won by the center-left *Ulivo* coalition led by Romano Prodi, the electoral threat posed by the autonomist movement still played an important role in shaping the agendas of the political parties and bringing attention to decentralization (Mazzoleni 2009; Massetti and Toubeau 2013; see also Chap. 3). The new governing coalition showed strong decentralist inclinations, which were translated into a strong commitment to decentralist reforms throughout Legislature XIII (1996–2001).

A first, albeit somewhat indirect, step in this new process of decentralization was the introduction of a regional tax on productive activities (IRAP, in Italian) with the passage of *decreto legislativo* (D.lgs.) 446/1997.[41] Although deeply controversial on economic grounds, this tax provided the regions with autonomous financial resources, reducing their dependence on state transfers (Baldi 2006, 92). Even greater financial autonomy was achieved three years later with the D.lgs. 56/2000,[42] which was explicitly (and significantly) titled "Rules concerning fiscal federalism." This act laid out plans for a shift from the system of state transfers to a mechanism for regional participation in revenue collection, such as with the VAT and excise tax (ibid.).[43]

The first decisive step toward enhanced decentralization, however, was represented by L. 59/1997, the so-called Bassanini reform.[44] It envisaged, "in compliance with the subsidiary principle," the transfer of "all the administrative functions and tasks concerning the interests and support of the development of the respective communities" to the regions and local authorities, "as well as [those] based in their respective territories" (Article 1 paragraph 2). The reform also made the State-Regions Conference's consultative role permanent rather than ad hoc, and its opinion compulsory for decisions concerning regional interests (Article 8 paragraph 1). In other words, intergovernmental cooperation, one of the defining features of a federation, started to become more institutionalized and would influence decision making more and more over time (Tamburrini 2011). Other laws, such as L. 127/1997 (Bassanini *bis*),[45] also played important roles in the decentralization of the country by thoroughly reforming the functioning of the local authorities (provinces and municipalities). These reforms pushed the process of decentralization further than it had ever gone before by substantially increasing the regions' administrative autonomy, and did it without changing the Constitution.

Nevertheless, it soon became clear that it would not be possible to achieve full-fledged decentralist reform, much less move toward a federalist system, without changing the provisions adopted by the Constitutional Assembly 50 years earlier.

2001: The Watershed Reform of Title V

The time for such a deep policy change was ripe during Legislature XIII, when two watershed constitutional laws were finally approved.

First, *Legge costituzionale* (L. Cost.) 1/1999 made important changes to the regional electoral system and the statutory autonomy of the regions.[46] It modified Articles 121–126 of the Constitution, which concerned the institutional organization of the ordinary regions. The main change was the introduction of direct election of the presidents of the regions, who were also referred to as governors (*governatori*). The political significance of this reform was in the increased stability and democratic legitimacy it conferred on the regional executives. Moreover, the constitutional law endowed the regions with the power to draft their own electoral laws. At the same time, a modification to Article 123 of the Constitution allowed the regions to write their own statutes without state approval through an ordinary legislative process, further increasing their statutory autonomy, though the central government reserved the right to question the constitutionality of these laws before the Constitutional Court.

At the very end of the legislative period, the center-left government radically reformed Title V of the second part of the Constitution with L. Cost. 3/2001.[47] Because the law did not obtain the qualified majority specified by Article 138 paragraph 3 of the Constitution (meaning two-thirds of Parliament), its approval was subject to a confirmatory referendum, which was heavily promoted by those on the center-right opposed to the reform. On October 7, 2001, Italian citizens were called, for the first time in Republican history, to vote on a constitutional law—and in a rather peculiar political context. In the five months that preceded the referendum, the center-right coalition, a renewed alliance between Silvio Berlusconi and the LN, won elections. However, the autonomist party was among the main opponents of the reform, together with its other center-right partners in the PdL, calling it a "useless" or "fake"[48] attempt at federalism, though some in the LN dissented[49] (see also Chap. 4). The reform was finally approved by 64.2% of voters, though with a very low turnout of 34.1%.[50]

The revised Title V was a watershed policy change in the process of decentralization in Italy. Although an exhaustive and detailed description of the reform would go beyond the purposes of this book, a few of its major changes require discussion.

First, it dramatically increased the legislative autonomy of the regions, which were endowed with exclusive legislative powers. In particular, the reform (Article 3) modified Article 117 of the Constitution by inverting the criteria governing the distribution of competencies between the state and the regions, taking inspiration from federal systems.[51] Contrary to the previous arrangement, the revised Article 117 now listed the policy areas in which the state had exclusive legislative power, including foreign and defense policy, immigration, law and order, social security, the environment, finance, electoral law, and judiciary policy. It spelled out areas that would be subject to concurrent legislative authority, in which regions would have the primary legislative power, though within the framework of general principles laid out by the central state; then it gave the regions "exclusive legislative power with respect to any matters not expressly reserved to state law." The revised Article 117 also eliminated the limit of the "national interest," which had constrained regional legislative activity.

Second, it deeply altered the administrative autonomy of the subnational levels. According to the new Article 118 of the Constitution as modified by the reform (Article 4), the municipalities would have the primary responsibility for administrative functions, in compliance with the subsidiary principle, while provinces, metropolitan cities, regions, and the state could play subordinate roles in carrying out these functions. This change implied that all the administrative provisions likely to affect people's lives would be adopted by the authority closest to the citizens.[52]

Third, changes to Article 119 of the Constitution (Article 5) enshrined both the revenue and spending financial autonomy of the subnational levels in the fundamental law, though this constitutional provision has still not been fully implemented (see also below).

Fourth, the reform repealed all those constitutional articles that provided for state control over the administrative and legislative autonomy of the regions (Article 9); it thereby eliminated the position of commissioner of the government (former Article 124 of the Constitution), the legitimacy of control governing the regions' administrative acts (first paragraph of Article 125 of the Constitution), the role of the "limits of the principles laid down by the general laws of the Republic" in determining the function of the subnational authorities (Article 128 of the Constitution), and regional control over the acts of local authorities (Article 130 of the Constitution).

Fifth, according to the new formulation of Article 127 of the Constitution, a region could question the constitutional legitimacy of a state or regional law before the Constitutional Court "when it deems that said law or measure infringes upon its competence" (Article 8).[53]

Finally, a revision to Article 114 of the Constitution (Article 1) put all the local authorities on the same level (institutional equality) so that regions no longer held a position of superiority, creating a "multi-polar architecture" (Baldi 2006, 98) of state power. Some power differences remained: regions were still endowed with exclusive legislative powers, for example. This formulation was unique among European democracies.

2002–2012: The "Rightist Flag" on Decentralization

The profound policy changes initiated by the Bassanini laws in 1997 and completed with the constitutional reform of 2001 were advocated by a center-left coalition. When a center-right coalition took over in Legislature XIV (2001–2006), it tried to put its own stamp on the reform process.

Encouraged by the federalist discourse of its autonomist coalition partner, the government proposed the so-called reform of the reforms, also known by the more British term *devolution*"(Massetti 2012a, b), which was translated into a constitutional law and approved on November 16, 2005 (bill n. 2544-D). As in 2001, it was an intrinsically partisan bill, passed with a relatively narrow majority; and, for the second time in four years, the Italian electorate was asked to vote to confirm a decentralist reform program on June 25 and 26, 2006. This time, however, more than half of eligible citizens turned out (52.46%); and 61.29%[54] voted against the reform, which was eventually rejected. This referendum took place in conditions similar to those of 2001, to the extent that, just two months before, the center-left coalition, which had opposed the reform, had come to power.[55] Scholars have since argued that the constitutional reform of 2006 would hardly have had the federalizing effects intended even if it had passed, as it included several recentralizing measures (Baldi 2006; Massetti 2012a). For instance, although it extended regional competence to include health, education, and local public security, it nevertheless reintroduced the principle of national interest to narrow the regions' legislative autonomy (Article 45). One argument used by supporters of the reform was that it introduced a so-called federal senate through the modification of Articles 56–57 of the Constitution (Articles 1–3). However, despite the federal label used in the bill, the composition of the body proposed was determined according to a principle of proportional representation of the regions based on their population; this is not consistent with the model of federal senates, which ensure equal representation for all of their territorial units regardless of population (Baldi 2006).

The subsequent Legislature XV (2006–2008) was too short to advance further decentralist reforms, but the decentralist drive reemerged in the following Legislature XVI (2008–2013), albeit with less intensity than in the past; the financial crisis overtaking Europe had become the first priority.

The center-right, once again allied with the LN, returned to power in 2008, with the LN emphasizing the issue of fiscal federalism in particular during the campaign (Chap. 3). However, despite apparent consensus among the mainstream parties on the need for genuine fiscal federalism, reform was once again conceptualized according to purely partisan logic (Massetti 2012b). A "fiscal federalism reform" law was adopted by the center-right coalition, with the main opposition party formally abstaining and the *Unione di Centro* (UDC) (Chap. 4) opposing; it passed as L. 42/2009.[56] The main goal of the law was the full implementation of local authorities' revenue and spending autonomy, defined by Article 119 of the Constitution and based on principles of "enhanced administrative, financial, and accounting responsibility of all the levels of governance" (Article 2 paragraph 2a). Municipalities, provinces, and regions would be endowed with their own autonomous resources, though these resources would be at the mercy of the country's principle of solidarity (Article 2 paragraph 2e). Concerning that solidarity, the law called for the creation of an equalization fund (*fondo perequativo*) to support the disadvantaged territories. Moreover, it provided mechanisms to reward or sanction the authorities concerned based on how they exercised their financial autonomy (Article 2 paragraph 2z). The underlying idea was to enhance efficiency and accountability in both the taxation system and public spending at the subnational levels (Scuto 2012).

However, since L. 42/2009 simply enabled the government to pass decrees implementing the reform, the actual policy changes were not immediately visible. In the meantime, the center-right coalition collapsed under the pressure of the scandals surrounding leader Silvio Berlusconi and the burden of the economic crisis. It was replaced by a new government made up of "technocrats" led by Mario Monti, who slowed down the implementation of decentralist reform. This political turmoil, as well as the country's financial concerns and the measures adopted to address them (ibid.), delayed the adoption of the decrees even further.

The early dissolution of Parliament before new elections on February 24 and 25, 2013, further complicated the full implementation of the reform. As of the end of 2017, 11 decrees have been adopted, most of them between 2010 and 2011.[57]

Leaving aside the specifics of such a complex reform program, the process involved represents an interesting example of the gap between political rhetoric and decision making. As Massetti (2012a) argues, one of the main supporters of the reform, the LN, had long championed the fiscal federalism frame and the need to keep resources where they are produced, opposing any form of financial redistribution outside the territory. The autonomist party nevertheless had to take into account the centralist and state-centric positions of its coalition partners, including AN. This tension forced the government to craft a compromise between the drive for autonomy, accountability, and responsiveness at the subnational levels (which was addressed by L. 42/2009) and a need for territorial solidarity (which was strengthened by the D.lgs. 68/2011[58] and D.lgs. 88/2011,[59] the latter explicitly addressing the problems of territorial cohesion and the need to reduce socioeconomic gaps across the regions). The result was a somewhat centralizing solution, with the government retaining the ability to exercise the substitutive power "in case of inertia or non-fulfillment by the public administrations ... in order to avoid the automatic release of the EU funds, the Government, in order to ensure the competitiveness, cohesion and economic unit of the country" (Article 6 paragraph 6 of D.lgs. 88/2011).

2013–2017: The 2016 Referendum: A Backlash Against Decentralization?

According to Carrozza (2017, 101), Italy's process of decentralization can be seen as a sort of inverse parabola. The issue began receiving more attention in the 1970s which built up until the 2001 reform, and then the descent began. The concurrent competencies the reform envisioned required the frequent intervention of the Constitutional Court to address conflicts, which often decided in favor of the state; as discussed, actual implementation of fiscal federalism has long been delayed, and the problems created by the global financial crisis encouraged a return to enhanced state centralization because a stronger state had more tools at its disposal (Romeo 2017). L. Cost. 1/2012, for instance, moved the "harmonization of public budgets" from the concurrent competences to the exclusive state competences.[60]

Against this backdrop, the government of Prime Minister Matteo Renzi, with the support of a center-left majority and the centrist parties, pushed for a far-reaching constitutional reform (referred to as the "Renzi-Boschi reform" from the names of its main proponents),[61] which was approved by Parliament on April 12, 2016. In many respects, it represents an unprecedented attempt to modify the Fundamental Charter. It proposed to repeal 2 articles and to amend 45 articles, though in some cases this was just a matter of rephrasing. Although many changes addressed the state–regions relationship specifically, decentralization was not the core issue of the reform; rather, its framers intended it to be a reform of the state structure as a whole, one whose basic aim was to enhance the efficiency and efficacy of the state machinery and to limit the costs of state institutions. As was the case with the reforms of 2001 and 2006, however, this proposal was unable to achieve the required two-thirds majority in Parliament and thus became a constitutional referendum, which was called on December 4, 2016.

The referendum was preceded by a harsh electoral campaign, which soon turned into a vote on Matteo Renzi's leadership.[62] The reform was eventually rejected by 59.12% of voters, with an exceptionally high turnout (65.48%),[63] and Renzi resigned from office. Since then, nothing has changed in the distribution of competencies between the state and local authorities.

However, it is interesting to look at how the territorial structure of the state would have been affected by this reform had it passed. An examination of the contents of the reform package can help assess whether the process of decentralization in Italy has stopped, reversed course, or merely slowed down.

One core element of the Renzi-Boschi reform was the creation of a Senate of the Regions, made up of 95 representatives of regional and local authorities; 74 would have been elected by the Regional Councils and the Councils of the Autonomous Provinces of Trento and Bolzano from among their own members, while the remaining 21 would be selected by the regions from among their mayors (Article 2). This new Senate would have given voice to the subnational authorities, making the territories more representative (as is typical of federal systems). However, reform proponents devoted more attention to an entirely different modification to the state's structure: the abolition of the so-called perfect bicameralism, or the equality of the functions and competencies held by the Chamber of Deputies and the Senate, respectively. This division of labor has often been blamed as one of the main causes of the system's gridlock and inefficiency. To avoid adding to the problem, the Senate of the Regions would have been endowed with different functions and competencies—for example, it was excluded from votes of confidence and would have carried out the same legislative functions as the Chamber of Deputies in only a limited number of areas, mostly related to territorial issues (Article 10).

The text of the reform also envisaged a deep reform of Title V (Articles 29–36). First and foremost, it eliminated the "concurrent competencies" held by both the state and the regions, removing one of the main causes of state–region constitutional conflict. This would have been achieved through a limited recentralization: some competences would have been returned to the state, such as labor and antitrust policy and strategic infrastructure; moreover, the new Article 117 would have introduced a so-called supremacy clause, according to which the state could intervene in areas of regional competence "when required in order to protect the legal or economic unity of the Republic, or the national interest" (Article 31).

It also removed the requirement of an absolute majority of the Chamber of Deputies to approve laws granting heightened autonomy to the regions pursuant to Article 116 (Article 30). However, it also introduced a requirement that the any such expansions first be assessed to determine how they would affect the state budget.

Finally, the reform would have constitutionally abolished the provinces[64] (Article 29). Once again, supporters of the reform claimed that this would have further limited the costs of the institutions.

The proposed reform was thus a compromise between centralist and decentralist forces. Regardless of the final result of the referendum, its structure shows the underlying tensions in the Italian political system on the issue of decentralization. The state has not been able to appease local authorities' demands for increased autonomy, and it has not yet fully complied with the subsidiary principle, though the Senate of the Regions represented an attempt in that direction. At the same time, the global financial crisis laid bare the weaknesses in the current regional structure, burdened as it is with conflicting competencies and regional inefficiencies, especially in the south. These facts have led to a centripetal movement back toward recentralization, rendering the future of Italian decentralization uncertain.

The Long and Winding Road Toward Decentralization

This chapter illustrated the Italian process of decentralization throughout its Republican history. This should set the scene for an account of the party politics dynamics that have featured prominently in this process. Nevertheless, two questions can already be answered based on these narratives.

The first one concerns the direction of the Italian path to decentralization: Is it moving toward federalism, as is often claimed in the political discourse and rhetoric? Is Italy an inherently centralistic state disguised as a decentralized one, or did the country pursue genuine regionalist and federalist ambitions?

The second question concerns the pattern taken by the evolution of the decentralizing process in Italy: Was it a regular, continuous, incremental process of policy change? Or has it been fitful, featuring peaks of change alternated by phases of stalemate?

Italy: A Centralist Tradition with Federalist Ambitions

Notwithstanding some prominent federalist voices, Italy was built in the nineteenth century as an intrinsically unitary state and preserved this structure until the fascist dictatorship. In the aftermath of World War II, the Constituent Assembly was actually pressed by two competing needs: on the one hand, the urgencies of the postwar recovery, which required a strong decisional center; on the other hand, the country's recent experience of totalitarian control. Either way, the country's cultural and socio-economic heterogeneity made the question of territorial autonomy essential from the beginning.

To address this tension, the Constitution of 1948 provided the foundations for a potential regionalist state, which nevertheless remained largely on paper until the 1960s. Since then, functional and identity pressures, as well as structures of political opportunity, have played a major role in shaping both party attitudes and institutional behavior, which have been translated into decentralist reforms that have transformed the unitary state into a decentralized one, articulated across three levels of authority: the regions, the provinces, and the municipalities. It is therefore undeniable that Italy has actually moved away from a centralist system, although it is questionable whether it has moved toward a federal structure. Indeed, the "federal" label, especially since the 1990s, has increasingly become a sort of *passe-partout* word, which has even been adopted in the official legislation to define the output of these reforms. At the same time, the process of transferring powers and competencies downward has been largely directed by the central government, in a top-down fashion, although the system's actual evolution as a hold-together federalism, rather than a process of mere decentralization, is not so clear.

Table 2.2 presents a checklist of some of the main defining features of a federal system, as outlined before (see section "Federal Systems"), and compares them to the territorial organization of the Italian political system over time by considering the main reforming phases as critical junctures.

From 1948 to 1970, the lack of implementation of the constitutional provisions of Title V resulted in a de facto centralized, unitary state, which remained frozen until the late 1960s.

The state structure that emerged from the two key decentralist reforms of 1968–1972 and 1975–1977 was a regional one, in which regions were increasingly granted legislative, administrative, and statutory autonomy through the gradual implementation of the constitutional provisions set out in 1948. The local autonomy enshrined in the Constitution was finally realized, though the subnational levels themselves were not given a role in the processes of constitutional reform apart from the opportunity to promote a constitutional referendum by five regional councils (Article 138 of the Constitution).

Table 2.2 Italy's forms of territorial structure (1948–2017)

Defining features of federations	*1948–1967*	*1968–1996*	*1997–2017*
Constitutionally granted autonomy of territorial levels	Formal	Yes	Yes
Residuals legislative competences assigned to subcentral units	No	No	Yes
Participation of territorial subunits in constitutional reform	No	No	No
Self-rule	No	Limited	Yes
Financial autonomy	No	Limited	Yes
Second chamber representing territorial subnational units	No	No	No
Independent judicial court	No	Yes	Yes
Form of state organization	Unitary centralized	Regional state	Decentralized multipolar system

Despite the formulation of Article 57 of the Constitution specifying that "the Senate is elected on a regional basis," there is no second chamber to represent the local autonomies, and the only regional element in the election of the Senate is the definition of the constituencies (Groppi 2007).

The legislative autonomy of the regions has also been somewhat narrowed by Article 117 of the Constitution, which limits their autonomy to the "fundamental principles established by the state" and allows its exercise only when it does not "conflict with the national interest"; furthermore, unlike in a federal system, the constitution allows for concurrent legislative competence on only a restricted set of issues, leaving all that remain to the central state.

Moreover, in its old formulation, Article 127 paragraph 3 of the Constitution called for regional laws to require the signature of the government commissioner and envisaged a sort of veto power to be wielded by the central government, which could return regional laws to the regional council if they were deemed to "exceed the jurisdiction of the region" or conflict with the "national interests." Other constitutional provisions (Articles 115, 124, 125 paragraph 1, and 128–130 of the Constitution) further constrained regional (as well as local) self-rule with a system of state controls over the acts of local authorities. Pursuant to the old Article 119 of the Constitution, their financial autonomy was rather limited, and they had only authority over spending and budgets. In this system, there were no provisions for intergovernmental cooperation among state and subnational units.

Finally, Article 127 of the Constitution gave the central government the ability to question the legitimacy of state laws before the Constitutional Court, while no similar power was enshrined in the Constitution for the regions. This system remained mostly unaltered for almost 20-years; until the mid-1990s there was limited policy change on decentralization.

After the decentralist thrust of 1997–2001 followed by the "fiscal federalism" reform of 2009, the structure of the country changed dramatically. It became more decentralized and "multipolar" (Baldi 2006, 98), featuring equal institutional roles for three tiers of authority: regions, provinces and municipalities. The regions have maintained a preeminent role in the state architecture, not least because this is the only subnational level that exercises legislative autonomy. The new Title V adopted a few ideal or typical elements of federal systems, such as the criterion by which legislative competences are redistributed; state competences are now enumerated, while the remainder are left to the regions. The self-rule of the subnational units has also increased, as provisions for state control over the acts of local authorities were repealed by the 2001 reform. The subnational units' financial autonomy, further strengthened by the 2009 reform, now includes the regions' revenue autonomy, even if, as previously discussed, the 2009 reform's actual federalism is somewhat controversial. Finally, the new formulation of Article 127 of the Constitution explicitly allows the regions to question the constitutional legitimacy of state laws before the Constitutional Court "when it deems that [they] infringe upon its competence."

Notwithstanding the two attempted constitutional reforms in 2006 and 2016, however, the Italian system has never introduced any kind of federal senate; moreover, the regions' participation in the process of constitutional reform has still been limited to the promotion of a constitutional referendum.

The Italian process of decentralization has been the result of a fundamental tension between contrasting forces: on the one hand the pressures for further decentralization to enhance efficiency and democracy, on the other hand the country's centralist culture (Massetti 2012b) and desire to preserve its hard-won national unity. Within this framework, a complex intertwining of institutional obstacles and political ambivalence have combined to make the path toward decentralization long and uneven. Federalist ambitions have so far largely remained nothing but rhetoric, and the country seems unsure which direction it even wishes to pursue—whether toward federalism or centralization.

Italian Gridlock: The "Punctuated Equilibrium" of Agenda-Setting

The historical account of the Italian process of decentralization provided in the previous sections shows short periods of dramatic change (1968–1972; 1975–1977; 1997–2001; 2009) and long periods of stability.

This pattern of policy change can be empirically measured with an index (Decentralization Index, or DI) made up of further indexes of the legislative, statutory, administrative, and financial autonomy of the local authorities. For the indexes on statutory, administrative, and financial autonomy, a yearly score is assigned,[65] ranging from "no autonomy at all" (0) to "high autonomy" (3); in the case of administrative autonomy, the score of "subsidiarity" has been added (4), which indicates an articulation of this autonomy for all the subnational levels. The design of these indexes is based on the literature and a qualitative assessment of the legislation. Legislative autonomy is calculated by considering, for each year, whether a set of policy areas (e.g., education, health, and tourism) is under exclusive state competence (0), concurrent competences (1), or exclusive regional competence (2); the mean of the yearly score of all the policy areas gives the index of legislative autonomy. The final DI is then the result of the sum of these four indexes on autonomy.[66]

The score on administrative autonomy was 0 from 1948 to 1972. Then, following the adoption of the legislative decrees of 1972, the level of administrative autonomy increased by one point and increased further after the decrees of 1977. It remained stable until 1997, when it became 3 (full autonomy) thanks to the Bassanini reform of 1997 (implemented in 1998); and it finally increased to 4 after the introduction of the subsidiary principle in 2001.

Statutory autonomy increased by two points in 1970, an effect of L. 1084/1970 repealing the former Legge Scelba, and remained stable until 1999 when L. Cost. 1/1999 eliminated the provision of Article 123 of the Constitution concerning the "approval by state law" of regional statutes.

Moving to legislative autonomy, the first increase, although modest, occurred in 1972 with the implementing decrees that transferred competencies to regions, pursuant to Article 117 of the Constitution. The areas of regional legislative competence remained unaltered until the watershed reform of 2001, when several matters became of exclusively regional competence. A small decline of legislative autonomy was registered in 2012, when L. Cost. 1/2012 shifted the "harmonization of public budgets" from a concurrent competence back to an exclusive state competence.

Measuring financial autonomy is less straightforward because the impact of the reform concerned has often been controversial. However, a qualitative assessment of the legislation can be supported by official statistics on financial autonomy and fiscal autonomy. The reform of 1970, which earmarked some tax revenue for the regional budgets, had a somewhat limited impact. Financial autonomy considerably increased between 1997 and 2000 following the implementing decrees of L. 662/1996 instituting the IRAP/IRPEF and the D.lgs. 56/2000. However, though the constitutional reform of 2001 enshrined the principle of financial autonomy in the Constitution and L. 42/2009 introduced so-called fiscal federalism, the actual impact of these reforms on the financial autonomy of the regions has been somewhat limited; some commentators even argue that it was reduced during the economic crisis.

The aggregate index obtained by combining these four indexes can be used to demonstrate annual policy change and is calculated as the yearly percentage variation of that index from 1948 to 2017. For instance, until 1970 the degree of decentralization of the country remained somewhat constant; accordingly, the yearly variation on the DI was zero.[67] After the first phase of reforms, the score of the DI shifted from 0 to 2, producing a percentage increase of 200% in 1970. It follows a period of further increase in subnational autonomy until 1977. Then, the DI remains stable throughout the 1980s, with no variation whatsoever. Other peaks of change occurred in 1997 (16% percentage increase) and subsequent years, until 2001 (17% percentage increase). Then, the index did not vary anymore, except for the little recentralization that occurred with the above-mentioned L. Cost. 1/2012.

As Fig. 2.1 shows, the frequency distribution of annual policy change on decentralization is strongly leptokurtic, exhibiting kurtosis equal to 56.77

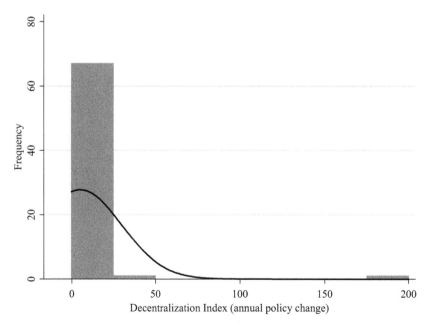

Fig. 2.1 Frequency distribution of annual policy change on decentralization

(N = 69), as most of the yearly scores cluster around a value of 0 (which means that little or no policy change occurred in those years), while the few outbursts of change result in the long tail of the distribution. It also displays positive skewness, as the process of decentralization has been progressively and incrementally oriented to the achievement of greater degree of regional autonomy, with no backsliding a part from that of 2012.

This confirms the scenario that emerged from the historical timeline of decentralization in Italy, with a few key moments of profound transformation of the state's territorial structure followed by long periods in which it remained generally unaltered. These "critical junctures" of change correspond to the lowest bars of the histogram, showing the development of the subnational autonomy over the time span considered, such as the 200% increase after the first phase of reforms and the 17% increase after the reform of 2001.

This intermittent flow of policy change might be dismissed as just another example of inefficiency and gridlock in the Italian political system. However, the punctuated equilibrium (PE) theory (Baumgartner and Jones 1993, 2009) suggests an alternative perspective to look at the process of policy change, one focusing on the role of political actors in setting the policy agenda as a precondition for reforms.

The following chapters seek to account for the political dynamics that underlie the process of policy change on decentralization by focusing on the key protagonists of Italian policy making: the political parties.

Notes

1. VV.AA (2016, 9) define territorial public authorities as "those authorities for which the territory does not only set the boundaries of the scope of competence and efficacy of the powers, but it is also its constitutive element." In Italy, they are the regions, the provinces, the municipalities, and the metropolitan areas.
2. *Padania* is the term used by LN propaganda to identify the alleged "territory of the north" that should be made autonomous from the rest of Italy. Ideally, it should include the regions in the area surrounding the Po River (the Padana Valley)—namely, Lombardy, Veneto, Piedmont, Liguria, and Emilia Romagna. The boundaries of such territory, however, are far from straightforward.
3. The Swiss constitution specifies that any constitutional change must be approved by a referendum, which must obtain both the majority of votes of the people and the majority of the cantons.

4. These pressures and triggering forces constitute the theoretical bases on which the list of frames, included in the coding scheme for content analysis, has been drawn (on frames, see also Chaps. 1 and 5).
5. VV.AA (2016, 27) classify the juridical autonomy of the territorial authorities as normative (further distinguished as legislative, statutory, and regulatory) administrative, and financial.
6. The Constitutional Commission was composed of 75 members of the Constituent Assembly ("Committee of Seventy-Five"), elected by and among its members, with the task of designing and proposing a draft constitution to be debated by the Assembly. The Committee of Seventy-Five was further divided into three subcommissions, each of them dealing with different aspects of the constitutional charter (Rights and Obligations of the Citizens; Constitutional Organization of the State, including the regions; Economic and Social Relations). A drafting committee ("Committee of Eighteen") had the task of harmonizing and coordinating the work of the subcommittees. The committee for the autonomies was composed of members of the second subcommittee and was charged with the task of working specifically on local autonomies. http://archivio.camera.it/patrimonio/archivi_della_transizione_costituzionale_1944_1948/atc04/documento/CD1700000456; http://en.camera.it/4?scheda_informazioni=24 (accessed October, 30 2017).
7. All the debates of the Constituent Assembly are drawn from the online archives at www.nascitacostituzione.it
8. This incident was recalled by Meuccio Ruini at the June 12, 1947, meeting of the Constituent Assembly to discuss Article 5.
9. During the second subcommission's discussion of Article 5, Umberto Nobile recalled the declaration of Andrea Finocchiaro Aprile, member of the Sicilian Independentist Movement, who argued that Sicilian autonomy was the first step toward the full independence of the island (meeting of November 15, 1946, of the second subcommission).
10. During the March 5, 1947, session of the Constituent Assembly, Renzo Laconi declared that "… it is undeniable that the creation of the region … allows [us] to bring the state machinery closer to the people and put it under its control. … But there is no doubt that when Regions are endowed with powers that go beyond the administrative ones … we cannot support it anymore. … We think it will lead to the fragmentation of the legislative power, to the disaggregation of the unity of the country" (pp. 1785–1786).
11. For the declarations of Pietro Nenni and Palmiro Togliatti on concerns related to the regions and the likely threat to the unity of the nation, see also the debate on Article 5 at the meetings of the Constituent Assembly on, respectively, March 10 and 11, 1947.

12. Amendment proposed by the socialists Angelo Carboni, Carlo Ruggiero, Luigi Preti, Giovanni Cartia, and Danilo Paris (session on March 22, 1947).
13. Meeting of March 24, 1947.
14. All the translations of the articles of the Italian Constitution that are still in force, when not specified otherwise, are taken from the translations provided by the website of the Italian Senate: www.senato.it/documenti/repository/istituzione/costituzione_inglese.pdf
15. This article was amended by Legge costituzionale (L.Cost.) October 18, 2001, n. 3. The translation of this version of this article of the Constitution of 1948 is taken from CODICES, the InfoBase on Constitutional Case Law of the Venice Commission. This source has been used for the translation of those articles that are no longer in force, when not indicated otherwise: www.codices.coe.int/NXT/gateway.dll?f=templates&fn=default.htm
16. Repealed by L. Cost. 3/2001.
17. In 1948, four constitutional laws set up the special regions—namely, Sicily, Sardinia, Trentino-Alto Adige, and Valle d'Aosta—pursuant to Article 116 of the Constitution. The fifth Special Statute Region, Friuli Venezia Giulia, was acknowledged with Legge costituzionale January 31, 1963, n. 1. Article 116 of the Constitution was amended by L. Cost. 3/2001.
18. Amended by L. Cost. 3/2001.
19. Amended by L. Cost. 3/2001.
20. Amended by L. Cost. 3/2001.
21. Amended by L. Cost. 3/2001.
22. Amended by L. Cost. 1/1999 and L. Cost. 3/2001.
23. Amended by L. Cost. 1/1999.
24. Amended by L. Cost. 1/1999.
25. Legge February 10, 1953, n. 62 "Constitution and functioning of the regional bodies." It was mostly repealed by Legge December 23, 1970, n. 1084.
26. Declaration of Giulio Turchi (PCI) at the meeting of the Chamber of Deputy on November 22, 1951 (Atti Parlamentari, 33392): "You [Christian Democrats] were strongly regionalists … until you were afraid that the development of the political events within and outside the country could bring you to a position of control and opposition and not of government; … you did not officially deny the regionalist position … and this is proven by the fact that we are voting on this law … but you deprived the regions as much as you could, to reduce it as a sort of big province, subjected to the will of the government."
27. The convergence of the PSI with the DC and its simultaneous estrangement from the PCI were first announced during the XXXII Congress of the PSI, held in Venice in 1957 and further affirmed at the XXXIV

Congress in Milan in 1961 (see www.dellarepubblica.it/congressi-psi/xxxii-congresso-venezia-6-10-febbraio-1957 and www.dellarepubblica.it/congressi-psi/xxxiv-congresso-milano-16-18-marzo-1961).
28. In the "Communication of the Government" in the meeting of the Senate on December 12, 1963 (Atti Parlamentari, 3954), the appointed Prime Minister Moro stated that the priorities of the new government included "the creation of the ordinary regions, a highest form of autonomy and moderation of the central power of the state ...," while also pointing out that "this reform would be difficult to implement in a political situation with no consistent majority to bear the burden of this innovation, namely avoiding the risk of dissolution of the state."
29. Legge February 17, 1968, n. 108 "Rules for the elections of the Regional Councils of the Ordinary Regions."
30. Legge March 18, 1968, n. 249 "Delegation to Government for the reorder of the State Administration, decentralization of the functions and the redefinition of the careers and retributions for state employees."
31. Legge May 16, 1970, n. 281 "Financial measures for the implementation of the Ordinary Regions."
32. They were essentially state transfers, as the law did not envisage any autonomous taxation power for the region, which had no income of its own.
33. Decreti del Presidente della Repubblica (DPR) N. 1-11 of 1972.
34. Legge October 28, 1970, n. 775 "Modifications and integrations to Legge 18 marzo 1968, n. 249." The law tasked the government with adopting decrees concerning the reordering of the central and peripheral administrations, taking into account the transfer of functions from the state to the regions.
35. Legge July 22, 1975, n. 382 "Norms on the regional rules and organization of public administration."
36. Decreto del Presidente del Consiglio dei Ministri October 12, 1983. More information on this institutional body is available on the State-Regions Conference website: http://www.statoregioni.it.
37. Article 12 of Legge August 23, 1988, n. 400 "Discipline of the Government activity and regulation of the Presidency of the Council of Ministers."
38. Legge June 8, 1990, n. 142 "Regulation of local autonomies."
39. In this period, other, minor reforms were adopted, such as one concerning the direct election of mayors (Legge March 25, 1993, n. 81 "Direct election of the mayor, president of the Province, of the Municipal Council and Provincial Council") and another implementing a new electoral law in the regions (Legge February 23, 1995, n. 43 "New dispositions for the election of the Ordinary Regions," also referred to as "Legge Tatarella"); the latter, however, was gradually replaced by statutes from the regions themselves, which now have the power to autonomously approve their own

electoral laws, pursuant to Article 122 of the Constitution, as amended by L. Cost. 1/1999 (see also below).
40. The PD was created after the DS merged with the centrist Democracy Is Freedom—The Daisy (heir to the Italian's People Party, which was created in its turn after a split within the left wing of the DC).
41. Decreto legislativo December 15, 1997, n. 446 "Institution of the regional tax on the productive activities, revision of the tax brackets, and Irpef deduction and institution of a regional personal income tax, as well as reorganization of discipline on local taxation" based on delegating law Legge December 23, 1996, n. 662 "Measures of rationalization of public finance."
42. Decreto legislativo February 18, 2000, n. 56 "Dispositions concerning fiscal federalism, pursuant to article 10 of Legge 13 maggio 1999, n. 133." Based on Legge May 13, 1999, n. 133 "Rules concerning the equalization, rationalization and fiscal federalism."
43. However, the decisional role of the state still remains relevant to the extent that the latter establishes the quotas for regional participation.
44. Legge March 15, 1997, n. 59 "Delegation to the Government for the transfer of functions and tasks to the regions and local authorities, for the reform of Public Administration and the administrative simplification." It was implemented with the Decreto Legislativo March 31, 1998, n. 112 "Transfer of functions and tasks to the regions and local authorities, pursuant to chapter I Legge 15 marzo 1997 n. 59."
45. Legge May 15, 1997, n. 127 "Urgent measures for the simplification of the administrative activity and of the decisional and control procedures."
46. Legge costituzionale November 22, 1999, n. 1 "Norms concerning the direct election of the President of the Regional Giunta and the statutory autonomy of the Regions."
47. Passed by Parliament on March 8, 2001, it was then adopted after the approval with Constitutional Referendum as Legge costituzionale October 18, 2001, n. 3 "Amendments to the Title V of part second of the Constitution."
48. Useless reform is the definition adopted by the governor of Veneto, Giancarlo Galan of the Casa delle Libertà ("Referendum inutile, non cambia nulla. Meglio la mia proposta di Statuto" in Corriere della Sera, October 8, 2001); likewise, the then-LN deputy Roberto Maroni defined it a fake reform ("Un referendum respingerà questo falso federalismo" in La Padania, March 7, 2001).
49. Not all the center-right politicians, however, shared this perspective on the reform. Roberto Formigoni, for instance, who was then the center-right governor of the northern region of Lombardy, supported the yes camp

("Formigoni: Sì al referendum ma niente guerre di religione" in La Repubblica of October 5, 2001).
50. Electoral data available at http://elezionistorico.interno.it/index.php?tpe l=F&dtel=07/10/2001&tpa=I&tpe=A&lev0=0&levsut0=0&es0=S&ms=S. Unlike for abrogative referenda, for confirmatory referenda it is not necessary to achieve a quorum of voters to validate a consultation.
51. It has been observed, however, that this distribution is far from clear and unambiguous. For instance, D'Atena (2006) argues that the field of education has been both an exclusive state competence and a concurrent one: the boundary between "general norms on education" (a state competence) and "education, without infringement of the autonomy of schools and other institutions, and with the exception of vocational training" (a matter of concurrent legislation) is difficult to define. The Constitutional Court, moreover, has contributed to these with its somewhat "creative" jurisprudence.
52. The reform also modified the so-called principle of parallelism of the functions, according to which regions could exert administrative powers in the matters where they had legislative (concurrent) competency. The new Article 118 established the primary administrative roles of the municipalities regardless of the distribution of competencies set by Article 117 Constitution.
53. Before then, however, regions might raise the question of constitutionality anyway, according to Article 2 of the Legge costituzionale February 9, 1948, n. 1.
54. http://elezionistorico.interno.it/index.php?tpel=F&dtel=25/06/2006&tpa=I&tpe=A&lev0=0&levsut0=0&es0=S&ms=S.
55. It should be pointed out that the since the 2006 election the electoral system has returned to the proportional rule.
56. Legge May 5, 2009 n. 42 "Delegation to Government on fiscal federalism, implementing article 119 of the Constitution."
57. An updated account of the process of implementation is provided on the Italian Parliament's website, www.parlamento.it/parlam/leggi/deleghe/09042ld.htm (accessed November 1, 2017).
58. Decreto Legislativo May 6, 2011, no. 68 "Norms concerning the revenue autonomy of the Ordinary Regions and the Provinces, as well as the determination of the costs and standard needs of the health sector."
59. Decreto Legislativo May 31, 2011, n. 88 "Norms concerning additional resources and special intervention for the removal of socio-economic gaps, pursuant to article 16 of the Legge 5 maggio 2009, n. 42."
60. Legge costituzionale April 20, 2012, n. 1 "Introduction of the principle of the balance of budget in the Constitution."

61. Legge costituzionale 16A03075 "Norms for the abolition of the perfect bicameralism, reduction of the number of parliamentarians, reduction of the costs of functioning of the institutions, abolition of the CNEL and reform of Title V of the second part of the Constitution."
62. Indeed, several commentators have pointed out that Renzi personalized this referendum when he announced that he would resign in the case of rejection.
63. http://elezionistorico.interno.it/index.php?tpel=F&dtel=04/12/2016 &tpa=Y&tpe=A&lev0=0&levsut0=0&es0=N&ms=S (accessed on November 1, 2017).
64. It should be stated that Legge April 7, 2014 n. 56 ("Legge Delrio") had already changed the role of the provinces, which were now second-order administrative authorities. Provincial Councils are no longer directly elected. It also turned some provinces into metropolitan areas.
65. This index considers the main subnational levels to be regions, which can be granted financial, administrative, legislative, and statutory powers; and municipalities and provinces (reformed with L. 56/2014), which can be granted financial and administrative autonomy.
66. The final index, obtained by adding up all the scores, shows a positive and significant correlation with the Regional Autonomist Index (RAI), which measures the autonomy of the subnational levels in 81 countries over the period 1950–2010 (Schakel 2009a; Hooghe et al. 2010, 2016) (Pearson pairwise correlation values r (63) = .99, $p < .001$). This correlation confirms the validity of the score used in this research.
67. Because dividing a number by zero is impossible, all values of DI were raised by 1 point to obtain valid values of the annual percentage change.

References

Baldi, Brunetta. 2006. *Regioni e federalismo. L'Italia e l'Europa*. Bologna: CLUEB.

Baldini, Gianfranco, and Brunetta Baldi. 2014. Decentralization in Italy and the Troubles of Federalization. *Regional & Federal Studies* 24 (1): 87–108.

Bartolini, Stefano. 2005. *Restructuring Europe: Centre Formation, System Building, and Political Structuring Between the Nation State and the European Union*. Oxford: Oxford University Press.

Baumgartner, Frank R., and Bryan D. Jones. 1993. *Agendas and Instability in American Politics*. Chicago: University of Chicago Press.

———. 2009. *Agendas and Instability in American Politics*. 2nd ed. Chicago: University of Chicago Press.

Berneri, Camillo. 1970. *Carlo Cattaneo federalista*. Pistoia: Edizioni RL.

Bull, Martin, and Gianfranco Pasquino. 2007. A Long Quest in Vain: Institutional Reforms in Italy. *West European Politics* 30 (4): 670–691.
Bulli, Giorgia, and Filippo Tronconi. 2011. The Lega Nord. In *From Protest to Power: Autonomist Parties and the Challenges of Representation*, ed. Anwen Elias and Filippo Tronconi, 51–74. Wien: Wilhelm Braumüller.
Carrozza, Paolo. 2017. The Paradoxes of the Constitutional Reform. *The Italian Law Journal*, Special Issue: 91–103.
D'Atena, Antonio. 2006. Giustizia Costituzionale e Autonomie Regionali. In Tema Di Applicazione Del Nuovo Titolo V. In *Corte Costituzionale e Processo Costituzionale. Nell'esperienza Della Rivista «Giurisprudenza Costituzionale» per Il Cinquantesimo Anniversario*, ed. Alessandro Pace, 270–285. Milano: Giuffrè Editore.
———. 2016. *Tra autonomia e neocentralismo: Verso una nuova stagione del regionalismo italiano?* Torino: Giappichelli Editore.
Duchacek, Ivo D. 1970. *Comparative Federalism: The Territorial Dimension of Politics*. New York: Holt, Rinehart and Winston.
Groppi, Tania. 2007. L'evoluzione Della Forma Di Stato in Italia: Uno Stato Regionale Senz'anima? 4. Federalismi.it.
Hooghe, Liesbet, Gary N. Marks, and Arjan H. Schakel. 2010. *The Rise of Regional Authority: A Comparative Study of 42 Democracies*. 1st ed. London/New York: Routledge.
Hooghe, Liesbet, Gary Marks, Arjan H. Schakel, Sandra Chapman-Osterkatz, Sandra Niedzwiecki, and Sarah Shair-Rosenfield. 2016. *Measuring Regional Authority. Volume I: A Postfunctionalist Theory of Governance*. Oxford: Oxford University Press.
Keating, Michael. 2001. *Plurinational Democracy: Stateless Nations in a Post-Sovereignty Era: Stateless Nations in a Post-Sovereignty Era*. Oxford: Oxford University Press.
———. 2008. Thirty Years of Territorial Politics. *West European Politics* 31 (1–2): 60–81.
———. 2009. *Second Round Reform. Devolution and Constitutional Reform in the United Kingdom, Spain and Italy*. SSRN Scholarly Paper ID 1550951. Rochester: Social Science Research Network.
Massetti, Emanuele. 2012a. La Riforma Federale: La Fine Dell'inizio o L'inizio Della Fine? In *Politica in Italia. Edizione 2012*, ed. Anna Bosco and Duncan McDonnell, 141–160. Bologna: Il Mulino.
———. 2012b. Federal Reform: The End of the Beginning or the Beginning of the End? *Italian Politics* 27 (1): 137–154.
Massetti, Emanuele, and Simon Toubeau. 2013. Sailing with Northern Winds: Party Politics and Federal Reforms in Italy. *West European Politics* 36 (2): 359–381.
Mazzoleni, Martino. 2009. The Italian Regionalisation: A Story of Partisan Logics. *Modern Italy* 14 (2): 135–150.

Mazzoleni Martino. 2009. The Saliency of Regionalization in Party Systems: A Comparative Analysis of Regional Decentralization in Party Manifestos. *Party Politics* 15 (2): 199–218.

Putnam, Robert D., Robert Leonardi, Raffaella Nanetti, and Istituto Carlo Cattaneo. 1985. *La pianta e le radici: il radicamento dell'istituto regionale nel sistema politico italiano*. Bologna: Il Mulino.

Putnam, Robert D., Robert Leonardi, and Raffaella Y. Nanetti. 1993. *Making Democracy Work: Civic Traditions in Modern Italy*. Princeton: Princeton University Press.

Riker, William H. 1975. Federalism. In *The Handbook of Political Science, Volume V: Government Institutions and Processes*, ed. Fred I. Greenstein and Nelson Polsby, 93–172. Reading: Addison Wesley.

Romeo, Graziella. 2017. The Italian Constitutional Reform of 2016: An 'Exercise' of Change at the Crossroad Between Constitutional Maintenance and Innovation. *The Italian Law Journal*, Special Issue: 31–48.

Schakel, Arjan H. 2009a. *A Postfunctionalist Theory of Regional Government—An Inquiry into Regional Authority and Regional Policy Provision*. Amsterdam: Vrije Universiteit Amsterdam.

———. 2009b. Explaining Policy Allocation over Governmental Tiers by Identity and Functionality. *Acta Politica* 44 (4): 385–409.

Scuto, Filippo. 2012. Il Federalismo Fiscale a Tre Anni Dalla Legge N. 42: Questioni Aperte E Possibili Sviluppi Di Una Riforma Ancora Incompleta. Centro Studi Sul Federalismo.

Stepan, Alfred. 1998. Democrazia E Federalismo. Un'analisi Comparata. *Rivista Italiana Di Scienza Politica* XXVIII (1): 5–53.

Swenden, W. 2006. *Federalism and Regionalism in Western Europe: A Comparative and Thematic Analysis*. Houndmills/Basingstoke: Palgrave Macmillan.

Tamburrini, Valentina. 2011. I Raccordi Cooperativi Nel Biennio 2008–2009: Il Ruolo Della Conferenza Stato-Regioni. In *Sesto Rapporto Sullo Stato Del Regionalismo in Italia*, ed. Antonio D'Atena. Milano: Giuffrè Editore.

Vandelli, Luciano. 2002. *Devolution e altre storie: paradossi, ambiguità e rischi di un progetto politico*. Bologna: Il Mulino.

VV.AA. 2016. *Compendio di diritto regionale e degli enti locali*. 18th ed. Napoli: Edizioni Giuridiche Simone.

CHAPTER 3

Salience: Putting Decentralization on the Agenda: The Role of Political Parties

The Process of Decentralization Between Deep-Rooted Obstacles and Agenda-Setting Dynamics

Over the 70 years of its Republican history, Italy has been a more or less permanent "work in progress" (Bull and Pasquino 2007; Farinelli and Massetti 2011, 687); it has rarely managed to make its political system efficient or accountable. This unfinished quality applies to several long-awaited reforms, including the differentiation of the competencies of the two parliamentary chambers, the strengthening of the prime minister's office, and reforms to the judicial system and the country's electoral law. Last but not least, there is the issue of the redistribution of competencies across territorial levels.

Scholars have already identified the main causes of the country's enduring deadlock and its inability to complete any significant systemic transformation. These include the fragmentation of the party system and the related weakness of the governments it produces; cumbersome legislative procedures (Fabbrini 2013); and the absence of a political class holding a clear, long-term blueprint for systemic reform (Bull and Pasquino 2007, 671). Despite these hurdles, Italian institutions have undergone profound changes and dramatic reforms over the years, even if the deep-rooted, institutional difficulties of the system are likely to leave these reforms frustratingly incomplete (ibid.).

© The Author(s) 2019
L. Basile, *The Party Politics of Decentralization*, Comparative Territorial Politics, https://doi.org/10.1007/978-3-319-75853-4_3

The process of decentralization is a perfect example of this pattern of upheaval, as it lacks a definitive, clear, and complete resolution. As described in Chap. 2, it has followed a somewhat uneven pattern, featuring short periods of intense reform activity followed by long intervals of deadlock. It took 20 years for Parliament to adopt laws to implement the ordinary regions; over the 50 years that followed, a number of laws and one constitutional reform (and two failed attempts) have not been yet able to clearly define the territorial structure of the country, leaving it dangling between its federalist ambitions and its centripetal temptations.

This is usually explained as yet another example of the country's structural inefficiencies. However, the punctuated equilibrium (PE) theory (Baumgartner and Jones 1993, 2009) suggests a less critical interpretation of the uneven and troubled process of decentralization. It posits that policy making, at least in some policy areas, is often characterized by long periods of stability, "punctuated" by outbursts of change, which are then followed by further long periods of equilibrium. This is due to the fact that political systems have a potentially endless number of issues to address, forcing political actors to select those they will pay attention to and put on the policy agenda. Policy change can occur only during those windows when an issue has seized the attention of political actors (Green-Pedersen and Walgrave 2014).

This argument recalls Carmines and Stimson's (1993) definition of *issue competition* as the struggle among political actors to decide which issues enter the political agenda. The use of words such as *competition* and *struggle* is not accidental: the authors, by adopting an evolutionary perspective founded in biological theory, conceive of issue competition as a process of "natural selection." According to their argument, issues originate when they emerge in the larger society, having won a harsh battle to become political priorities. The authors consider this process of issue origination a product of complex environmental dynamics that are difficult to study, much less predict; indeed, they choose to focus on what comes after an issue has achieved prominence—that is, the development of the issue or, in their words, "how do some issues thrive against the heavy odds of competition for scarce attention" (ibid., 153). Even after they are selected, issues must continue "fighting" with other issues to preserve their place in the political agenda.

The agenda-setting literature studies precisely those actors, mechanisms, and dynamics that allow an issue to seize the attention of political actors and rise in the political agenda, triggering policy change (Jones and

Baumgartner 2005). This area of research has developed furthest in the United States, and its main theories are modeled on that political system; as a result, relatively limited attention has been paid to the role of political parties in the so-called politics of attention because they play a limited role in US politics compared to interest groups, think tanks, and policy entrepreneurs (Baumgartner et al. 2006). However, in a parliamentary system like Italy's, the central role of political parties cannot be ignored (Green-Pedersen 2007).

This chapter applies an agenda-setting approach to explain the uneven path of decentralist reforms in Italy by focusing on the role of political parties and their politics of attention on decentralist issues. Adopting this perspective to explain policy change (and its obstacles) should not be seen as an attempt to shift blame from the above-mentioned deeply rooted causes of gridlock; however, it offers an alternative, complementary interpretation of the process of policy change, one that focuses on the dynamics of party competition, in keeping with this book's goal of telling the story of the Italian process of decentralization from the backstage of politics.

This study uses a model that describes party strategies as the simultaneous communication of three messages—namely salience, position, and frame (Chap. 1). This chapter deals with the first component of party strategy, salience, defined here as a political party's decision to pay attention to a policy issue or not; in other words, the decision to make an issue a part of its agenda. Using the agenda-setting approach, this chapter then examines whether a policy change on decentralization actually occurred after it achieved simultaneous prominence in the agendas of the majority of the political parties, and thus across the entire political spectrum.

After assessing the impact of the (party) politics of attention on the process of reform, this chapter then moves to inevitable follow-up questions: why and how did the party system decide to pay more attention to an issue at a given point in time? Which actors, if any, drove this process?

To address these questions, this chapter attempts to explain the dynamics of party competition that are likely to influence the agenda of the parties; in particular, it looks at those actors that are able to promote a specific issue and, under specific circumstances, compel other parties to pay attention to it as well. The ultimate goal of this analysis is to suggest a theoretical model for the analysis of policy change, one that points out the role that political parties and party competition play in triggering reforms through their impact on the party system agenda.

Do Parties Have an Impact on Decentralist Reforms? An Agenda-Based Model of Policy Change

Whose Attention Deserves Attention?

Baumgartner and Jones (1993, 2009) described the punctuated equilibrium framework of policy change as featuring brief, dramatic outbursts of change followed by long periods of stalemate. The authors argue (Jones and Baumgartner 2005) that when such a pattern is present the amount of annual policy change will be empirically represented by a leptokurtic distribution—that is, a distribution in which most of the data points are clustered around a single point, resulting in a high peak. If one graphs the amount of annual policy change in a PE scenario with a histogram, most of the yearly scores will cluster around a value of zero, indicating little or no policy change, which will form the central peak of the value distribution; on the other hand, the occasional punctuations of policy change will result in the long tails (Baumgartner et al. 2006, 2009). This is exactly the pattern of distribution found when plotting the Italian process of policy change on the territorial dimension, which featured at least three key periods of change (1968–1977, 1997–2001, and 2009) followed by long periods of stalemate (see Fig. 2.1).

This raises the question of why policy change, at least in some areas, is so intermittent and uneven. As has been previously argued, part of the explanation lies in the structural and institutional frictions of the political system; the Italian process of decentralization provides an outstanding example of these counterbalancing forces.

There is, however, an alternative explanation, one that might provide more insight than a broad reference to systemic inefficiencies. In this alternative (yet complementary) explanation, which appears often in the agenda-setting literature, a PE-like scenario is the most likely result of the "bounded rationality" of the decision makers: since these decision makers can pay attention to only a limited number of issues at a time, they have to ignore most policy areas and include only a few in the policy agenda. Policy change will therefore only occur in those issue areas that, at a given point in time, get decision makers' attention (ibid., 960). Going a step further with this argument, the agenda-setting literature seeks to explain the mechanisms and processes that cause shifts in attention to policy issues—that is, the "politics of attention" (Jones and Baumgartner 2005).

Most of the agenda-setting theories meant to explain attention shifts and related policy changes, however, are hardly applicable to parliamentary systems like the Italian one. Indeed, as mentioned earlier, because these theories developed predominantly in the United States, they focus on those actors and dynamics that reflect the peculiarities of that political system, in which the role of parties is less significant than in the parliamentary systems of Europe. In parliamentary systems, however, the parties play a crucial role in the dynamics of policy change and reform.

Italy represents a good example of a multiparty, parliamentary system in which parties have always exerted a strong influence over political institutions and decision making, an influence that was reduced but not eliminated by the electoral and political changes of the early 1990s (Fabbrini 2009). As Bull and Pasquino (2007, 671) point out, in Italy "reforms were generally dictated by the need of parties themselves, or at least they were not willing to tolerate reforms which might undermine their own bases." Paraphrasing an old saying, this argument could be summarized as "not a reform stirs but political parties will it." Indeed, the crucial role parties play in shaping the reforming process was emphasized by then-president of the Republic Francesco Cossiga in his often-cited message to Parliament on June 26, 1991. In his controversial message, the president rebuked Italian parties for failing to translate popular demands for change into reforms.[1]

Within this framework, the Italian process of decentralization has been shaped by partisan logic too (Mazzoleni 2009b): "regional matters tended often to become bargaining points between the parties at [the] national level" (Bull and Pasquino 2007, 682).

Working under the assumption that political parties matter, recent comparative approaches have sought to adapt the insights of agenda-setting literature to the European parliamentary systems (Green-Pedersen 2007) by emphasizing the role of political parties and party competition in the process. The most interesting contributions in this direction are the studies that have tested the "mandate theory" by adopting a policy-agenda approach. The mandate theory, originally formulated in the context of the US case, argues that party agendas are likely to influence the legislative agenda in that "the electoral program of the winning party gets translated into government policy" (Budge and Hofferbert 1990, 112). Agenda-based approaches to the mandate theory, which have focused on both majoritarian parliamentary systems like the United Kingdom (Froio et al. 2016) and multiparty parliamentary systems with coalition governments like Italy (Borghetto et al. 2014), have challenged this argument, showing that external pressures like the impact of mass media and public opinion, as well as institutional frictions, weaken the connection between a party's electoral pledges and its actual policy making.

Both the original mandate theory and the policy-agenda approaches focus on the electoral platforms of governing parties,[2] as their main research question is whether parties fulfill their electoral pledges once in government by translating their policy priorities into legislative priorities. They compare different issues at the same time, assessing the likelihood that any given issue among several that come up during an electoral campaign will eventually become the subject of legislation. The implicit assumption of all of these studies is that an issue can be only present or absent in a party manifesto, and it is merely this presence or absence that warrants scrutiny.

As the following sections illustrate, however, there are cases in which a policy issue, like decentralization, is always present in the majority of party manifestos, those of the governing parties and those of the opposition parties, and the relevant question is not *whether* parties pay attention to the issue, but *how much* attention they pay. The argument presented here is that *variation of the salience* of the issue of decentralization in party agendas is likely to have an impact on the future legislative agenda. Once this argument is established, this work will then explore whether and to what extent the dynamics of party competition are likely to influence such variations in attention—and, as a result, the prospective for policy making—by paying more attention to issues that would have otherwise been neglected.

It's the Party System, Not the Party!

To better understand the argument and finally bring parties into the agenda-setting approach (as well as examine their influence on the initiation of policy reforms), it is useful to first make a distinction between the individual party agendas and the *party system agenda* (PSA) (Green-Pedersen 2007; Green-Pedersen and Krogstrup 2008; Green-Pedersen and Mortensen 2010). Individual parties have their own agendas, meaning their ideological platforms in which they decide whether and how much attention to pay to certain issues (i.e., salience) for both ideological and strategic reasons. At the same time, parties are part of a broader party system with an agenda of its own—the PSA, which in turn is shaped and defined by the parties themselves. The PSA can be defined as the hierarchy of issues that, at any given point in time, are established among the parties of a political system; in other words, it is the set of policy priorities recognized at the systemic level, a set determined by the sum of the choices of the individual parties and their strategic interactions (Green-Pedersen and Mortensen 2010). Each party tries to ensure that the issues it emphasizes the most in its own agenda are at the top of the PSA, for ideological reasons, electoral reasons, or both, by deciding its own policy priorities (ibid.).

The process of deciding which issues to prioritize is one of the many forums in which the parties compete with each other (Chap. 1). As Steenbergen and Scott (2004, 167) argue, "[P]arty competition often takes the form of a battle over agenda control. Parties try to affect the issues that are on the agenda, by selectively emphasizing those issues that are favorable to them ... and de-emphasizing those that are unfavorable. Thus, party competition involves the definition of the political space—i.e. what is salient and what is not".

Parties will seek to prioritize those issues that are more favorable to them, while pursuing their preferred policy direction on those issues (Chap. 4) and setting the terms of debate (Chap. 5). Success in this competition largely depends on a combination of variables, including external events, the party's electoral strength, and the way in which the party frames the issues and, of course, on the dynamics of party competition. Whatever the reason for the successful party's victory, placing an issue at the top of the PSA will have crucial effects on both policy and party competition. An issue's prominent position on the agenda will actually increase its chances of being included in the decision-making agenda and eventually achieving policy change. Moreover, if the latter occurs, the "proponent party" will likely take credit for it, assuming the change goes in the party's preferred direction, in order to gain electoral advantages in the following elections at the expense of the other parties.

Against this backdrop, let's see how party competition represents a crucial tool for understanding how the PSA is determined, how its priorities are defined, and how policy change is triggered.

First, issues are usually introduced into the party competition by the proponent parties that champion them, either for ideological reasons (parties as policy seekers) or because they hope to win the support of the electorate as a reward for decision making in that area (parties as vote seekers) (Basile 2016, 12); the two motivations can obviously also coexist. When competing parties realize that a proponent party has strong chances of succeeding in elections, they are forced to make a decision on the issues it has championed, one that minimizes their potential loss of votes to the proponent party. First, they can ignore it, although this strategy can be costly if it means leaving a potentially appealing issue to competing actors (neglecting strategy); second, they can recognize and emphasize the issue by accommodating the same policy solutions promoted by the proponent party (accommodative strategy); and third, they can take the issue up, but oppose the proponent party's solutions (adversarial strategy)[3] (Meguid 2005, 2008; see also Chap. 4). When most of the parties within a system opt for the two latter strategies of party competition, the intensity of political debate on the issue is heightened, further contributing to its rise to the top of the PSA. Once an issue has reached a high position within the PSA, the governing party (or the coalition parties in coalition governments) cannot ignore it any longer in their actual policy making, increasing the likelihood of policy change even further.

Of course, the process described above is purely theoretical; a policy issue can be promoted by more than one party at a time, and many contextual factors, such as crises, media coverage, and shifting public opinion (Froio et al. 2016) interact to affect the political debate and the legislative agenda beyond parties' electoral pledges. However, despite the potentially unlimited complexities of the actual dynamics of issue attention, this model provides a theoretical framework for investigating the impact of political parties and party competition on agenda setting and policy change.

Party Competition and Policy Change in the Italian Process of Decentralization

The theoretical model outlined above represents a useful framework for formulating two baseline hypotheses to explain the role and impact of party competition on the uneven and intermittent process of decentralization in Italy.

The first hypothesis posits that "major decentralist reforms in Italy occurred in those legislatures that were preceded by electoral campaigns in which decentralist issues were highly salient in the PSA, to the extent that most political parties paid significant amounts of attention to them" (H1: the politics of attention hypothesis). In other words, reforms took place only after parties made this issue hot in the political debate. This hypothesis, as already observed, relies on the assumption that the process of decentralization in Italy followed a PE pattern—that is, an uneven path featuring short outbursts of change followed by long periods of stalemate.

If such a relationship between party system attention and policy change is found, the follow-up question would be, Who drives the PSA's attention on decentralization? Accordingly, the analysis will shift to the dynamics of party competition that are likely to favor the rise of an issue in the PSA. As already argued, party competition over issues is based predominantly on the dynamics and interactions between a proponent party and its competitors, which decide to take up a certain policy dimension when dismissing it could prove costly in electoral terms. In the case of decentralization in Italy, the role of proponent party was played mostly by a specific group of niche actors (Meguid 2005, 2008)—namely the autonomist parties, whose very raison d'être consists of demands for greater autonomy for the subnational levels.

In Italy, autonomist parties have contested elections since the creation of the Republic, including the *Partito Sardo d'Azione, the Südtiroler Volkspartei,* and the *Union Valdôtaine.* However, the *Lega Nord* (LN), which emerged in the early 1990s, can be considered the first autonomist party to obtain a significant share of votes at the state level, compete for governing positions, and pose a serious electoral threat to the other national statewide parties. Nonetheless, even before the rise of the LN, other political actors, including the Italian communist and socialist parties, championed the issue of decentralist reform, in part because they had strategic interests in the creation of subnational levels of administration (Alonso 2012).

Based on these arguments, the second hypothesis posits that: "the issue of decentralization rose in the PSA in parallel with the electoral success of the parties—both leftist and autonomist—that have promoted decentralizing reforms in their own agendas" (H2: the entrepreneurial agent hypothesis).

Change Requires Salience

The first hypothesis argues that decentralist reforms in Italy occurred in those legislatures that were preceded by electoral campaigns in which this issue was particularly high in the PSA. Accordingly, the overall salience, at the system level, of decentralization is the main independent variable, which should have an impact on policy change, which is therefore the dependent variable.

The TERRISS Dataset contains information on the emphasis each party placed on the decentralist issues, measured as the percentage of quasi-sentences related to the subject from each party's entire manifesto (the salience;

Chap. 1). The amount of attention paid to decentralist issues in the PSA during a given election is calculated as the median[4] of the salience of decentralization in party manifestos. High median values of the salience in the PSA indicate that during that election most parties paid a significant amount of attention to decentralist issues, fostering political debate on it at the party system level. Policy change, meanwhile, is measured in terms of both legislative and substantial change. Legislative change is assessed by examining the reforms adopted in each legislature, according to the account provided in Chap. 2, distinguishing between major reforms (those that had a significant impact on the process of decentralization) and minor reforms (including legislative acts with limited impact on decentralization). Substantial change, on the other hand, evaluates the degree of decentralization achieved after each reform and is measured according to the Decentralization Index (DI) (Chap. 2). The need for this distinction is straightforward: the adoption of laws and decrees regarding decentralization does not immediately produce concrete autonomy for the subnational levels, and it takes time before institutions and actors adapt themselves to new rules.

How Much Is Enough?

The first hypothesis asserts that the main explanatory factor of policy change is shifts in the amount of attention paid to decentralization; it is implicitly assumed that this issue has always been present in the PSA, varying only in the degree of significance. This is in line with the extant literature (Putnam et al. 1993; Mazzoleni 2009a, b; Massetti and Toubeau 2013), according to which Italian political debate has always addressed issues related to the reorganization of the state's territorial structure.

Nonetheless, a topic's presence within the PSA is not a binary condition; it remains necessary to determine a threshold of attention that indicates that an issue is relevant to the agenda and among the political system's top priorities. In other words, how much party attention is enough to consider an issue highly ranked in the PSA? Before examining the impact of the variation of salience in the PSA on policy change, this study will make a brief preliminary aside to determine a yardstick for relevance and evaluate whether and to what extent the issue has actually been present in the agenda of the individual parties, as well as in the PSA as a whole, in each electoral campaign from 1948 onward.

The literature has not yet provided common parameters to establish how much attention is enough to consider an issue relevant, and setting any threshold of relevance necessarily implies a certain degree of arbitrariness. According to Alonso (2012, 67), a minimum value of 2% salience in a manifesto can render an issue relevant,[5] and a salience score above 4% in manifestos indicates a high amount of attention.

TERRISS Dataset shows that only 18 out of 120 coded documents contain no statement related to territorial issues at all, while in about 70% of the manifestos they have a salience score above 2%. The median salience of this issue in the entire corpus analyzed is 3.3%, while the mean is 4.4%, with a standard deviation of 5.7%. Values range from (apart from zero salience) 0.2% for the joint document of *Centro Cristian Democratico* (CCD), and *Cristiani Democratici Uniti* (CDU) of 1996 to 41% for the programmatic document of LN 2008. Moreover, party manifestos included statements on regions and local authorities since the first elections of the Italian Republic in 1948. Thus it can be said that the issue of decentralization has been relevant in Italian party manifestos in general over the entire period considered.

A synoptic map of the salience of decentralization in Italian manifestos can be obtained by recoding the salience score into a categorical variable. This study set the boundaries for each category by considering the median and the percentiles as parameters, while a separate group includes those manifestos that pay an exceptionally high amount of attention to decentralization, which are considered outliers.[6] Based on this recoding, while 15% of the documents neglect the issue entirely, more than half of the documents display a somewhat high amount of attention, with 25% (n = 30) of the documents displaying "medium-high" salience (values between 3.3% and 5.7%), 20.8% (n = 25) displaying "high" salience (values between 5.7% and 11.9%), and 4.2% (n = 5) being outliers (values above 11.9%). On the lower end, 25% (n = 30) of the documents feature "medium-low" attention (from 1.5% to 3.3%), and 10% (n = 12) feature "low attention" (from 0.1% to 1.5%).

These findings reveal that decentralization has featured in most party manifestos over the entire time span considered, with most documents displaying a somewhat high degree of salience of this policy dimension; only a few parties ignored it entirely. With this background on the salience of decentralization in party manifestos complete, the analysis can now shift to the system level in order to address the first hypothesis: how much attention did decentralization receive at the party system level in elections from 1948 onward? And did that level of attention vary over time in parallel with the uneven path of reform?

Did the Party System Agenda Prompt Decentralist Reform?

The box and whisker plot (Fig. 3.1) shows the variation of median salience over all the electoral campaigns[7] that have taken place in the history of the Italian Republic as well as the range of salience scores—that is, the cohesion among parties on the amount of attention paid to decentralization. It is evident that the level of attention paid to decentralization has not been consistent over time at the party system level.

To test the assumption of H1, these variations should be compared to progress made on reforms.

A Gradual Rise in Attention as a Prelude to Major Reforms

On the eve of Legislature I (1946–1953), all parties except the *Partito Liberale Italiano* (PLI) and the *Movimento Sociale Italiano* (MSI)

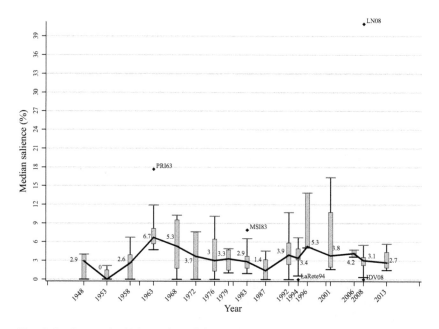

Fig. 3.1 Box and whiskers plot of the median value of salience of decentralization in Italian party manifestos for each election (1948–2013) (%)

(salience score 0) included statements on decentralization in their manifestos, resulting in an overall median salience of 2.9%, with percentages of attention ranging from 2.9% for the *Democrazia Cristiana* (DC) and the *Partito Socialista dei Lavoratori Italiani* (PSLI) to 4% for the *Partito Repubblicano Italiano* (PRI). These statements were mostly vague references to the need for actual implementation of the autonomy of the municipalities (*Fronte Democratico Popolare* [FDP], which was a joint federation between the *Partito Comunista Italiano* [PCI] and the *Partito Socialista Italiano* [PSI]); to "the division of competencies across the state, the regions, and the municipalities" (PRI 1948); or to the "increase of the regional life, especially in the *Mezzogiorno*" (DC 1948). This lack of a clear blueprint for how to actually implement Title V of the Constitution resulted in limited legislative activity on decentralization and the meager autonomy granted to local authorities by L. 62/1953 (Legge Scelba; see also Chap. 2).

This was the prelude to a period of widespread neglect of this topic; in fact, its median attention in the PSA dropped to 0% in 1953. Apart from the PLI and MSI, which were firmly against the regional structure (Chap. 4), the PSI was the only party to mention the need to "fully and effectively implement the Special Statutes of Sicily and Sardinia" (PSI 1953) in its manifesto. Amid general silence from the main political forces, the project of reforming the territorial structure of the country sunk into oblivion and was not addressed at all in Legislature II (1953–1958).

At the end of the 1950s, however, the time was ripe for renewed interest in the regions and the process of decentralizing the country. As argued in Chap. 2, there were several functional pressures that triggered a desire for greater autonomy for local authorities, among them the drive to overcome the inefficiency of the central state. Moreover, the administrative elections of the 1950s revealed strong electoral support for the leftist parties, especially in some areas of the country that would gain governing authority if the regions were finally implemented.

Reflecting this new scenario, the median attention paid in 1958 elections rose up to 2.6%, ranging from 2.3% for the MSI to 6.8% for the PSI, which strongly advocated the "rapid adoption of the necessary laws to implement regions in the entire nation," which were defined as an "essential instrument for the democratic development of the country" (PSI 1958). Likewise, the PCI demanded the fulfillment of the constitutional provisions concerning the regions, and the PRI was also a passionate supporter of decentralist claims. Nonetheless, the DC, which considerably increased its share of the votes in the election, paid limited attention to the financial autonomy of the local authorities; and with the main governing party showing little interest, no significant action was taken on territorial reform between 1958 and 1963.

The scenario changed dramatically in the elections of 1963, in which parties generally paid a high amount of attention to decentralist issues, with a median salience of 6.7% and a percentage increase of 158% from the previous election. No party among those that entered Parliament in that period ignored the topic of decentralization, with salience scores among the parties ranging from 4.7% for the PLI to 17.6% for the PRI. The PCI strongly called for the "urgent implementation of the ordinary regions" (PCI 1963), with an electoral manifesto that also included explicit references to the competencies of the local authorities concerning agriculture and health. The PSI also devoted a large part of its manifesto to the topic, rebuking the DC for its failure to comply with the political commitments it had made with the PSI itself to adopt a law creating the ordinary regions; the party actually made this an essential condition for any further coalition agreement with the DC.

In light of this pressure from the left, the DC could not neglect the issue anymore, and announced its support for "the greatest form of autonomy envisaged by our Constitution, namely the regions, corresponding to our original insight," while to "this reform, which has not been abandoned[,] ... it should be applied that criterion of prudent gradualism that should underlie the full implementation of the Constitution, albeit necessary" (DC 1963). With its usual rhetorical strategy, which often used a wait-and-see approach, the DC acknowledged the need for prompt reform, although under "conditions of real political stability." The impressive rise of the issue of decentralization in the PSA was not in vain, as it presaged the adoption of L. 108/1968 on the implementation of the regions at the end of Legislature IV (1963–1968). This law represented an important, albeit not sufficient, step toward decentralization, and decentralist parties kept their attention focused on the issue to ensure adequate follow-up to this preliminary reform. As a result, in the 1968 electoral campaign the overall salience of the issue remained somewhat high (with a median salience of 5.3%), with a 21% decrease from 1963 as well as a less cohesive pattern of salience among parties (with values ranging from 1.8% for the PCI to 10.3% for the MSI and with the *Partito Socialista Italiano di Unità Proletaria* [PSIUP] ignoring the issue entirely). The PCI, one of the most passionate supporters of the reform, seemed to pay less attention to the regions than in the previous election (1.8%; see also following sections), though it firmly called for their implementation "with no more delays, by 1969" (PCI 1968). The regionalist front was nevertheless well represented by the PSI, which was then allied with the *Partito Socialista Democratico Italiano* (PSDI) to form the *Partito Socialista Unificato* (PSU). The PSU paid a high amount of attention to the issue, with 5.2% of its statements referring to decentralization and the need to spur on the reform process. At the same time, in response to the reformist dynamism of the main political parties, the MSI—the fiercest opponent of the regions—also paid increased attention to this issue (10.3%). The relevance of decentralization in the PSA actually resulted in a season of intense reforms, which reached its peak with L. 281/1970 and the adoption of the related implementing decrees in 1972.

The 1970s saw a decrease in the overall attention paid to decentralization, although it remained a relevant issue at the system level. In 1972 the median salience of the issue was 3.7%, with a percentage change of −31% from 1968 (with values ranging from 1.7% for the PRI to 7.6% for the PCI and the DC). The main advocates of decentralization, such as the PCI and the PSI, still kept a high amount of attention focused on it, devoting 7.6% and 5.7% of their statements to the topic, respectively. They called for the complete and full implementation of the regions, which was still largely a work in progress whose outcomes were far from clear. At the same time, the DC also devoted a large part of its manifesto to the topic (7.6%), acknowledging the need to complete the reform process begun in 1968. The consistent amount of attention the parties devoted to decentralization on the eve of Legislature VI (1972–1976) led to the major reform adopted with L. 382/1975 (though it was actually implemented only in the following legislature, with the decrees of 1977). It is interesting that the two fiercest opponents of regionalism, the MSI and the PLI, completely ignored the issue that year.

The Years of Gridlock

With the constitutional provisions finally implemented, the thrust of reform began losing steam. In the elections of 1976, the median attention paid to the issue of decentralization in the PSA was 3%, an 18% decrease from the previous election, with values ranging from 0.5% for the *Democrazia Proletaria* (DEM.PROL.) to 10.1% for the DC. The most prominent voices were the main governing party, the DC (10%), and the main opposition party, the PCI (6.4%). Both programs emphasized the need to concretely empower the regions once the reforms were finally adopted. The DC's manifesto, for instance, listed the interventions necessary to complete the transfer of autonomy to the regions in the areas of education, culture, and health. Moreover, it claimed credit for the progress achieved with the reforms of the 1968–1975 period: "Legislature VI has seen the program of the DC and of the Government concerning the creation of the regional legislation largely met," while also reinforcing the need to "rapidly implement the legislative delegation pursuant to L. 382/1975" (DC 1976). Likewise, the PSI, with 8.4% of its electoral program devoted to the regions, pointed out the need to address "the very serious problem of the finances of the local authorities" and the "full implementation of the regional legislation" (PSI 1976). Similar claims were also made by the PCI, although it also blamed the DC for not having accomplished the reform of the regions' financial autonomy and for its "resistance to go ahead in the process of the reforms and autonomies, to the full development of the regions" (PCI 1976). Other parties like the MSI completely ignored the issue, while still others paid it little attention, such as the Democrazia Proletaria DEM. PROL. (0.5%) and the PLI (1.3%).

As these examples show, the main concern at the time was the need to translate the legislative changes made on decentralization between 1968 and 1975 into substantial change. With this focus on implementing existing laws, there was a considerable increase in the autonomy of the local authorities during Legislature VII (1976–1979), mostly due to the implementing decrees of 1977 and the regions' achieving financial autonomy. This progress is also shown by the DI, which increased one point during this legislature (from 4.3 in 1976 to 5.3 in 1979).

The salience of decentralization in the PSA remained almost stable in 1979 (3.3%, a percentage increase of 9 from 1976). Unlike in previous elections, there was no significant difference between the parties in the amount of attention they paid to the territorial issue: no party's manifesto devoted more than 5% of its statements to the territorial issue (PSDI), and the PRI manifesto mentioned it the least, at 1.1%. During that electoral campaign, the DC devoted 4.1% of its manifesto to reminding voters about its leading role in the process of decentralization, saying the "implementation of L. 382/1975 ... remain[s] one of the main qualifying aspects of the regionalist vocation of the DC"; as for the controversies surrounding the reforms, it maintained that they were mostly due to the "lack of some framework laws postponed to a later time whose adoption we have hoped to achieve since the very beginning of the new legislature."

The main governing party was aware of the need to practically implement the laws and decrees that had already been adopted and strengthen the financial autonomy of the local authorities (DC 1979). The PCI (salience 4.7%) blamed centralist tendencies for constraining the full autonomy of the regions and municipalities and supported enhanced efforts to empower local authorities. Similar claims were made by the PSI (salience 2.1%): "it should be overcome this stalemate, by allowing regions to fully carry out their tasks"; the socialists also called for the "rapid adoption of the framework laws to complete the process of decentralization initiated with Law 382/1975" (PSI 1979). Notwithstanding these claims, however, it was evident that the "regionalist euphoria" that had taken hold of the parties was starting to diminish and that it was no longer an attractive issue for party competition.

In the 1983 elections, attention paid to decentralization dropped to 2.9%. Salience was low among most of the parties individually, ranging from 1% for the PSDI to 7.9% for the MSI, which mentioned the issue that often only to criticize the regional system: "The MSI observes that the reservation and concerns advanced at the moment of the implementation of the ordinary regions, unfortunately found confirmation in the reality after 10 years, and this is not a crisis, but the failure of the regional experience" (MSI 1983). In line with this diminished salience, during Legislature VIII (1979–1983), no significant steps toward enhanced decentralization were taken. As argued in Chap. 2, regional legislation lagged behind expectations, centralist tendencies reemerged in the decision-making process, and the autonomy of local authorities was constrained by state activity. This was the beginning of the stalemate on decentralization that would last throughout the 1980s.

The salience of decentralization in the PSA reached a nadir in 1987, with a median value of 1.4%. Even the primary opponent of decentralization, the MSI, ignored the issue, and the two leftist regionalist parties limited the issue to, respectively, 1.5% (PCI) and 1.1% (PSI) of their manifestos. The DC kept paying some attention to the need to complete the reform of the regions and the local authorities (3.2%); similar statements could be found in the manifesto of the PLI, which was the party that devoted the most space to decentralist issues in its manifesto that year (4.6%). Regardless of party, references to the topic were more often references to the unsatisfactory results of the process of decentralization up to that time and its incompleteness rather than concrete plans to return the issue to the top of the policy agenda. The process of decentralization experienced a further setback.

Renewed Attention to Decentralization and the Season of Partisan Reform

The situation changed dramatically in the 1990s. In 1992, the median salience of the territorial issue in the PSA rose again, reaching a value of 3.9%, representing a 175.1% increase from the previous election. Obviously, the LN, which was just entering the electoral arena, led the debate, with 10.8% of its manifesto devoted to decentralist issues. Attention was also high among the other parties, such as the *Partito Democratico della Sinistra* (PDS) (4.4%), the center-left heir to the communist party, and the more radical leftist *Rifondazione Comunista* (RC) (2%) and even the centralist MSI (8.5%). On the eve of the new millennium, the political discourse apparently abandoned the need to complete the regionalist legislation of the 1968–1975 period. Instead, there was a push for new reforms and even a drive for changes to the Constitution, including a proposal to transform the Senate into a Chamber of the Regions; forces like the LN were blamed for wanting to "break the unity of the nation" (PDS 1992, Chap. 5).

The political instability of those years led to early elections, and it became impossible to achieve any reform whatsoever. In the elections of 1994, however, decentralization maintained a significant position in the PSA, with a median attention of 3.4% in a political scenario that had been completely rewritten by the new electoral rules and a radically different party system (Chap. 2). Decentralization was relevant in the manifestos of new parties, such as the emerging *Forza Italia* (FI) (3.2%); likewise, it was emphasized in the manifestos of the successors of old formations, such as the *Alleanza Nazionale* (AN) (4.1%), which was formed from the dissolution of the rightist nationalist MSI, and the *Partito Popolare Italiano* (PPI) (6.1%), founded after the crisis of the DC. At the same time, established parties, such as the PDS (4.9%), RC (3.4%), and, of course, the LN (6.7%), paid significant attention to the issue. Once again, however, reform efforts, including fiscal federalism, the Chamber of the Region" (FI 1994), and "regional governance with strong federalist inspiration" (PDS 1994), were thwarted by the early interruption of Legislature XII (1994–1996).

The decentralist issue nevertheless consolidated its position in the PSA, reaching 5.3% median salience in the 1996 elections (55% increase from 1994). Even leaving aside the LN (13.9%), references to decentralization, federalism, and the regions occupied significant portions of the party manifestos of both competing coalitions in 1996. The center-right *Polo delle Libertà* (PdL) coalition, which combined FI with the nationalist AN, paid a noteworthy amount of attention to decentralization, reaching 5.3% of salience. The coalition delivered a manifesto containing several references to federalism, which became a huge part of the political lexicon of the 1990s, while advocating a "presidential-federal system" and full fiscal federalism based on enhanced autonomy for the regions. At the same time, the manifesto of the center-left coalition *Ulivo* coalition—which included the PDS, Verdi, *Rinnovamento Italiano* (RI), and PPI, and allied with RC—included references to decentralization in 5.1% of its statements. The center-left coalition actually spelled out a detailed plan for decentralization, which envisaged, among other things, the "attribution to the regions of the legislative competence, except for those issues explicitly conferred to the central State" (Ulivo 1996). This provision should sound familiar: the attribution of exclusive legislative competencies to the regions and the explicit identification of state matters were among the main innovations introduced by the watershed constitutional reform carried out by the center-left majority in 2001. In the aftermath of this rise of decentralization in the PSA, Legislature XIII (1996–2001) featured, as seen in Chap. 2, the most intense period of decentralist reforms since 1968, whose cornerstones were L. 59/1997 and L. Cost. 3/2001, which was also the first purely "partisan" decentralist reform, advanced by the governing coalition despite the fierce objection of the opposition (Chap. 4).

In the elections held in May 2001, the amount of attention paid to territorial issues dropped to 3.8% (a percentage decrease of 28%), although decentralization remained a somewhat salient issue in the PSA. At the time of the elections, the constitutional reform of 2001 was still awaiting popular confirmation by constitutional referendum, which was held a few months later in October 2001. It is surprising that its main proponent, the *Ulivo*, devoted just 2.4% of its manifesto to decentralist issues. It nevertheless claimed credit for the adoption of the constitutional reform, defined as a "great success" and "incomprehensibly not voted by the opposition" (Ulivo 2001); it also announced the need to proceed further in the process by creating the Chamber of the Regions and enhancing efforts toward creating a federal system. Meanwhile, the *Casa delle Libertà* (CdL), the new name of the former PdL, had allied with the LN, and decentralist statements made up 5.2% of its manifesto. It is interesting that the manifesto of the CdL strongly promoted the "devolution of powers … from the state to the regions" and the full application of the subsidiary principle (CdL 2001), although it campaigned against the constitutional reform that introduced most of these changes. The center-right coalition eventually won the 2001 elections and pushed for another intrinsically partisan constitutional reform, which was adopted in Legislature XIV (2001–2006); this time it was opposed by the center-left coalition, and was eventually rejected in the constitutional referendum of 2006 (Chap. 2).

The two coalitions kept attention focused on decentralization in the 2006 elections as well, and the issue's median salience moderately increased to 4.2%. The CdL focused mostly on fiscal federalism, devoting 3.6% of its manifesto to the issue. At the same time, the large center-left coalition, which was renamed *Unione*, delivered an exceptionally long electoral program of 281 pages, 4.7% of which dealt with decentralization. With the early termination of Legislature XV (2006–2008), however, no reforms were adopted.

In the 2008 elections, decentralization remained relevant with an overall median salience of 3.1%, though there were signs that interest was declining (−27% from 2006). Leaving aside the LN, which at 41% was an outlier, the attention paid to territorial issues among the main competing parties ranged from 2.3% on the center-left (making up the newly founded *Partito Democratico* [PD], which merged the PDS with the center-left Catholic parties) to 3.6% from the *Unione di Centro* (UDC). As in the previous elections, the center-right, which had formed a new party, *Popolo delle Libertà* (PDL), confirmed its support for fiscal federalism, the topic that occupied most of the sections of its manifesto devoted to decentralization (salience 3.1%). The PD, while acknowledging the need for fiscal federalism, called for a new constitutional reform to overcome the conflict between the regions and the state after the reform of 2001 and once again promoted the creation of a Chamber of the Regions. In Legislature XVI (2008–2013), the winning center-right majority, spurred on by its autonomist ally the LN, eventually implemented the fiscal federalism reform, which became L. 42/2009.

The amount of attention paid to decentralist issues remained almost constant in 2013 (2.7%), with a slight decrease from the previous election (12% decrease): the new *Movimento Cinque Stelle* (M5S) party paid less attention to the issue (1.5%), as did another new centrist actor, *Scelta*

Civica (2.3%); 5.7% of the manifesto of the PDL referred to decentralization, compared to 3.1% of the manifesto of the PD. This constant, if muted, attention to decentralization in the last two legislatures reveals that the party system still considers the reform of subnational authorities a relevant policy issue, although they are less focused on it than in the periods preceding the key reforms of 1969–1975 and 1997–2001. It seems, however, that decentralization is now considered a part of a broader project of reforming the system that can no longer be delayed, especially in light of the impact of the global financial crisis that began in 2008; the attempted constitutional reform of 2016 was one more step in this direction.

Uneven Attention in the PSA and an Uneven Path of Reform

In line with the expectations of H1, the data presented above show that when the topic of decentralization was prominent in the PSA during an electoral campaign, major reforms followed—namely, the legislative changes and the "spikes" in the amount of substantial policy change[8] on the territorial redistribution of competencies over time (Fig. 3.2). This relationship between party system attention and policy change, both legislative and substantial, is particularly evident during the two key seasons of reforms, 1968–1975 and 1997–2001, and to a lesser extent during the third season from 2008 to 2013.

The peaks in attention during the elections of 1963 and 1968 were followed by the adoption of two major reforms (L. 108/1968 and L. 281/1970) and two minor reforms (L. 775/1970 and L. 1084/1970) during Legislature V, which represented another outburst of legislative change. Meanwhile the adoption of the implementing decrees of 1972, made the DI increase from 0 in 1968 to 3.3 in 1972, indicating a substantial policy change of +330% from one election to another (if one considers the annual change between the two electoral years, it was 200% in 1970 and 44% in 1972). Another 23% increase in substantial policy change occurred in 1973, when the effects of the financial autonomy following L. 281/1970 became tangible; likewise, the 1979 elections were held after the 19% increase in substantial policy change occurred in 1977 as an effect of the implementing decrees of 1977.

It is interesting to note that since 1972, the salience of decentralization in parties' discourses declined, while the process of decentralization increased. This can be explained by the fact that, once reforms were part of the policy agenda, parties lost interest in increasing the attention they

88 L. BASILE

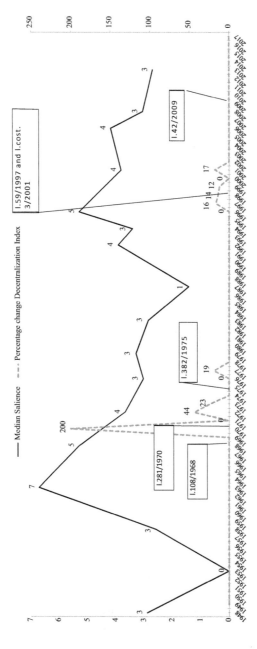

Fig. 3.2 Median salience for each election (left axis, %) and percentage change on the Decentralization Index for each electoral year (right axis, %)

paid to this policy dimension; although these issues remained relevant in the party discourse, legislative change was no longer a compelling issue of the political debate. However, the legislative reforms had triggered a process of substantial change, and it took some time before the regionalist legislation became fully operative and entrenched in the state machinery. Accordingly, one could conclude that, while legislative change depends on a political discourse that devotes significant attention to decentralization, the peaks in substantial change are usually delayed and tend to overlap with declining phases of interest.

The dramatic drop in the 1980s in the attention paid to decentralist issues in the PSA coincided with a period of limited substantial policy change; no major reforms were adopted that decade, and the only legislation concerning decentralization consisted of minor reforms.

The early 1990s saw a new swell of attention to the decentralist issue in the PSA, which reached its height in the 1996 elections. Mirroring the pattern of the first phase of reform, this peak of attention was followed by the adoption of key reforms in Legislature XIII, which were later substantiated into actual policy change: from 1996 to 2001 the DI rose 16%, 14%, 12%, and 17% in 1997, 1998, 1999, and 2001, respectively, as an effect of the Bassanini laws and the constitutional reform.

In the 2000s the amount of attention paid to decentralization declined again, although the issue seemed to still "thrive against the heavy odds of competition for scarce attention" (Carmines and Stimson 1993, 153). Indeed, the Legislatures XIV–XVII each featured a fiscal federalism reform and a failed attempt at a constitutional reform, though their actual impact in terms of substantial policy change was somewhat limited, and, in some respects, remains to be seen (Chap. 2).

Party Competition and the PSA: Who Takes the Lead?

The previous section showed that an increase in the attention paid to decentralist issues in the PSA seems to effect actual policy change. Accordingly, it is crucial to understand which actors and dynamics are likely to cause such shifts in attention.

As discussed in Chaps. 1 and 2, there are triggering pressures (functional and identity pressures and opportunity structures) that prompt governments to decentralize their political systems. It would be beyond the scope of this book to explain why, when, and how these pressures emerge at a given point in time; instead, this study will treat the existence of these pressures as a given, and assume that, because parties' main task is the representation of social demands within the political arena, shifts in parties' attention might be explained by these underlying pressures in society.

However, this explanation ignores the crucial role party competition plays in setting the agenda of the PSA, and implies that all parties respond to these demands at the same time and in the same way. On the contrary, parties differ from each other dramatically in their ideology, electoral base, geographical strongholds, government responsibilities, and so on. Accordingly, this work argues that there are some parties that are more likely than others to capture certain emerging needs, such as decentralist claims, and bring them into the political debate. Depending on their electoral strength, these parties are sometimes able to force competing parties to take up this policy dimension in their political discourse, causing it to rise in the broader PSA (H2: the entrepreneurial agent hypothesis).

In Italy, two party families have played this proponent role, though for different reasons: the autonomist parties and the leftist parties.

Jumping on the Autonomist Bandwagon

Most of the extant research on territorial party politics has explained parties' attention to decentralization by focusing on the electoral threat that autonomist parties have posed to mainstream parties.

These works have largely relied on Meguid's position, salience, and ownership (PSO) theory (2005, 2008), which describes party competition as a mainstream-niche contraposition. This theory is based on the assumption that new, electorally competitive niche parties refuse to compete on extant dimensions of policy; instead, they seek to place their own core policy issues on the political agenda (Meguid 2008, 3–4). Their success in doing so depends on the strategic choices of the mainstream parties. To avoid losing votes to niche actors, these mainstream parties must choose to either include the new issue in their own agendas by staking out accommodative or adversarial positions or dismiss the issue entirely. The underlying idea of the PSO theory is that the "giants" of the political system are compelled to adjust their strategies when challenged by political "dwarves" on the terrain of a new policy dimension (Basile 2015, 888).

Within this framework, electorally relevant autonomist parties, which emerge from the center–periphery cleavage (Lipset and Rokkan 1967), can be thought of as niche actors who own the issue of decentralization, because their core purpose is to achieve further autonomy for the subnational levels. These parties seek to force such demands into the political agenda.

In Italy, although there is a long tradition of autonomist movements in the party system, it was only with the rise of the LN that a representative of this party family posed a serious electoral threat while prioritizing the issue of decentralist reform. According to this theoretical framework, one would expect that both the party's electoral success and the salience of decentralist discourse in its communication would increase the attention paid to decentralization in the PSA.

Figure 3.3 shows the attention paid to decentralization in the PSA alongside the attention paid by the LN and its electoral performance from 1992 onward. In the 1992 elections, the LN experienced its first electoral success when it took 8.7% of the vote in the Chamber of Deputies while strongly promoting decentralization in its manifesto (with a salience of 10.8%); at the same time, the median salience score of the territorial issue in the PSA increased considerably, climbing 175.1% (percentage change) from the previous election. In 1994, the LN campaigned with the FI and AN and slightly softened its secessionist rhetoric; this coincided with a decline in its share of the vote. However, the effects of the strong secessionist rhetoric it had introduced nearly two years before persisted in the PSA, which showed a fairly constant level of attention being paid to decentralist issues. In 1996, the LN, which did not join the rightist coalition, further radicalized its political discourse on decentralization and was rewarded with its best electoral result ever. Its 1996 manifesto, for which it chose the significant title "Electoral Manifesto of the Padania," devoted 13.9% of its statements to the LN's blueprint for a federal government, while warning against "the false prophets of the federalism ... who seek to sell as federalism a mere autonomy or decentralization" (LN 1996). During this campaign, the attention paid to decentralization increased further at the PSA level, presaging a new season of reforms.

In 2001 the LN presented a joint document with the PdL (the so-called *Patto Lega Polo*, or Lega-Polo agreement) that paid particularly high attention to the issues of federalism and local identity. In this election, however, its share of the vote was cut in half, coinciding with a decline in interest in center–periphery issues in the PSA.

After the hiatus of 2006 when the LN did not issue any manifesto of its own, the party published a programmatic document featuring radically decentralist discourse in 2008, in which the territorial issue was highly

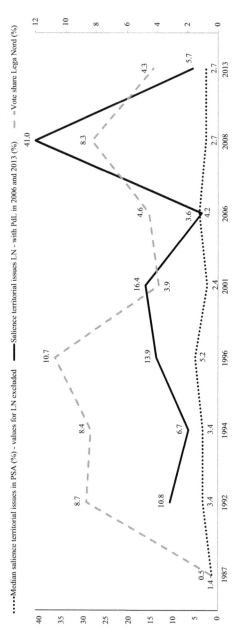

Fig. 3.3 Median salience in the PSA and salience in LN's manifestos for each election (left axis, %); vote share LN (right axis, %) (Note 1: Median salience was calculated by excluding the values for LN's documents. Note 2: For the 2006 and 2013 elections the salience values for LN are those of the CdL and the PdL coalition manifestos, respectively, because the LN formally joined these documents.)

salient (41%), which was rewarded by the electorate. Unlike in the 1992 and 1996 elections, however, neither the LN's renewed decentralist rhetoric nor its electoral success drew much attention to the decentralist issue at the system level; in fact, it declined slightly. By this point, the secessionist threat the LN posed in the early 1990s had lost most of its impact. Under Umberto Bossi the party had been part of the government, assuming governing roles in the much-maligned "robber Rome" for two legislatures, and the constitutional reform it had promoted when it was in government had been rejected two years earlier. Accordingly, the LN of the late 2000s seemed to have a reduced ability to take the lead on decentralization in the party competition.

In the 2013 elections, the LN dramatically reduced its emphasis on decentralist issues. Having joined the electoral program of the PDL, the party released a manifesto in which it devoted only 5.7% of statements to decentralist issues; its eventual share of the vote dropped to 4.3%. The party's reduced focus on the very issues that traditionally formed the centerpiece of its ideology was in keeping with its new ideological profile, developed under the leadership of Matteo Salvini, which was markedly populist, with an emphasis on anti-EU and anti-immigration issues. In the 2010s, the party had become "less a macro-regionalist party and more a national populist party, ... shifting to the right and away from federalist issues" (McDonnell and Vampa 2016, 121). This has actually reduced its ability to emphasize decentralization in the party system.

According to these data, the LN exerted some influence on the PSA by forcing the decentralist issue into the political discourse, especially in the early 1990s, while its impact seems to have dropped in the 2010s.

However, the variation in attention over time shows that that the topic of decentralization has been present to some extent in all Italian electoral campaigns from 1948 onward, well before the emergence of an autonomist electoral threat. How can this finding be reconciled with the PSO theory? Moreover, does it meet with the assumptions of the entrepreneurial agent hypothesis (H2) to explain the peak in attention before 1992?

Recent advances in the literature of niche parties have pointed out that, contrary to the PSO assumptions, niche actors do not necessarily campaign on new issues. Rather, they are likely to revitalize old topics that have been neglected by their competitors (Meyer and Miller 2015, 3); decentralization represents a typical case (Wagner 2012, 852). Nevertheless, the core question remains: who took the lead on decentralization before the rise of the LN? Which political party was better able to interpret and bring into the political discourse social demands for expanded local autonomy in the absence of a credible autonomist electoral threat?

The Left Side of Territorial Reforms

As already argued, one possible answer to the question just raised is suggested by Alonso (2012, 160), who points out that the PCI actually represented a "functional equivalent to a peripheral party threat" before the appearance of the LN. Indeed, this party had geographically concentrated support in the so-called red belt (Tuscany, Emilia-Romagna, and Umbria),[9] and generally supported decentralist reforms. Beyond ideology, this support for greater autonomy for the subnational levels had a purely political purpose. Throughout the first Republic, the PCI was the second largest party in the country in terms of votes, but was permanently excluded from the government (a rule often referred to as the *conventio ad excludendum*). The creation of the regions would have allowed the PCI to at least secure power in its regional strongholds. The PSI was also able to gain votes in these same geographical areas by supporting their autonomy (ibid.).[10]

As Chap. 4 will discuss, the TERRISS data confirm that the PCI and its successors the PDS/PD, and PSI have traditionally been decentralist parties, and all strongly promoted decentralist reforms well before the politicization of the autonomist demands of the LN. It remains to be ascertained whether they played a role in compelling competing parties to pay attention to these issues as well.

Figures 3.4 and 3.5 show the evolution of the salience of decentralization over time in the manifestos of these two leftist actors, in parallel with their electoral fortunes and the overall relevance of the policy dimension in the PSA.

In 1948, the PCI, united with the PSI in the FDP, presented a short manifesto in which 3.9% of statements dealt with local autonomies, although it referred predominantly to the municipalities; in the following elections in 1953, all references to decentralization disappeared from the PCI's political rhetoric. As earlier observed, little attention was paid to this policy dimension at that time, even at the system level. The scenario changed in 1958, when 2.6% of the communist's manifesto referred to decentralization, mirroring a similar rise in the PSA. The real boost, however, occurred in 1963: alongside its increasing electoral strength, the PCI delivered a manifesto devoting 6.1% of its space to the creation of the ordinary regions and the strengthening of local autonomies; as one would

SALIENCE: PUTTING DECENTRALIZATION ON THE AGENDA: THE ROLE... 95

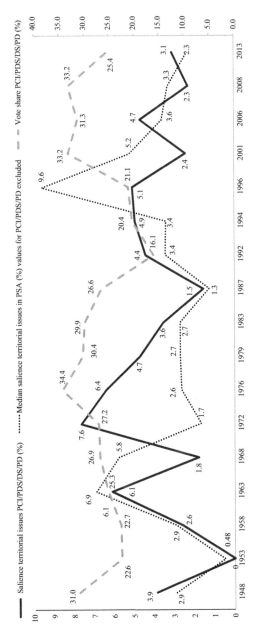

Fig. 3.4 Median salience and salience in PCI/PDS/Ulivo/PD's manifestos for each election (left axis, %); vote share PCI/PDS/Ulivo/PD (right axis, %) (Note: Median salience was calculated by excluding the values for PCI/PDS/Ulivo/PD's documents.)

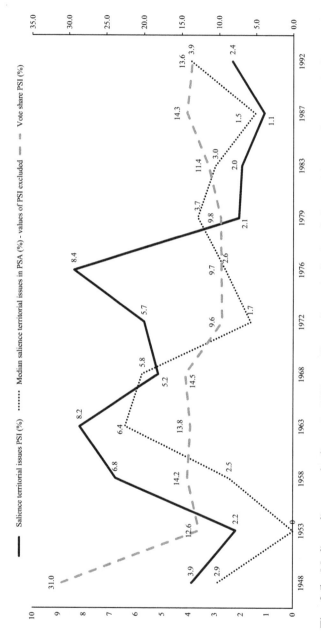

Fig. 3.5 Median salience and salience in PSI's manifestos for each election (left axis, %); vote share PSI (right axis, %) (Note: Median salience was calculated by excluding the values for PSI's documents.)

expect, this enhanced emphasis coincided with an exceptional rise of the issue's prominence at the PSA level.

While from 1948 to 1963 the salience of decentralization in the PSA seemed to track variations in the communists' political discourse, the trends diverge in the 1968 and 1972 elections. In the 1968 elections, the PCI issued a short manifesto containing only limited references to decentralization (1.8%); it was still relevant at the system level, though its importance was slightly declining. It should be noted, however, that Italy was in the middle of a political crisis at the time: student protests were introducing new issues to the policy agenda, from the reform of the education system to opposition to US intervention in Vietnam. The PCI used a "strategy of attention" in addressing this unrest, which explains an electoral manifesto focusing on the issues that were most important to the movements (Höbel 2004, 439–440), which reduced the space for other topics.[11] After that pause, the trend reversed course in 1972: the PCI paid high attention to the then-ongoing territorial reform process (7.6%), while its salience declined in the PSA. At the time, the PCI expressed the dissatisfaction of the regionalist front with the reform of 1970, claiming the need to "overcome the limits of the functions assigned [to the regions] so far" (PCI 1972). However, by this point the process of reform had already been established as a part of the institutional routine, which might explain why the attention of the entire system was no longer as focused as it had been.

From the second half of the 1970s through the 1980s, the PCI reduced its attention to regionalism, and the same decline can be observed at the system level: from 6.4% in 1976 it dropped to 4.7% in 1979 and 3.6% in 1983, and reached a nadir in 1987 of 1.5%. Over this period the party experienced varied electoral success, with periods of electoral strength, like 1976, alternating with periods of relative weakness, as in 1987. This declining trend mirrored the system level, seemingly realigning the communist political discourse on this dimension with the overall PSA.

In the early 1990s, the successor to the PCI, the PDS, was able to capture the increasing social demand for autonomy as well as the new opportunities created by the European Union with the Treaty of Maastricht in 1992. It emphasized decentralization once again (4.4%), mirroring a similar rise in the PSA. The PDS kept its attention focused on territorial matters in the two close elections of 1994 (4.9%) and 1996 (5.1%; *Ulivo* manifesto). This pattern of political discourse matched the electoral growth of the party, which entered the government in 1996. The PSA reflects this heightened attention to decentralization, though in those years the party system was also driven by LN's influence, as seen in the previous section.

In the 2000s the salience of the issue of decentralization within the DS-PD started at 2.4% in 2001, rose in 2006 (4.7%; manifesto of the *Unione* coalition), declined in 2008 (2.3%), and rose again in 2013 (3.1%). It is interesting that the prominence of the decentralist issue in the PSA followed the same trend as the main center-left party's electoral strength.

Shifting to the PSI, between 1948 and 1968, variations in the attention the party paid to decentralist issues paralleled trends at the system level. In 1948, as discussed previously, it presented a joint manifesto with the PCI, in which the two leftist movements advanced decentralist arguments. But attention decreased in 1953 (2.2%) before rising dramatically in the elections of 1958 (6.8%) and 1963 (8.2%). At this point, the party was preparing to enter the government, and the creation of the regions was part of the agreement it had struck with the DC (Chaps. 2 and 4).

The party paid less attention in 1968 (5.2%; joint manifesto with the PSDI) and 1972 (5.7%), corresponding with diminishing interest at the system level.

It 1976, the trend mirrors that of the PCI in the previous elections: regardless of the emphasis paid by the PSI (8.4%), the party system agenda paid less attention to decentralization. As already mentioned, once the process of reform was a part of the institutional program, it ceased to be a matter of political competition among the parties, though its main leftist proponents worked to keep attention focused on the actual implementation of the legislation adopted in the previous two legislatures.

The pattern reversed course in 1979 when the PSI paid less attention to center–periphery relations than the median attention in the PSA; other actors, including the PSDI and the MSI, made the issue a higher priority. The 1980s were characterized by declining attention to territorial issues, both at the system level and in the PSI's individual agenda, while the electoral strength of the PSI grew considerably, consolidating its role in the government. In 1992, the PSI displayed more interest in decentralist issues, marking the onset of a renewed phase of emphasis on territorial issues. However, this was the last election before the political turmoil that followed the corruption scandals, and the PSI disbanded in 1994.

The data in this section reveal that, before the surge of the LN, other entrepreneurial agents, including the territorially based leftist parties, played a role in stoking social demands for stronger local autonomy, which also drew the attention of the competing parties to these issues. This driving effect is particularly evident in the early stages of the reform process.

A Chicken and Egg Situation?

At this point the reader might be puzzled by this account of the driving effect, especially when it concerns the alleged role of the leftist parties before the rise of the LN. How can one be sure that overall salience in the PSA rose because of the influence of the PCI and PSI and not for other reasons, either external or internal to the party system?

While the figures show that, at least in certain periods, the salience of decentralization has increased simultaneously in both the agendas of these parties and the PSA, it is hard to be certain that these two parties actually drove the others and were not simply following the same external driving forces as their competitors. In other words, it is a sort of chicken and egg situation, where it is difficult to say whether the leftist parties shifted the system's awareness toward decentralization or were simply carried along with the tide. Indeed, if one looks at the salience of decentralization by party families, it emerges that, in the period between 1948 and 1992, the Christian Democrats paid more attention to decentralization overall than other party groups, including the socialists and leftists, before 1992, with a mean salience of 4.6% (standard deviation 2.9), followed by the communists (3.8%; standard deviation 2.4) and the socialists (3.5%; standard deviation 2.8). So why not argue that, for instance, the DC government played a key role in influencing the PSA, rather than the PCI and the PSI? In fact, as it was the main party with a stable ruling majority, it would be reasonable to argue that it had the power to set the agenda more than its competitors, especially the PCI.

A partial answer to this puzzle is that these empirical findings basically support a reading of history that is commonly acknowledged by the literature and historical accounts concerning the Italian process of decentralization: there is general agreement that the leftist parties played a leading role, followed by the autonomist party in the 1990s, in influencing the PSA. The analyses in the previous section could be considered an attempt to express this reform narrative in numbers and figures.

However, further empirical analysis should confirm that the leftist parties exerted a pulling effect on the party system, calling attention to decentralist issues even before the breakthrough of the LN.

One way to begin this analysis would be to examine the parties' directional intensity on decentralization, rather than just the issue's salience. In the TERRISS Dataset, directional intensity measures not only how much parties talk about decentralization but also their stance—positive, negative, or neutral—by multiplying salience for directional certainty. If a party is a genuine supporter of decentralist positions, the issue's salience will take a clear, positive direction; all of its statements on decentralization will be coded as decided endorsements of reform, with a positive sign. Conversely, a centralist party's statements concerning decentralization will express its adversarial stance, which will result in a negative sign; in some cases, an adversarial party has been compelled by other driving actors to address this issue, even if it would prefer to exclude it from the agenda. In between these two poles there are those parties whose positions on decentralization are ambiguous and vague (Chap. 4). They might incorporate the issue in their own agendas, but its salience in their political discourse would be weakened by contradictory or blurring statements. If a party devotes 3% of its manifesto to this policy area, for example, but half of its statements are vague or contradictory references, the actual intensity score will be much lower than 3%. Indeed, such behavior is likely to be adopted by those parties that have been compelled by other actors to deal with a topic when they have not yet developed a blueprint for it. If the argument of leftist influence holds true, one would expect a higher directional intensity among the communists and socialists than the Christian democrats, at least before 1992.

And indeed, looking at the values of directional intensity for all the party families before 1992, the Christian Democrats had a mean score of 2.6 on this measure (standard deviation 1.5), that is to say 2 points less than the party's mean saliency score. On the other hand, the communist party family took the lead, with an average score of directional certainty of 3.5 (standard deviation of 1.9), in line with its saliency score, followed by the socialists (average score of directional intensity 2.9; standard deviation 2.3). As will be discussed at length in Chap. 4, the political discourse of the DC on decentralization often featured a certain ambivalence and tendency toward rhetorical acrobatics (Mazzoleni 2009b, 137). The PCI and PSI, on the other hand, have clearly supported territorial reform, especially on the eve of the reforming season of 1968–1975.

In the post-1992 period, the scene has clearly been dominated by the autonomist party family. For two decades, the LN has taken the lead on the political discourse on territorial matters in Italy; still, the social democrats, represented by the PDS/Ulivo's manifestos, seem to have taken up the mantle of the PCI, to the extent that they have continued to express their clear support for decentralization, keeping attention focused on this policy area.

An ANOVA was also used to examine the effect of belonging to a party family on salience and directional intensity, and showed a statistically significant difference between family groups on both the values of salience [$F(10, 120) = 2.24, p < 0.05$] and directional intensity [$F(10, 102) = 3.66, p < 0.001$)].[12]

To further strengthen these arguments, Fig. 3.6 shows the variation of the intensity of the political discourse on decentralization over time from the PCI, the PSI, and the main governing party, the DC, and compares these scores to the median salience at the PSA level. The DC's emphasis on decentralization was higher than that of the PCI, but lower than that of the PSI in 1958 elections, which was mostly due to the fact that the DC expressed the need to implement the constitutional provisions after the adoption of the law of 1953. The issue, however, was not yet relevant in the PSA. As previously discussed, it became relevant in the PSA only in the following elections, when the intensity of the political discourse of both the PCI and the PSI superseded that of the governing party, with a parallel rise in attention in the PSA. Once the reforming process had begun, the issue of reform was already a part of the agenda, which explains the higher intensity of the political discourse coming from the governing party in 1968. The dissatisfaction of the regionalist front in early 1972, however, was visible in the renewed, intense attention the leftist actors paid to the reforms throughout the 1970s, while at the party system level it was no longer an issue of party competition. When the process of reform was accomplished, even with all its limits, the PCI and the PSI dramatically reduced the attention they paid to the issue, and the theme of reform ceased to be as relevant as it was in the 1960s. It was the leftist party that once again raised awareness of decentralization in the early 1990s, but by then it had to share the driver's seat with the LN.

These findings help confirm that the leftist parties were likely the driving actors that, according to the entrepreneurial agent hypothesis, played a role in increasing the party system's attention to decentralization.

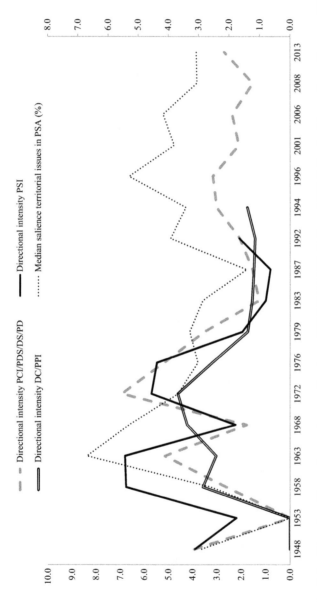

Fig. 3.6 Directional intensity on decentralization of PCI/PDS/PD, DC, and PSI (left axis, %); median salience at PSA level (right axis, %)

Concluding Remarks: The Reforming Process, Between Gridlock and Party Attention

It is easy to find fault with the process of decentralization in Italy: it has been uneven and incomplete, and it is still unclear whether the country is moving in a federalist direction or not. In many respects, it is just another example of an Italian pattern when it comes to structural reform—there is a strong desire for change, but it is often frustrated by deep-rooted causes of gridlock.

This chapter, however, advances an alternative yet complementary viewpoint on the process of decentralization. Using an agenda-based approach, the alternating short, intense periods of policy change and long phases of stalemate can be explained as a result of the bounded rationality of the political actors involved, including the political parties. It is only when most of the actors within the party system have simultaneously emphasized decentralization that the issue has risen to the top of the PSA and policy change has become likely. The findings discussed in this chapter also showed the importance of the dynamics of party competition and party strategies in influencing the PSA. In particular, empirical data support the widely believed argument that assigns a prominent role to the leftist and autonomist parties in influencing the party system and bringing attention to decentralist reforms.

This analysis does not test the impact of other external forces and pressures like mass media and public opinion. Although this constitutes a potential weakness of the analysis, the primary reason for not including this information is that it would not be feasible to collect reliable, comprehensive, and consistent data on these forces for the entire period considered. Notwithstanding this shortcoming, the systematic analysis of the dynamics of party competition vis-à-vis the path of policy change conducted in this chapter still yields important results, showing the existence of a relationship between an increase in the amount of attention paid to decentralization in the PSA and the process of reform. As already argued, this basically conforms with the prevailing accounts of the process of decentralization proposed by scholars and commentators.

Nonetheless, the goodwill of political parties is a necessary but not sufficient condition for reform to occur. Once the issue is transferred from the PSA to the legislative agenda, it must be supported by the governing parties and then get the support of the majority of the political forces represented in Parliament to become a full-fledged reform. Accordingly, the next chapter will illustrate the patterns of party support and opposition to decentralization in Italy by looking at the second component of party strategies: position.

Notes

1. Document I, n. 11 "Message to the Chambers by the President of the Republic," transmitted to the presidency on June, 26 1991.
2. Froio et al. (2016, 8) also test the hypothesis of responsiveness of the legislative agenda to both government and opposition party agendas but find only partial evidence of such a correlation.
3. These dynamics of party competition were originally described by Meguid (2005, 2008), although she refers exclusively to new, niche parties as the main proponents of new issues (Basile 2015).
4. The median has been preferred to the mean because it is less sensitive to the outliers. In this way, it was possible to also include the manifestos of the LN (for which territorial issues represent the raison d'être) in the calculation of the overall salience in the PSA at a given point in time.
5. This value is obtained by computing the mean saliency score of all the 56 categories included in the content analysis carried out by the Comparative Manifesto Project (CMP) in four countries (Italy, Belgium, the United Kingdom, and Spain), which is 1.6%, with a standard deviation 1.54%. Alonso finds that only 16% of the categories included in the CMP display average saliency scores above 2% (e.g., "Welfare state" has a mean value of 6%). She therefore argues that "percentages above four are already quite large and rare, if we look at the totality of manifestos" (Alonso 2012, 67). Moreover, based on her analysis, the issue of "decentralization" is the fourth-most mentioned category, with 4.9% average mentions.
6. The threshold for considering something an outlier is based on the computation used to obtain the box and whisker plot of the salience of the territorial dimension in all the manifestos included in the dataset. Conventionally, outliers are all those data points below the first interquantile −1.5 multiplied for the interquartile range or above the third interquartile +1.5 multiplied for interquartile range. In this case, all the manifestos with a saliency score for decentralization above 11% can be considered outliers. They are mostly the manifestos of the *Lega Nord*.
7. For 1996, the TERRISS Dataset coded both the manifestos of the two main coalitions (*Ulivo* and *Polo delle Libertà*) and the manifestos of their member parties. To avoid double counting parties, the calculation of the median includes only the two coalition manifestos. The median value including all documents for 1996 is 5.19%, while by considering only the

coalition manifestos and that of the LN it is 5.30%. Likewise, the joint document of the CCD-CDU of 2001 has been excluded from the calculation of that year's median because the program of these parties was included in the manifesto of the coalition *Casa delle Libertà* (the median including the CCD-CDU document was 2.4%, while it was 3.8% without this document).
8. As in Chap. 2, policy change has been calculated by adding 1 to the DI score to avoid null values.
9. The PCI obtained 25.26% of the vote in the 1963 elections, but the vote share for the party was respectively 39.5% in Tuscany, 35.8% in Emilia-Romagna, and 36% in Umbria. The mean of the votes for the Chamber of Deputies in the constituencies of Tuscany (Siena, Arezzo, Grosseto; Firenze, Pistoia; Pisa, Livorno, Lucca, Massa Carrara), Emilia Romagna (Mantova, Cremona; Parma, Modena, Piacenza, Reggio Emilia; Bologna, Ferrara, Ravenna, Forlì) and Umbria (Perugia, Terni, Rieti). Author's own elaboration of data from http://elezionistorico.interno.it/index.php?tpel=C&dtel=28/04/1963&tpa=I&tpe=A&lev0=0&levsut0=0&es0=S&ms=S (accessed March 29, 2017). In Emilia-Romagna, if one excludes the vote in Mantova-Cremona (26.5%), the mean of the vote rises up to 40.5%.
10. The PSI obtained 13.84% of the vote in the 1963 elections, with a vote share of 16.3% in Tuscany and 14.7% in Emilia-Romagna.
11. This strategy was actually rewarded by younger voters, as Höbel (2004) recalls, as the PCI gained 1.6% points in the Chamber of Deputies from the previous election, with an increase of voting among younger people. Among younger voters, the PCI reached 43.5%.
12. The ANOVA was also run controlling for the interaction effect of the period of observation, both before and after 1992.

References

Alonso, Sonia. 2012. *Challenging the State: Devolution and the Battle for Partisan Credibility: A Comparison of Belgium, Italy, Spain, and the United Kingdom.* Oxford: Oxford University Press.

Basile, Linda. 2015. A Dwarf Among Giants? Party Competition Between Ethno-Regionalist and State-Wide Parties on the Territorial Dimension: The Case of Italy (1963–2013). *Party Politics* 21 (6): 887–899.

———. 2016. Measuring Party Strategies on the Territorial Dimension: A Method Based on Content Analysis. *Regional & Federal Studies* 26 (1): 1–23.

Baumgartner, Frank R., and Bryan D. Jones. 1993. *Agendas and Instability in American Politics.* Chicago: University of Chicago Press.

———. 2009. *Agendas and Instability in American Politics.* 2nd ed. Chicago: University of Chicago Press.

Baumgartner, Frank R., Christoffer Green-Pedersen, and Bryan D. Jones. 2006. Comparative Studies of Policy Agendas. *Journal of European Public Policy* 13 (7): 959–974.

Baumgartner, Frank R., Christian Breunig, Christoffer Green-Pedersen, Bryan D. Jones, Peter B. Mortensen, Michiel Nuytemans, and Stefaan Walgrave. 2009. Punctuated Equilibrium in Comparative Perspective. *American Journal of Political Science* 53 (3): 603–620.

Borghetto, Enrico, Marcello Carammia, and Francesco Zucchini. 2014. The Impact of Party Policy Priorities on Italian Lawmaking from the First to the Second Republic, 1983–2006. In *Agenda Setting, Policies, and Political Systems: A Comparative Approach*, ed. Christoffer Green-Pedersen and Stefaan Walgrave, 164–182. Chicago: University of Chicago Press.

Budge, Ian, and Richard I. Hofferbert. 1990. Mandates and Policy Outputs: U.S. Party Platforms and Federal Expenditures. *The American Political Science Review* 84 (1): 111–131.

Bull, Martin, and Gianfranco Pasquino. 2007. A Long Quest in Vain: Institutional Reforms in Italy. *West European Politics* 30 (4): 670–691.

Carmines, Edward G., and James A. Stimson. 1993. On the Evolution of Political Issues. In *Agenda Formation*, ed. William H. Riker. Ann Arbor: University of Michigan Press.

Casa delle Libertà. 2001. Piano di governo per un'intera legislatura. In Lehmann, Pola, Theres Matthieß, Nicolas Merz, Sven Regel, and Annika Werner. 2017. *Manifesto Corpus*. Version: 2017-2. Berlin: WZB Berlin Social Science Center.

Democrazia Cristiana. 1948[1968]. Appello della Democrazia Cristiana al Paese. In *Atti e documenti della DC 1943–1967*, 377–378. Roma: Cinque Lune. 4 Marzo 1948.

———. 1963[1968]. Programma elettorale della DC per la IV Legislatura. In *Atti e Documenti della DC 1943–1967*, 1473–1519. Roma: Cinque Lune.

———. 1976. Il programma della Democrazia Cristiana. *Biblioteca della Libertà* Anno XIII (61/62): 85–127.

———. 1979. Il programma elettorale della DC. *Il Popolo*, May 12, 1979.

Fabbrini, Sergio. 2009. The Transformation of Italian Democracy. *Bulletin of Italian Politics* 1 (1): 29–47.

———. 2013. Political and Institutional Constraints on Structural Reforms: Interpreting the Italian Experience. *Modern Italy* 18 (4): 423–436.

Farinelli, Arianna, and Emanuele Massetti. 2011. Eppur Non Si Muove? Prospects for Constitutional Reforms in Italy After the 2009 European and 2010 Regional Elections. *Journal of Modern Italian Studies* 16 (5): 685–704.

Forza Italia. 1994. Cinque obiettivi per quarantacinque proposte. Febbraio 1994.

Froio, Caterina, Shaun Bevan, and Will Jennings. 2016. Party Mandates and the Politics of Attention: Party Platforms, Public Priorities and the Policy Agenda in Britain. *Party Politics,* January.

Green-Pedersen, Christoffer. 2007. The Conflict of Conflicts in Comparative Perspective. Euthanasia as a Political Issue in Denmark, Belgium, and the Netherlands. *Comparative Politics* 39 (3): 273–291.

Green-Pedersen, Christoffer, and Jesper Krogstrup. 2008. Immigration as a Political Issue in Denmark and Sweden. *European Journal of Political Research* 47 (5): 610–634.

Green-Pedersen, Christoffer, and Peter B. Mortensen. 2010. Who Sets the Agenda and Who Responds to It in the Danish Parliament? A New Model of Issue Competition and Agenda-Setting. *European Journal of Political Research* 49 (2): 257–281.

Green-Pedersen, Christoffer, and Stefaan Walgrave. 2014. Political Agenda Setting: An Approach to Studying Political Systems. In *Agenda Setting, Policies, and Political Systems: A Comparative Approach*, ed. Christoffer Green-Pedersen and Stefaan Walgrave, 1–16. Chicago: University of Chicago Press.

Höbel, Alexander. 2004. Il Pci Di Longo E Il '68 Studentesco. *Studi Storici* 45 (2): 419–459.

Jones, Bryan D., and Frank R. Baumgartner. 2005. *The Politics of Attention: How Government Prioritizes Problems*. Chicago: University of Chicago Press.

Lega Nord. 1996. In *Programma elettorale. Elezioni politiche del 21 aprile '96*, A cura dell'Ufficio Legislativo Federale Lega Nord. Milano: Lega Nord.

———. 2008. Parlamento del Nord. *Risoluzione federalismo*, marzo 2, 2008.

Lipset, Seymour Martin, and Stein Rokkan. 1967. *Party Systems and Voter Alignments: Cross-National Perspectives*. New York: Free Press.

L'Ulivo. 1996. Tesi per la definizione della piattaforma programmatica de L'Ulivo. 6 dicembre 1995. Retrieved from http://www.perlulivo.it/radici/vittorieelettorali/programma/tesi/. Accessed 10 Apr 2018.

———. 2001. *Rinnoviamo l'Italia, Insieme. Il programma dell'Ulivo per il governo 2001/2006 presentato da Francesco Rutelli*. Roma: Newton & Compton Editori.

Massetti, Emanuele, and Simon Toubeau. 2013. Sailing with Northern Winds: Party Politics and Federal Reforms in Italy. *West European Politics* 36 (2): 359–381.

Mazzoleni, Martino. 2009a. The Saliency of Regionalization in Party Systems: A Comparative Analysis of Regional Decentralization in Party Manifestos. *Party Politics* 15 (2): 199–218.

———. 2009b. The Italian Regionalisation: A Story of Partisan Logics. *Modern Italy* 14 (2): 135–150.

McDonnell, Duncan, and Davide Vampa. 2016. The Italian Lega Nord. In *Understanding Populist Party Organisation: The Radical Right in Western Europe*, ed. Reinhard Heinisch and Oscar Mazzoleni, 105–129. London: Palgrave Macmillan.

Meguid, Bonnie M. 2005. Competition Between Unequals: The Role of Mainstream Party Strategy in Niche Party Success. *American Political Science Review* 99 (3): 347–359.

———. 2008. *Party Competition Between Unequals: Strategies and Electoral Fortunes in Western Europe*. Cambridge: Cambridge University Press.

Meyer, Thomas M., and Bernhard Miller. 2015. The Niche Party Concept and Its Measurement. *Party Politics* 21 (2): 259–271.

Movimento Sociale Italiano. 1983. Il Messaggio degli Anni '80. *Il Secolo d'Italia*, January 23, 1983.

Partito Repubblicano Italiano. 1948. Il Programma del partito repubblicano per le elezioni del 18 aprile. In Lehmann, Pola, Theres Matthieß, Nicolas Merz, Sven Regel, and Annika Werner. 2017. *Manifesto Corpus*. Version: 2017-2. Berlin: WZB Berlin Social Science Center.

Partito Socialista Italiano. 1953. Il PSI agli elettori. Vota alternativa socialista garanzia di progresso e di pace. *Avanti!*, April 26, 1953.

———. 1958. *Per una politica di alternativa democratica*. Roma: Seti.

———. 1976. La proposta politica del PSI. *Biblioteca della Libertà* Anno XIII (61/62): 299–314.

———.1979. Idee per un programma. *Avanti!*, May 27, 1979.

Partito Comunista Italiano. 1963. Battere la DC. Rafforzare il PCI. Il Programma elettorale del PCI. *L'Unità*, March 3, 1963.

———. 1976. Partito Comunista Italiano. E' necessaria una nuova guida politica e morale. *Biblioteca della Libertà*, Anno XIII, 61/62: 161–166.

———. 1968. E ora di cambiare, si può cambiare: appello programma del PCI. *L'Unità*, May 12, 1968.

———. 1972. Il programma dei comunisti: per un governo di svolta democratica. *L'Unità* (Special issue), March 26, 1972.

Partito Democratico della Sinistra. 1992. Costruiamo una nuova Italia. PDS opposizione che costruisce. *L'Unità (supplemento)*.

———. 1994. *Per ricostruire un' Italia più giusta, più unita, più moderna. Dieci grandi opzioni programmatiche*. Roma: l'Unità.

Putnam, Robert D., Robert Leonardi, and Raffaella Y. Nanetti. 1993. *Making Democracy Work: Civic Traditions in Modern Italy*. Princeton: Princeton University Press.

Steenbergen, Marco R., and David J. Scott. 2004. Contesting Europe? The Salience of European Integration as a Party Issue. In *European Integration and Political Conflict. Themes in European Governance*. Cambridge: Cambridge University Press.

Wagner, Markus. 2012. Defining and Measuring Niche Parties. *Party Politics* 18 (6): 845–864.

CHAPTER 4

Position: Sharp Conflict or Shared Consensus?

Getting to Reform: A Search for Consensus or Party Competition?

The discussion of the "party politics of attention" in Chap. 3 argues that the greater the emphasis placed by parties on an issue during the electoral campaign, the higher the likelihood that a reform concerning it will be passed during that Legislature. However, attention is not enough to produce policy change. In modern democracies, reforms are the result of complex bargaining processes among decision makers, veto players, and stakeholders, which take place within the framework of a system's institutional procedures and veto points; in parliamentary democracies, political parties are likely to play a crucial role. Reforming processes ultimately result in bills that require the approval of the majority, whether simple or qualified, of the parliament's members to be passed. To obtain this approval, it is necessary for the main political actors to reach agreement.

To provide a full-fledged account of the reforming processes, however, the peculiarities of different kinds of reform must be taken into account. The main distinction here is between two categories of reform: structural reforms, which make long-term alterations to a state's economy or legal system to address complex challenges and crises, such as the global financial crisis; and laws that are intended to set the rules of the game in a

© The Author(s) 2019
L. Basile, *The Party Politics of Decentralization*, Comparative Territorial Politics, https://doi.org/10.1007/978-3-319-75853-4_4

political system, such as electoral regulations and, in keeping with this book's purposes, territorial reforms (Bull and Pasquino 2007; Sorens 2009).

According to a common belief, the latter kind of reform requires broad consensus among political forces. The advantages of "drafting the rules of the game together"[1] rather than basing sweeping reforms on thin majorities[2] have always been espoused by political leaders and political commentators to ensure decisions concerning democratic rules, fundamental rights, and individual freedoms are not left to the arbitrary will of a temporary majority (Fabbrini 2013). Some scholars argue, however, that when institutional reforms are supported by broad consensus among the political forces they lack internal coherence, consistency, and ambition, because "when a project must be tuned to too many and conflicting interests, its quality is going to be poorer and poorer in direct proportion to the number of actors involved. Higher consensus equals more constraints" (Fusaro 1998, 70). Instead, a strong, cohesive political majority is sufficient to advance a project of reform, ideally one embedded within a broader, coherent scheme, which can then be submitted to debate and the proposals of the opposition (ibid.; Paolazzi and Sylos Labini 2012). The normative debate on the preferability of consensual or majority reform and the quality of the output resulting from each of the two approaches is beyond the aims of this book. Nonetheless, as the patterns of conflict and agreement between parties are crucial in explaining the final outcomes of the processes of reform, this chapter investigates whether, how, and to what extent the dynamics of party competition have affected the pattern and output of decentralist reforms in Italy. Indeed, as Fusaro (1998, 70) argues: "In ordinary circumstances, no goodwill can prevent constitutional and electoral reforms from becoming the ground and the weapon of the competition within the political system." In particular, this chapter will explore whether the path to decentralist reform in Italy has been supported by a shared, consensual approach among the political actors, or has served as a battlefield for party competition, with decision making led by the party majority in power.

In discussing party competition on the territorial dimension, this empirical analysis makes a necessary distinction between two concepts: a party's *electoral position*, as expressed in its party manifestos before the elections within the electoral arena, and the *voting positions* parties actually adopted when forced to vote on decentralist reforms in Parliament.

This chapter pursues a threefold purpose: (1) to ascertain whether the main political forces have converged, at least in their electoral programs, on the need to proceed with the decentralization of the country; (2) to analyze whether and to what extent the concrete aspects of the country's territorial restructuring have been subjected to political debate, conflict, and negotiation; and (3) to assess whether parties have been coherent with the preferences they have expressed in their electoral campaigns when they were asked to vote on decentralist reforms in Parliament.

The chapter is structured as follows: the next section introduces the theoretical model and a set of working hypotheses to predict the pattern—consensual or conflicting—of party competition on decentralization in electoral and parliamentary debates. Then TERRISS data on directional certainty (Chap. 1) are used to map party positioning on decentralization over time. Finally, the last section compares party electoral rhetoric on decentralization with actual voting behavior on the major reforms that shaped the territorial redistribution of powers in Republican Italy from 1948 until the present.

Parties' Strategic Considerations When Setting the Rules of the Game: A Framework for Analysis

As seen in Chap. 3, when a policy issue is introduced into the political agenda, parties must first decide whether to include it in their own agendas or neglect it. If they choose the former, they must also choose among the available positions, in this case, either to accommodate demands for decentralization (accommodative strategy) or oppose them (adversarial strategy) (Meguid 2008, 27–30). Political actors can also choose to express less clear-cut positions on an issue (Basile 2016). There are at least two forms of such strategic ambiguity. When using a "blurring strategy" (Rovny 2013), parties issue intentionally vague statements that do not make their support or opposition entirely clear. This strategy is often adopted by parties when they have not yet developed a clear preference on a certain policy issue that has nevertheless entered the party system agenda (PSA) or when adopting a clear stance in either direction might deter a share of potential voters holding differing preferences (Basile 2015). When a party adopts a "broad appeal" (Somer-Topcu 2015) or "contradictory" strategy, on the other hand, it takes contradictory stances on different aspects of the same topic (Basile 2016).

What does this theoretical model say about party strategies on decentralization in Italy? Did parties generally follow accommodative, adversarial, or ambiguous strategies when a political actor—whether an emerging, niche actor or an established political force (Chap. 3)—championed such an issue in the PSA? Did this vary over time, especially between the First and Second Republics? And, moreover, which factors are likely to explain these party strategies?

Existing research has not produced consistent findings; some authors believe that major parties have tended to converge on accommodative strategies (Mazzoleni 2009), while others have pointed out that this apparent agreement conceals unspoken disagreement about the actual competencies to be redistributed, as well as the path to follow, paving the way to inherently adversarial and contradictory strategies (Keating and Wilson 2010; Farinelli and Massetti 2011; Palermo and Wilson 2013). Massetti and Toubeau (2013, 359) have argued that in Italy, at least since 1992, the territorial dimension has become a divisive issue of party competition, with parties adopting conflicting stances and adversarial strategies. Little systematic research has been conducted to ascertain whether the pattern of party competition has been even over time or has instead alternated between periods of shared consensus and others of sharp dissent.

To examine the pattern of party competition on decentralization in Italy, some initial hypotheses can be made. The first set of hypotheses deals with party electoral positioning (hypotheses H1a–c), while the second set of hypotheses focuses on parties' voting behavior, and postulates that this behavior is influenced by parties' electoral positions and governing roles, while acknowledging that these factors are also likely influenced themselves by the secular features of the party system (hypotheses H2a–d).

This study also proposes innovate ways of approaching the idiosyncrasies of both the issue of decentralization and the nature of the Italian party system; for the case under scrutiny, a one-size-fits-all model would not be effective for conducting research. As argued elsewhere in this volume, decentralization is not "just another policy output" but rather an integral part of how the state sets the rules of the political game (Sorens 2009, 268); accordingly, it would be pointless to adopt the same theoretical assumptions that would apply to other policy issues, which are more tailored to win votes than reshape state institutions over the long term (ibid.). Likewise, the Italian party system has its own peculiarities that render it an exceptional quasi-experimental environment. Over its 70 years of Republican history it has developed at least four different party systems

(Cotta and Verzichelli 2016), which allows an investigation of whether and how different party systems are likely to affect party strategies on issue competition.

As previously observed, the underlying assumption of the analysis conducted in this chapter is that party electoral strategies are likely to differ from their parliamentary strategies. Accordingly, the hypotheses will be presented within two separate theoretical models, one for each of two arenas.

Why Do Parties Talk as They Do? Party Competition in the Electoral Debate

As already argued, the main assumption concerning party strategies on decentralization is that they should not be conceived as binary questions of support or opposition; rather, party strategies stake out positions along a continuum that ranges from accommodative to adversarial and includes different nuances of ambiguity (blurring or contradictory strategies). Based on this premise, the first set of hypotheses argues that a party's electoral strategy on the territorial dimension hinges on the interaction of two factors—namely, the party's actual stances on decentralization, and its strategic considerations.

A party's stances are the result of a combination of substantial and ideological factors. Substantial support for decentralization can stem from several arguments in favor of decentralization, such as the idea that redistributing competencies downward creates further governing opportunities for political actors and increases the flexibility of policy making and the accountability of policy makers (Chap. 2). On the contrary, a party might have significant reasons for not supporting the state's decentralization—for instance because it fears decentralization could open further government opportunities to competing parties, or because it would jeopardize the efficiency of the state machinery; or, alternatively, the party might not have developed a clear preference on the issue yet itself.

However, political parties also have to take into account the plausibility and credibility of their attitudes in the context of their historical traditions and ideologies; indeed, a party's support for decentralization should be consistent with its overall ideological platform and its stances on other related issues (Toubeau and Massetti 2013; Toubeau and Wagner 2015). A relevant example is that of the national conservative parties, such as the *Movimento Sociale Italiano* (MSI)/*Alleanza Nazionale* (AN), which oppose decentralization and consider the preservation of the state identity and central authority part of their ideological cores. Other party families have to reconcile their ideologies with their stances on decentralization to make the latter as credible as possible. For instance, the Christian Democrats have a long tradition of supporting principles like subsidiarity, and Luigi Sturzo, one of the fathers of the *Partito Popolare Italiano* (PPI), the precursor to the *Democrazia Cristiana* (DC), was a passionate advocate of local autonomy and federalism (Gargano 1999). Nonetheless, when the DC came to power in 1948, these autonomist ideals clashed with the party's need to slow down the process of decentralization to prevent the communists from securing governing positions in their regional strongholds (Chaps. 2 and 3). Parties from the left side of the political spectrum, meanwhile, should theoretically oppose any redistribution of powers downward because of their commitment to the practice of state intervention in the economy; nonetheless, the *Partito Comunista Italiano* (PCI) was forced to reconcile its ideological preferences with its emerging strategic interests by supporting decentralization with equally plausible leftist arguments, such as the need to strengthen alternative avenues of democratic representation and government. These examples suggest how important it is for a party to connect its ideological background with its position on a specific policy dimension. Parties often achieve this by using another strategic tool—namely, frames, which will be discussed in Chap. 5.[3]

Parties also have to take into account strategic considerations such as the electoral strength of the party (or parties) promoting decentralization and the popular support for the issue among the electorate[4] before defining their final electoral strategies on decentralization. Strategic considerations, in this respect, resemble what Harmel and Janda (1994, 261) define as "external stimuli" that explain party change: "decisions to change a party's … issue positions or strategy face a wall of resistance common to large organizations. A successful effort to change the party usually involves … a good reason (which, granted, often does involve the need to take account of environmental changes)." According to the authors (ibid., 267), "external stimuli include numerous factors," such as "constitutional reforms … [and] birth of relevant new parties" and the distribution of votes among parties. Based on this definition, the above-mentioned strategic considerations can be considered external stimuli influencing party strategies.

Against this backdrop, it can be argued that a party will pursue an accommodative, decentralist strategy when it agrees with most of the substantial arguments in favor of decentralization, and its stance is supported by its ideological background. This hypothesis, however, holds only in the presence of specific strategic considerations—namely, that decentralization is popular among the electorate and that its proponents are likely to gain electoral advantages from it; on the contrary, even a strongly decentralist party might opt to somewhat blur its position when strategic conditions are not favorable to outright accommodation (see hypothesis H1c). Accordingly, the first hypothesis posits that "The more a party holds substantial and ideological reasons to support decentralization, the more likely it is to adopt an accommodative electoral strategy, assuming the presence of strategic conditions favorable to decentralization" (H1a: the accommodative strategy hypothesis).

Hypothesis H1a, however, needs to be further refined. In particular, it can be argued that when different parties coalesce around a decentralist position, a party's voters might be confused to see its programmatic platform moving too close to that of its adversaries. Parties are therefore required to differentiate their political proposals to some extent from those of the other parties. In the case of decentralization, for example, a party might support a transfer of competencies in some areas, such as education or health, while affirming the need to keep state authority in others, thereby adopting *an accommodative strategy with differences.* Hence hypothesis H1a could be reformulated by arguing that: "on multidimensional policy issues like the territorial dimension, competing parties sharing substantial and ideological support for the overall purposes of decentralization will be likely to nuance their attitudes, even holding contradictory stances on different aspects of the same dimension" (H1a-*bis*: the contradictory strategy hypothesis).

The second hypothesis explores the converse scenario in which parties are substantially and ideologically opposed to decentralization. In this case an adversarial strategy is likely. Once again, this strategy also requires that a specific condition is fulfilled—namely, that the issue of decentralization is not popular among the electorate and that this strategy would not imply any loss of votes to a proponent party. When an outright adversarial strategy could prove politically costly, a party might decide to blur its adversarial stance (see hypothesis H1c): "The more a party holds substantial and ideological reasons to oppose decentralization, the more likely it is to adopt an adversarial electoral strategy, assuming the presence of strategic conditions unfavorable to decentralization" (H1b: the adversarial strategy hypothesis).

Finally, the third hypothesis explains party strategies in those remaining cases in which either the party is supportive of decentralization but strategic considerations prevent it from expressing such support or, on the

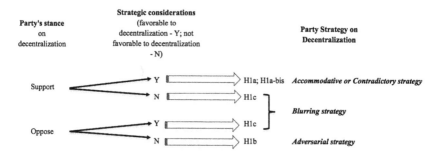

Fig. 4.1 Party electoral strategies on decentralization and determinants

contrary, the party opposes decentralization but that would not be strategically convenient. Hence the argument posits that when a party's stance (either supportive or adversarial) on decentralization runs counter strategic considerations, the party is likely to ambiguously blur its position: "The greater the distance between a party's stance and the strategic conditions, the more a party will seek to blur its electoral strategy on decentralization" (H1c: the blurring strategy hypothesis).

Figure 4.1 summarizes all the determinants of a party's strategy (a party's stances and its strategic considerations), and the possible scenarios that can result from their interaction.

Why Do Parties Vote as They Do? Party Competition in the Parliamentary Arena

Shifting to parties' behavior in Parliament, one would expect that parties would tend to stick to the preferences expressed in their manifestos once they enter the institutional arena. However, things are often less straightforward when political advantage is at stake, and parties' coherence with their own pledges cannot be taken for granted. This premise raises the first question concerning party behavior in parliamentary votes on decentralist reforms: Are parties[5] coherent with their electoral rhetoric on the territorial dimension?

The opening section of this chapter introduced another relevant topic—namely, that of political actors' goal to set the rules of the game when adopting reforms concerning the institutional architecture of the state, including decentralization. Without taking any position in the normative debate on the preference of consensual or majority reforms, an analysis of the parliamentary arena poses a second question: Were decentralist reforms in Italy approved consensually or were they contested reforms?

To answer these questions, this section formulates some hypotheses to explain party voting behavior on decentralist issues. These hypotheses will connect the ideas of coherence and consensual reforms, as they are closely interrelated; a desire for coherence might lead an opposition party to vote in favor of a bill supported by the majority, leading to the approval of broadly supported laws.

In the parliamentary arena, voting strategy is likely to be influenced by a number of factors, more than can be listed here.[6] First, there are obviously party preferences on specific policy issues, as expressed in their electoral rhetoric; second, there is a party's role in government; and third, there are the features of the party and political system of a country, such as whether the party system is bipolar or fragmented, how much the government sets the agenda, what the relationship between the executive and the legislative powers is, and what decision capacities the government possesses (Cotta and Marangoni 2015). Moreover, even in the institutional arena the peculiarities of the issue of decentralization seem to matter, and in particular its potential to achieve a far-reaching reform and define the key rules of the functioning of the state.

The influence of party preferences on voting behavior seems to be rather straightforward, to the extent that a political actor, once in Parliament, will likely pursue the political objectives it claimed to support during the electoral campaign. This leads to a baseline hypothesis based on party preferences: "The more a party expresses decentralist preferences during the electoral campaign, the more likely it will be to support decentralist reforms in the parliamentary arena" (H2a: the party preferences hypothesis).

The pursuit of policy goals in the institutional arena, however, hinges on a party's role in government, because the latter heavily affects the party's actual influence on policy making. As mentioned in Chap. 3, mandate theory (Budge and Hofferbert 1990) argues that parties seek to fulfill their electoral pledges to the greatest extent possible once in office, although other studies have questioned this argument (Froio et al. 2017; Borghetto et al. 2014). The logic underlying mandate theory is that a party that wins elections on the basis of certain promises is then "bound (both morally and by fears of retribution at the next elections) to carry through the program on which it has been elected" (Budge and Hofferbert 1990, 111). Failing to meet expectations might prove costly at the following elections.

When decentralist reforms are at stake, a counterargument might be that it would make sense in principle for incumbent parties to oppose the creation of further layers of authority at the subnational level, as this would reduce the strength of their political position (Sorens 2009). However, when there is a strong popular demand for territorial reform, an adversarial strategy can prove risky for an incumbent party as it risks a loss of votes to decentralist parties in the following elections. The latter, in fact, would have reason to criticize the party in government for failing to implement what is generally perceived as a necessary reform. Accordingly, it can be more effective for a governing party to propose and support a bill on decentralization, allowing it to claim credit for making progress itself and simultaneously avoid being vilified by the opposition in the following elections. Based on this argument, the first baseline hypothesis might be refined, positing the existence of a direct relationship between a governing party's preferences on decentralization and its vote on territorial reforms: "The more a party supports decentralization during the electoral campaign the more likely it will be to support decentralist reforms once in government" (H2b: the decentralist governing party hypothesis).

This argument is based on the assumption that the governing party has expressed a decentralist preference in its electoral campaign. There are also the cases of coalition governments in which one partner has expressed centralist positions during the electoral campaign and the other has supported territorial reforms. The review of the vast literature on coalition governments' policy making goes beyond this book's purposes. It should nevertheless be pointed out that when parties in multiparty and divided governments have different policy preferences, compromise becomes necessary for policy change, although this might result in the loss of votes in the following elections (Fortunato 2017). Indeed, a coalition partner has to make a cost–benefit evaluation, weighing its office-seeking goals (i.e., its desire to remain in government) against its vote-seeking goals (i.e., its desire to minimize vote losses in subsequent elections). This leads to a bargaining process meant to find a compromise with the government's allies when a bill is sponsored, one that minimizes the distance between the party's own preferences and the proposed legislation. In practical terms, in the case of territorial reforms the bargaining between centralist and decentralist parties in coalition governments can result in the introduction of amendments preserving national unity and the role of the central state authority to mitigate the effects of a transfer of competencies downward. Hypothesis H2b might therefore be adapted to the case of governing parties holding centralist positions within coalition governments sponsoring territorial policy change: "Centralist parties in a (coalition) government will be likely to vote in favor of territorial reforms sponsored by the government, while seeking a compromise to reduce the distance between their original party preferences and the final bill" (H2b-*bis*: the centralist governing party hypothesis).

The main limit of mandate theory is that it mostly focuses on the role of the governing parties. Attention, however, should also be paid to the voting behavior of those actors that form the opposition, which express their preferences on bills promoted by governing actors. There are even cases in which the opposition is faced with a bill sponsored by the government that promotes policies initially demanded by the opposition party itself in the electoral campaign. This requires a discussion of the impact of party roles in government on voting behavior. The choice facing a decentralist opposition party when responding to a decentralist bill proposed by a governing party is particularly challenging. If a party has championed the issue of decentralization in its electoral campaign, either for ideological reasons or because it sees a strategic opportunity to gain power at the subnational level, it will find itself at a crossroads: On the one hand, it should support legislation on decentralist reforms, as that would be coherent with its electoral stance and its strategic reasoning. On the other hand, it could opt to oppose decentralist legislation and blame the governing party for shortcomings in a reform plan in the following election. According to De Giorgi (2017), an opposition party's support for bills decreases when the distance between the opposition's and the government's policy preferences on an issue increases, the bill is proposed by the government, and the bill deals with complex issues—the so-called mesopolicies (Cotta 1996) concerning long-awaited reforms, which tend to feature a greater level of political competition. Some of these elements should be constants in the analysis of decentralist reforms; they are in fact complex reforms concerning crucial issues and the bills under scrutiny are all government initiatives.[7] Therefore the role of policy preferences needs to be considered, with the assumption being that governing and opposition parties might support the same bill simply because they share a policy preference on that issue (De Giorgi 2017; Giuliani 2008). Accordingly, one could formulate the following hypothesis concerning the voting behavior of opposition parties: "The more an opposition party supports decentralist positions, the more likely it will be to vote in favor of decentralist reforms, even if they are promoted by the government" (H2c: the opposition party preferences hypothesis).

To add even further complexity, the nature and the characteristics of the party system must also be taken into account. Polarized multiparty political systems and bipolar systems are particularly likely to drive different party strategies. In the former case, a consensual democracy is likely to develop, with reforms mostly adopted after mediation and compromise among the main political forces. Since no single party is likely to achieve a majority in Parliament, each one is forced to rely on the votes of other actors, even the opposition. In a bipolar system, on the other hand, one party or coalition holds 50+1% of the seats in Parliament. Accordingly, it might proceed with reforms regardless of the support of the opposition. This system would therefore be more likely to emphasize conflict, leaving little room for opposition to maneuver (De Giorgi 2017).

The Italian case is particularly interesting in this respect because the country's party system changed profoundly between the First and Second Republics. In the First Republic, the purely proportional electoral system led to an enduring multipolar, fragmented party system, with the DC playing a pivotal role (leading Sartori to call it "polarized pluralism" in 1976). This system produced large coalition governments without alternation in power, the result of postelectoral bargaining between the DC, which never obtained an absolute majority in Parliament, and other smaller parties from both the center-right and center-left, like the *Partito Repubblicano Italiano* (PRI), the *Partito Liberale Italiano* (PLI), the *Partito Socialista Democratico Italiano* (PSDI), and the *Partito Socialista Italiano* (PSI). The second largest party, the PCI, was permanently excluded from government. Scholars argue that within this framework Italy developed a form of consensual democracy, featuring mediation and compromise among the main parties and interest groups before government decisions were adopted (Fabbrini 2009, 35). The scenario changed dramatically after 1994 with the adoption of the so-called Mattarella law, which was mainly majoritarian with proportional elements (Chap. 2). Although the new electoral rules did not reduce fragmentation (Bull and Pasquino 2007), they nevertheless paved the way to a bipolar party system in which power alternated between two main preelectoral coalitions—namely the center-right and the center-left, with the leader of each intended as a candidate for the role of prime minister (Fabbrini 2009). The bipolar system survived further changes to the electoral law in 2006, when the Mattarella law was replaced by a proportional electoral system featuring large constituencies,[8] closed lists, and the possibility for parties to campaign as coalitions.[9] In the 2013 elections the emergence of new actors on the political scene, especially the *Movimento Cinque Stelle* (M5S), along with increased political volatility resulted in a new party system featuring three poles (center-right, center, and center-left) plus the M5S (Cotta and Verzichelli 2016). Leaving aside the changes that have occurred over the last few years, the "fragmented polarization" that has existed since 1994 has actually reinforced tendencies toward partisan reforms: first, there is a stronger link between legislative performance and productivity and policy-making activity, with the government more associated with adopted legislation than in the past (Cotta and Marangoni 2015, 199). Second, in this new system the level of competition has increased (ibid., 205), with the opposition generally more likely to vote against reforms proposed by the governing coalition (Massetti and Toubeau 2013). Moreover, it was only in the Second Republic that constitutional reforms failed to reach the qualified majority required, rendering these laws an area of sharp contestation (Giuliani 2008). Scholars have nevertheless argued that, notwithstanding the undeniable changes that occurred in the Italian party system between the First and the Second Republic, patterns of consensus still exist (ibid.; Cotta and Marangoni 2015; De Giorgi 2017). According to Giuliani (2008, 76), part of the explanation lies in the fact that decades of consensual practices have left a certain "imprinting" on the political system, reinforcing bipartisan tendencies in the legislative process; moreover, most of the "consensual" bills concern issues that are not politically controversial, micro-issues featuring low levels of dissent. On the contrary, decentralist reforms, as already argued, concern the rules of the game, where conflict is more likely, especially in majoritarian systems. Accordingly, another hypothesis would argue that: "The more the political system tends toward a consensual model (as in the Italian First Republic), the more territorial reforms will be adopted with a wide consensus among most of the main parties from both the government and the opposition, assuming they share the same preferences on decentralization; conversely, the more the political system leans toward a majoritarian model (as during the Second Republic), the more decentralist reforms will become battlefield between the government and opposition parties, even if they share the same decentralist preferences" (H2d: the party system hypothesis).

Based on these premises, one would expect that decentralist governing parties would be likely to support decentralist reforms in the parliamentary arena when they can gain electoral advantage from them; in coalition governments, even centralist allies should vote in favor of these reforms, although they will seek to reach a compromise to mitigate their decentralizing

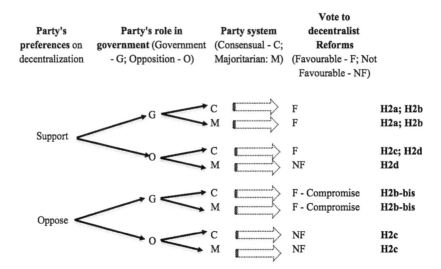

Fig. 4.2 Party voting behavior on decentralization and determinants

effects. On the other hand, decentralist parties in the opposition have to choose between remaining coherent with their decentralist claims (and therefore voting in favor of reforms) or adopting an adversarial stance so that they might later blame the incumbent party for flaws in the reform proposed. In both cases, however, strategic considerations are dictated in part by the nature of the party system, and a multiparty system appears to be more likely to encourage cooperation than a bipolar one. Figure 4.2 provides an overview of the likely scenarios resulting from the interaction of the three factors of parties' original preferences, their role in government, and the party system.

Mapping Party Electoral Strategies on Decentralization

Before proceeding with the empirical assessment of the hypotheses, it is necessary to provide an overview of electoral party strategies on decentralization as expressed in party documents over time, which represent the main dependent variable in hypotheses H1a–c and a key independent variable in hypotheses H2a–d. Strategies might be conceived as a combination between two elements: position, either decentralist or centralist, and salience—that is, whether the party pays a lot or a little attention to the issue, if any.

In the TERRISS Dataset, directional certainty measures party position—that is, whether a party has adopted an accommodative (values close to +1), adversarial (values close to −1), or blurred/contradictory (values close to 0) stance on decentralization. The latter group might be further divided between those leaning toward an adversarial stance (negative values), those leaning toward an accommodative stance (positive values), and those manifestos with scores of 0 on directional certainty. The data show that 102 documents out of 120 contained at least one statement on decentralization (i.e., the salience value is not zero; see Chap. 3),[10] and that these documents cover all the possible positioning options, ranging from −1 to +1. Nonetheless, the values' distribution is negatively skewed (skewness −1.09) because most of the documents display scores close to +1; moreover, there is also a relevant number of documents with position values that are positive but close to 0. The mean and median are, respectively, 0.5 (standard deviation 0.5) and 0.6. All these measures seem to support the finding that most parties in Italy have generally adopted an *accommodative stance in their electoral rhetoric or at least provided ambiguous support for decentralization.*

To provide a full-fledged picture of party strategies, the two tools at parties' disposal—salience and position—can be combined into a typology (Table 4.1). Saliency scores can be collapsed into categories, the boundaries of which are based on the median and percentiles (Chap. 3): "no attention" (values of 0%), "minor attention" (values between 0.01 and 3.3%), and "major attention" (from 3.3% upward). Values of directional certainty, ranging from −1 to +1 including zero, can be categorized as follows: values between −1 and −0.5 and between 0.5 and +1 correspond to, respectively, adversarial and accommodative strategies; values between −0.5 and 0 and 0 and 0.5 indicate ambiguous documents leaning either in a centralist or a decentralist direction, respectively; finally, documents coded as 0 are purely ambiguous.

The first group of the typology includes the "neglecting" parties, those 18 documents that completely ignored the issue of decentralization, indicating that these parties opted for a neglecting strategy. This group mostly comprises manifestos issued in the First Republic; 8 of them date back to the period preceding the 1963 elections, while the other 10 cases represent the manifestos of relatively small or fringe parties with strictly focused

Table 4.1 Typology of documents according to the salience and directional certainty on decentralization (cell percentages: number of documents in brackets.)

	Negative direction	Leaning negative	Ambiguous	Leaning positive	Positive direction
No attention			**Neglecting** 15% (18) Dismissal strategy		
Minor attention	**Mild centralist** 2.5% (3) *Moderate adversarial strategy*	centralist 3.3% (4)	**Reluctant** neutral 5% (6) *Moderate ambiguous strategy*	decentralist 5% (6)	**Mild decentralist** 19.2% (23) *Moderate accommodative strategy*
Major attention	**Strong centralist** 1.7% (2) *Adversarial strategy*	centralist 5% (6)	**Empty talkers** neutral 1.7% (2) *Ambiguous strategy*	decentralist 12.5% (15)	**Strong decentralist** 29.2% (35) *Accommodative strategy*

ideological profiles, such as the *Partito Radicale* (PRAD) in 1992 and *Italia dei Valori* (IdV) in 2008, parties that felt less compelled by strategic interests to emphasize an issue that was not among their core concerns. Aside from this small group, all remaining documents expressed a more or less clear-cut strategy on decentralization.

Some Say No …

The number of parties using a *tout-court* adversarial strategy is very small, including only those parties that expressed a negative position (directional certainty between −1 and −0.5) and either low (mild centralist) or high (strong centralist) salience. This category includes only five documents, mostly from the First Republic Among them, three were issued by the right-wing nationalist conservative MSI (in 1958, 1968, and 1979), whose ideological profile actually demanded opposition to bestowing competencies to the subnational levels, which it saw as weakening the central state and national identity. Likewise, the PLI (in 1963), a right-wing, conservative, free-market party, has traditionally been skeptical about decentralization, considering it responsible for increasing the inefficiency of state bureaucracy by creating overlapping centers of decision making. In the Second Republic, outright aversion to decentralization almost disappeared, with the only exception being the M5S in 2013; and even then, M5S made only a limited reference to the transfer of state competencies related to healthcare.

While sharp opposition has been relatively rare in Italian electoral rhetoric, a slightly larger group of documents (10) reveals ambiguous centralist stances, with values that are close to zero but clearly negative (directional certainty between −0.5 and 0). Depending on how much attention these documents devoted to decentralization, they can be classified as either "reluctant centralist" or "empty talkers centralist"; but either way, they expressed a certain openness to softening their initially critical stances toward the redistribution of powers. The centralist documents of the First Republic include the manifestos of the nationalist MSI in 1963, 1983, and 1992 and the rightist conservative PLI in 1953, 1968, and 1979. The PRI's manifesto from 1979 is the only nonrightist document in this group: despite its traditionally decentralist stance, the party issued a document that year in which decentralization was treated as a rather minor issue, focusing instead on the importance of the central state's ability to guide regional activity and the "national interest" in harmonizing the regions' positions. On the contrary, in the Second Republic doubt was voiced by the communist *Rifondazione Comunista* (RC) in 2001 and the Christian Democratic *Unione di Centro* (UDC) in 2008, while rightist opposition is represented only by a document released by the MSI's successor, AN in 1994. Looking closely at the documents, it is clear that RC was ideologically influenced by leftist support for strong state intervention in productive activities. The UDC meanwhile treated the territorial issue with the kind of hesitant ambivalence typical of its party family, supporting some decentralist reforms (e.g., the Senate of the Regions and fiscal federalism) while calling for other policy areas, such as "transports, energy, communication and labor" (UDC 2008), to be returned to state competency.

...But (Almost) Everyone Says Yes (or So)

The vast majority of parties could be classified as supporters of decentralization, whether mild or strong, with 58 documents showing positive directional certainty ratings above 0.5. All the main political parties, ranging from left to right, appear in this category at some point in the time period considered.

On the other hand, a significant share of documents (21) can be classified as reluctant decentralist or empty talkers decentralist, even if they lean toward decentralist stances. Within this group of ambiguously accommodative strategies there are 6 documents from the Christian Democrat party family (DC 1963, 1976, 1979, and 1987; PPI and *Patto per l'Italia* [Patto] 1994; and *Scelta Civica* [SC] 2013); the leftist parties, meanwhile, are responsible for 3 documents from the First Republic (*Partito Socialista Unitario* [PSU] 1968; PCI and PSI 1983) and 2 from the second Republic—namely, PDS 1992 and *Unione* 2006 (the latter was a broad coalition overburdened with different ideologies, ranging from the far left to the center). The remaining documents come from smaller, centrist parties (such as PRI 1968 and 1983 and PSDI 1979) or the rightist AN in 1996, which was at the time facing the electoral threat posed by autonomist former ally *Lega Nord* (LN). Surprisingly enough, the empty talkers decentralist group includes the manifesto of *Popolo delle Libertà* (PDL) from 2013, which was also endorsed by the LN. In this document, besides the usual decentralist references to the federal senate, the Europe of the Peoples, and a federal Italy, there were also statements pointing out those competencies that should not be bestowed to subnational levels, such as "foreign policy, public debt and national equalization," proposing instead that "25% of the tax revenues [be] used by the State to sustain the administrative expenditures" those competences incur (PDL 2013).

Parties at the Crossroads: Blurring and Contradictory Strategies

The data presented thus far suggest widespread support for decentralization, at least in the electoral arena, over the time period considered. Nevertheless, the slightly crowded gray area of the reluctant and empty talkers decentralists on both sides of the territorial continuum as well as the eight neutral documents presenting *tout-court* directional certainty scores of 0 (i.e., "reluctant neutral" and "empty talkers neutral"), deserve more attention, especially because they constitute a 32.5% share of the entire corpus analyzed. This is a heterogeneous group: among the purely neutral, there are both mainstream political parties such as the DC in 1948 and the PRI in 1972, and smaller fringe parties like *Democrazia Proletaria* (DEM.PROL.) in 1976 and RC in 1994 and 1996. Likewise, reluctant and empty talkers documents, both decentralist and centralist, are to be found for a variety of parties, as seen in the previous sections.

But what does this ambiguity mean? As Rovny (2013, 5–6) argues, "parties may strategically avoid stances on some dimensions of multidimensional political conflict. ..." When confronting issues that are not part of their core ideology, parties "may attempt to project vague, contradictory or ambiguous positions on these issues" rather than simply remaining mute or denying their salience. "The aim of the strategy is to mask a party's spatial distance from voters in order to either attract broader support, or at least not deter voters on these issues." Similarly, Somer-Topcu (2015, 3) indicates that parties might attempt to appeal to a broader electorate with different preferences by purposefully clouding their policy positions.

Although their motivations might be similar, there is nevertheless a substantial difference between those parties intentionally expressing blurred messages and those expressing clear but contradictory stances on different aspects of the same issue. The former is a concealing strategy, used to avoid making specific commitments on a topic to the electorate without alienating either supporters or opponents. A contradictory strategy, on the other hand, represents a nuanced approach to an issue. In the specific case of decentralization, this usually means a party is endorsing the transfer of competencies downward in certain policy areas, while at the same time confirming state control of others. This strategy might prove effective in attracting decentralist votes without alienating those who are skeptical about a profound territorial reorganization of the state; or as seen in hypothesis H1a-*bis*, it could be a way to differentiate a party's policy platform from that of its adversaries when they all share the same underlying support for decentralization.

A closer look at the TERRISS Dataset reveals that ambiguous scores in Italian party manifestos result more often from contradictory stances than blurring stances. Table 4.2 shows those documents with directional certainty values of 0, which indicates an ambiguous strategy that might also be either blurring or contradictory. There are only two documents among this group that feature exclusively neutral statements and can be classified as blurring, and both of them are from the First Republic: the manifesto of the DC in 1948 and that of PRI in 1972. The former referred to the issue with only a vague commitment to further action "to increase of the regional life, especially in the Mezzogiorno" (DC 1948), which actually left unanswered the question of whether the party was willing to implement the constitutional provisions on decentralization; similarly, the latter

Table 4.2 Documents with value 0 on directional certainty (ambiguous strategies: blurring and contradictory strategies.)

Type of ambiguous strategy	Salience	Directional certainty	Total number of statements on decentralisation in document	Number of neutral statements in document	% of neutral statements in document	% of neutral statements out of statements on decentralization	Party/year
Blurring	2.94	0	1	1	0.03	100.00	DC 1948
	1.66	0	4	4	0.02	100.00	PRI 1972
	6.27	0	18	16	0.06	88.89	PRI 1976
Contradictory	3.42	0	25	5	0.01	20.00	RC 1994
	1.47	0	2	0	0	0	MSI 1953
	0.46	0	2	0	0.00	0.00	DP 1976
	0.95	0	4	0	0.00	0.00	PSDI 1983
	3.02	0	12	0	0.00	0.00	RC 1996

Note: the first three parties are those classified as purely blurring, as their documents contain exclusively (or mostly, as in the case of PRI 1976) neutral statements and scoring 0 on directional certainty. Following are those parties with value 0 on directional certainty as well, but it is the result of contradictory decentralist and centralist statements that annul each other.

document made only a generic reference to a health reform project, saying it should be conceived by "respecting the State and Regions' competencies through a framework law," to the need to reorganize the administrative activity of the presidency of the Council of Ministers concerning regional administrative activity, while urging for a law that indicated a single template for the administrative action of the regions (PRI 1972). From these generic references to regional competencies, it is not at all clear whether these parties favored strengthening or weakening that tier of authority.

In cases like these, in which all statements on decentralization are 100% neutral, parties were pursuing typical blurring strategy, avoiding taking any one clear stance on the territorial policy dimension. Another example of a blurring strategy, albeit one with contradictory elements, is the 1976 PRI manifesto. This document earned a position score of zero; 16 out of 18 statements on the territorial dimensionwere neutral, mainly vague references to the need to reorganize state bureaucracy in light of the then-recent decentralist reform; the remaining 2 were, respectively, a critique concerning the decentralization of welfare and a statement supporting the fiscal autonomy of the municipalities.

The other five purely neutral documents with directional certainty scores of 0 can be classified as contradictory. The 1953 MSI manifesto, for example, called for the "entire repeal of the Title [of the Constitution] on the regional structure ...," on the one hand, while on the other hand proposing the "implementation of an effective and efficient decentralization of the administrative functions of the local authorities" (MSI 1953). Likewise, the 1996 RC manifesto contains no neutral statements whatsoever, but earns a directional certainty value of 0 thanks to its combination of support for the "decentralization of decision making ... of the legislative power" and affirmation of central authority over "the areas of defense, foreign policy, justice and macroeconomic issues" (RC 1996). Indeed, it seems that the party, caught in a heated decentralist debate triggered that year by the LN (Chap. 3), wanted to keep pace on autonomist demands, while at the same time comforting voters concerned that the unity of the nation was in jeopardy.

By extending the analysis of the gray zone to all those party documents with position scores between −0.5 and +0.5—that is, those documents labeled reluctant or empty talkers on either the decentralist or centralist side—it is possible to distinguish those parties using blurring strategies from those employing contradictory strategies by setting a threshold of

60%, meaning that if 60% of the total quasi-sentences on decentralization are neutral statements, the party is using a blurring strategy. The data show that only four additional documents meet this criterion—namely: PRI in 1983 (0.10 directional certainty; 75.9% neutral statements) and in 1979 (−0.33; 66.7%), SC in 2013 (0.18; 63.6%), and PLI in 1979 (−0.13; 60%). The remaining cases of ambiguity are generally the result of contradictory strategies, as in the above-mentioned case of RC in 1996, in which the parties seemed to opt for a "yes, but ..." strategy. The strategic implications of a contradictory stance will be thoroughly discussed later on in this chapter, in section "The Devil Is in the Details: Is There Conflict Behind the Surface Consensus?".

Party Strategies over Time: A Diachronic Analysis

Hypotheses H1a–c argue that party positioning on decentralization is influenced by both substantial factors, such as sincere support for transferring competencies downward, and strategic ones, meaning the fear of losing votes to a party championing the issue of decentralization. Besides these factors, parties also have to take into account any constraints imposed on their positioning by their ideological backgrounds. To empirically assess these hypotheses, the TERRISS data on party positioning can be diachronically examined, providing detailed data drawn from secondary sources on parties' ideological backgrounds, the substantial reasoning on decentralization, and the strategic conditions surrounding each electoral contest.

Figures 4.3 and 4.4 show the directional intensity for each electoral campaign from 1948 onward. As argued in Chap. 3, directional intensity "multiplies" the number of pro-, neutral and antidecentralist positions expressed in a document (i.e. the salience) by the directional certainty of this policy dimension, thereby providing a more nuanced description of overall party strategy in line with the typology proposed in Table 4.1. The figures do not display those documents that neglected the issue entirely. (For details on the scores on each variable for all of the analyzed documents, see Table A.1 in the Appendix.)

The First Republic

In the first two electoral campaigns of the Italian Republic, as seen in Chap. 3, the issue of decentralization was not a subject of significant party conflict. In 1948, the two leftist actors, PCI and PSI (which had combined to form the *Fronte Democratico Popolare* [FDP]), were strongly decentralist,

POSITION: SHARP CONFLICT OR SHARED CONSENSUS? 131

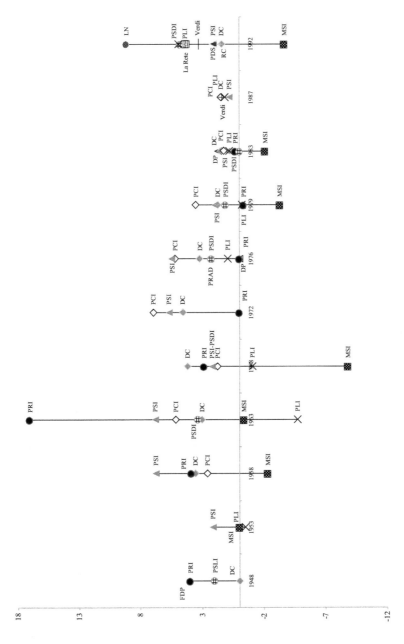

Fig. 4.3 Directional intensity of party manifestos (salience per directional certainty): 1948–1992

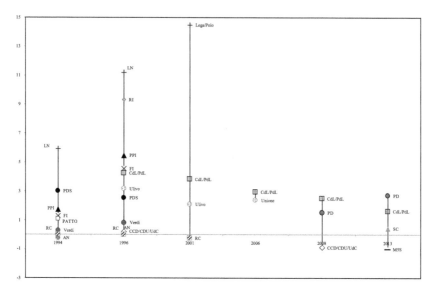

Fig. 4.4 Directional intensity of party manifestos (salience per directional certainty): 1994–2013 (values for LN 2008 omitted.)

and the *Partito Socialista dei Lavoratori Italiani* (PSLI) was generally decentralist as well, although their references to local autonomy were at the time limited to the role and competencies of the municipalities. The DC, on the other hand, had not yet begun to substantially support a regional structure for the state, instead using a blurring strategy on the topic and including only one vague statement referring to decentralization in its manifesto (see above). Indeed, only the PRI, a small centrist party, explicitly mentioned the need to implement "the division of the competencies between the State, the Regions, and the Municipalities" (PRI 1948), though no party expressed outright dissent on this issue. In 1953 only the PSI expressed a clear, if moderate, decentralist profile, promoting the full implementation of the Special Statutes; at the same time, moderate but resolute opposition to regional reform was beginning to emerge in the form of the rightist PLI, and the MSI presented a merely neutral document on decentralization featuring contradictory statements. The first republican elections were held in a period when the issue of decentralization held limited strategic significance for electoral dynamics. Accordingly, party positioning tended to reflect both substantial support for decentralization and its overall plausibility within the framework of party ideology.

The scenario changed in the late 1950s and early 1960s. As the public became more aware of the topic of regional reform, decentralization became increasingly salient in the political discourse, and thus more strategically relevant, although the public remained somewhat divided on the issue. According to a survey reported in Putnam et al. (1993, 68),[11] 51% of Italians had no opinion on the topic in 1960, while only 19% said decentralization would entail "more benefit" and 20% said it would entail "more detriment."[12] In 1963 the percentage of those favorable to regional reform rose to 31%, while the share of those skeptical remained generally stable (22%) and the share of those with no opinion dramatically decreased (30%).[13] Within this context, as noted in Chap. 3, both the PSI and PCI had compelling substantial reasons to push for the creation of the regions related to the opening of further centers of power at the local level, which they reconciled with their ideological backgrounds. Accordingly, they both released decidedly decentralist programmatic platforms. The 1958 and 1963 manifestos of these two parties show clear decentralist profiles: in 1958, the PCI stated: "It is necessary to proceed with the full implementation of the Constitution. ... The basis of such political reform, for the communists, is the creation of the Regions, which gets rid of the old structures of the oppressive and centralizing State" (PCI 1958); and in 1963 the party called for "the urgent implementation of the Ordinary Regions" (PCI 1963). Likewise, in 1958 the PSI blamed the DC for having "held back the demands of autonomy of the local authorities, with the bureaucratic centralization" (PSI 1958); moreover, the party's 1963 manifesto clearly proclaimed its strong support for decentralization, calling it a preliminary condition for any potential agreement with the DC: "the socialist party declared that it declined any proposal for an agreement during the Legislature, until the not implemented points of the government's program are carried out, and first of all the implementation of the Regions," defined as "a fundamental part of the Constitution" (PSI 1963). Confronted with such a solid decentralist front, the DC was compelled to adopt a direction in the territorial debate. Ideologically, decentralization was consistent with the Christian Democratic principle of subsidiarity. The DC took a wait-and-see approach, however, predominantly out of fear that the regions would open new governing opportunities to the communists. Accordingly, in 1958 the DC employed its usual rhetorical acrobatics to both confirm its commitment to "the gradual implementation of the regional structure" but do so "in the full respect of the unitary integrity of the State"—a statement with centralist undertones—

while advancing a number of concrete proposals concerning local financial and administrative decentralization (DC 1958).

The electoral campaign of 1963 was preceded by the first center-left government in 1962. Created at the end of Legislature II and led by Amintore Fanfani (DC), the center-left coalition was based on an agreement with the PSI, which had abstained from the vote of confidence; part of this agreement called for the creation of the regions. Nevertheless, this step was delayed again due to the approach of the 1963 elections. The moderate wing of the DC, headed by Mariano Rumor and Emilio Colombo, was afraid that further concessions to the center-left, which is how regionalist reform would have been seen, would alienate the conservative electorate (Taviani 2004). Right-wing propaganda already depicted regional reform as a product of the center-left alliance, one that could have potentially harmful consequences for the country. One example of this centralist campaign, which included a thinly veiled anticommunist message as well, can be found in the page of the 1963 PLI manifesto titled "Why we say NO to the Regions" (capital letters in the original). The page shows a map of Italy in which the regions with leftist majorities are colored in red, underlined by a final message: "Regions are one of the ways through which people from the center-left seek to gain the political and economic power" (PLI 1963). The MSI also adopted a clearly centralist adversarial strategy in keeping with its nationalist ideology in 1963.

The DC, caught between leftist decentralist demands and pressure from conservative voters and forced to act by the increasing awareness of regionalist issues among the electorate, delivered a manifesto in 1963 that featured a "empty talking" decentralist strategy and is a perfect example of the party's circumspect approach in general. It began by saying, "we confirm we are in favor, according to our original intuition, of the local autonomies ..."; but then it continued: "... to this reform, which has not been abandoned and, on the contrary, has made significant steps towards its implementation, *should be applied the criterion of prudent gradualism* that should underlie the necessary and full implementation of the Constitution. We thereby confirm that it is necessary a condition of political stability ... to carry out the reform, which should be presided ... by a democratic majority to carry the burden and guarantee the constructive and unitary value of the watershed reform. *There is no contradiction between the willingness to do and willingness to do well,* that is to say in the best time and ways ..." (DC 1963, italics added).

Translated from the jargon typical of the DC's moderate wing (the so-called *dorotei*), the DC was committing itself to meeting the socialists' demands in the form of a new agreement in Legislature IV, while reassuring the most conservative voters that it would ensure the integrity and stability of the institutions, which meant, in the language of the DC, that it would prevent the communists' rise to power.

The 1958 and 1963 elections reveal a pattern consistent with the model shown in Fig. 4.1. Indeed, those parties with substantial reasons to support decentralization adopted clear accommodative strategies—as was the case with the PCI and the PSI, which were also able to reconcile their ideological backgrounds with this stance (Chap. 5)—in line with the expectations of hypothesis H1a. The DC, despite sharing most of the substantial reasons to support the regionalization of the state, was strategically torn: on the one hand, it needed to accommodate the decentralist stances promoted by the leftist actors, which had become increasingly popular among the electorate; on the other, it wanted to avoid alienating the still relevant share of conservative voters, who were skeptical about the regions and the advantages they might bring the communists. As a result, the party opted for an ambiguous (mostly contradictory) strategy, to a certain extent diluting its support for decentralization, as posited by hypothesis H1a-*bis*. Finally, and again in line with hypothesis H1b, those parties that referred to ideologies predisposing them to outright opposition to any weakening of the central state (namely the MSI and the PLI) used adversarial strategies.

In the 1968 elections, however, the DC surpassed even the leftist parties in the intensity of its support for decentralization, shifting toward a clear accommodative strategy, which it maintained in the subsequent 1972 election; it kept an accommodative stance in 1976, and the ambiguity of the value of directional certainty (0.3) is mostly due to contradictory statements aimed at differentiating its policy proposal (see also section "The Devil Is in the Details: Is There Conflict Behind the Surface Consensus?" in this chapter). After the reform of 1968 (Chap. 2) the DC could actually claim credit for the recent "approval of the law for the election of the regional councils," which it defined as "one of the most significant steps of the last legislature" (DC 1968), thereby conferring to the DC a strategic interest in supporting the process it had itself initiated. The MSI and PLI, meanwhile, remained opposed on ideological grounds. This shift was also made possible by the changed strategic conditions. In the 1970s the regions were finally beginning to take shape, and Italians were gradually growing accustomed to the new state structure. According to a survey conducted by the DOXA and reported in Putnam et al. (1985, 303), the percentage of Italians who had heard "a lot" about the regions or were "somewhat" familiar grew from 35% in 1972 to 44% in 1977.[14] In this context, the pattern of party competition remained generally stable. The PCI and the PSI were still at the forefront of the decentralist group, demanding the completion "of the implementation of the regional structure" (PCI 1972; PSI 1976) and calling for the full transfer of "the functions that are still carried out by the national authorities in those matters of article 117 of the constitution and the implementation of the framework laws" (PCI 1972). The DC, for its part, reaffirmed its commitment to carrying out the necessary steps to complete the process of reform while retaining its usual prudence and gradualism, saying: "the DC considers the development of the regional and local autonomies as decisive for the full implementation of the constitutional framework of the democratic state, whereas Parliament and Government are put under the condition of seeing to the fundamental tasks of the national and international politics with authority and prestige." (DC 1976) Turning to the opposition, the MSI remained hostile to the creation of the regions, alternating between a strategy of neglect and one of open opposition in electoral campaigns. The PLI shifted from a neglecting strategy to moderate support for decentralization in 1976, proposing a regional Senate and the "completion of the transfer to the Regions of the functions of their competencies ..." (PLI 1976) before returning to a more critical, although blurring, approach in 1979, in line with H2c.

Indeed, in those years most parties saw a strategic advantage in adopting an accommodative stance on decentralization, in part because most parties had grounds to claim credit for the ongoing process of reform (see below); at the same time, awareness of the regions was gradually increasing among the electorate, and the growing complexity of the state structure was creating substantial reasons to support its decentralization. In this context, in line with the suggested hypotheses, an adversarial strategy was feasible only for those rightist conservative parties with clear ideological constraints, and even they had to slightly mitigate their opposition in this evolving political climate.

In the 1980s the regions were finally an established reality for many Italians. According to the above-mentioned time-series survey question reported by Putnam (1993, 68), the number of Italians who said "Don't know" when asked to evaluate the regions[15] dropped from 51% in 1960 to 5% in 1987; at the same time, the number of Italians expressing a positive impression of the decentralization process ("the reform of the Region entails more benefit") remained generally stable in the early 1980s (31%), and increased in 1987 (41%). Moreover, the leftist parties confirmed their strength in their strongholds in central and northern Italy in the 1980 and 1985 regional elections, achieving one of the main goals that had motivated their decentralist move. Looking closely at the content of the manifestos, we see the primary consequence of this "normalization" of the regional structure was the depletion of the topic's political relevance, and decentralization began to slip in the PSA (Chap. 3). Alongside this overall decline in attention, party positions tended to converge on moderate support. During this period, references to decentralization consisted mainly of rhetoric concerning the need for "enhancing the regionalist system" (PCI 1987) or the need to "develop the potentialities" (DC 1987) of the regions, which were not yet fully implemented or functional. In other words, most parties chose an accommodative strategy for both strategic and substantial reasons, which were shared by the political system's main actors. Even the ideologically adversarial MSI slightly moderated its opposition because it was no longer strategically convenient. It is interesting that the traditionally centralist PLI presented empty decentralist documents in the 1980s, representing a shift in the party's attitude.

In the 1992 election, however (the last of the First Republic), the entrance of an electorally relevant peripheral party upended the discourse on the territorial structure of the country. Despite the fact that the LN's "autonomist project … pursued the institutional reform in a federal direction" based on the creation of "macro-regions …, basic units of the Europe of the Regions" (LN 1992), the DC failed to revisit its own statements on the issue, instead basically repeating its proposals from the last elections.[16] The *Partito Democratico della Sinistra* (PDS), on the other hand, took up the challenge posed by the LN, advancing a proposal for an "almost federal State" endowed with a "Senate of the Regions" and grounded on enhanced regional financial autonomy, while simultaneously chastising the divisive autonomist claims of the LN (PDS 1992; see also Chap. 5). Although most political parties at the time shared a more or less pronounced decentralist attitude, the MSI remained the last bastion of opposition to the regions, vowing to "relentlessly struggle to alleviate their disastrous consequences" by pursuing their abolition[17] (MSI 1992). It is interesting that even the PLI, which had been a fierce opponent of the regional reforms of the 1960s and 1970s, now turned to firm support for reforming the regions within the framework of a federal Europe, which would develop the subnational communities (PLI 1992).

The autonomist challenge posed by the LN, on the eve of a new decade, had made an accommodative approach more strategically convenient for most Italian parties.

The Second Republic

In the Second Republic the political discourse on decentralization was dominated by a revitalized debate on the topic (Chap. 3), one that drew on new arguments (Chap. 5) and focused on proposals for a deep shift of the state's structure in a federalist direction (Chap. 2). Party competition was influenced by the harsh autonomist rhetoric of the LN, whose emphasis on this policy dimension was decidedly above the average of the other parties in all the electoral campaigns except those in which it joined an official coalition program (2006 and 2013).

Indeed, in the 1990s a diffuse sense of dissatisfaction with the current structure of the state emerged among Italians, along with emerging support for strengthening the subnational authorities. According to a survey conducted between 1995 and 1996 and reported by Barlucchi (1997, 354), less than half of Italian citizens thought that the current state structure was good (45.2% in September 1995; 38.9% in May 1996), while 38.2% were in favor of the empowerment of the regions, the federal state with its current regions, macro-regions, or a confederation of macro-regions (percentages obtained by aggregating these four "regionalist" options were 38.2% in 1995 and 48.1% in 1996).[18]

In this context, a centralist stance was not electorally advantageous. Parties had a strategic interest in joining the autonomist push, converging in general on accommodative strategies (although, as will be pointed out later, they were often compelled to differentiate their political discourse on decentralization from that of their adversaries, in line with the expectations of hypothesis H1a-*bis*). During this period, the centralist opposition almost disappeared, with only moderate centralism expressed by AN, the successor to MSI, in 1994.

In the novel two-coalition system, the main poles actually shared a fairly clear decentralist attitude. In 1994 elections the PDS presented a program that promised "a strong federalism, with federalist inspiration ... which is something different from a mere decentralization" (PDS 1994). This message was reaffirmed by both the party's electoral brochure and the coalition program published by *Ulivo* in 1996. In the latter, the coalition set out some of the key points that were then included in the constitutional reform of 2001, such as the attribution of legislative competencies to the regions, the transformation of the Chamber of the Regions into a permanent body, and fiscal federalism (Ulivo 1996). On the right side of the political spectrum, *Forza Italia* (FI), headed by the tycoon Silvio Berlusconi, tried to accommodate both the secessionist claims of the LN and the nationalist heritage of AN in its 1994 Popolo delle Libertà (PdL) coalition. FI's lack of a political past made it easier to find elements of cohesion and compromise between the two allies, but LN nonetheless withdrew its support in 1995, and the rightest pole did not propose another coalition with Bossi's party in elections the next year. However, the documents presented by both FI itself and the PdL coalition show firm support for federalism, and the center-right echoed its main adversary's proposal to create a Chamber of the Regions. On the eve of a new decade, state reform finally took place. In the 2001 elections, held a few months before the constitutional referendum, *Ulivo* claimed credit for the reform, which was "incomprehensibly not voted [for] by the opposition," while committing itself to continued efforts toward federalism, which needless to say meant overcoming bicameralism with the creation of the Chamber of the Regions.

Federal reform enjoyed widespread support among Italian citizens, who voted in favor in the referendum of October 2001. According to a preelectoral survey conducted by ITANES in 2001,[19] the federal reform was perceived as important by 60% of Italians;[20] moreover, 77.6% believed that "more autonomy should be given to regions," and 57.6% agreed with the statement that "tax money should be given to regions which will administrate these funds on their own."[21] Against this backdrop, it would have been costly for the rightist opposition to openly campaign against the reform approved at the end of the Legislature. As a result, the 2001 manifesto of the PdL, which had allied once again with the LN, basically ignored the pending reform of Title V, while laying down the key points of the "devolution." This indeed became the party's new slogan, and a part of the political discourse on the structural reform of the state. The only voice against decentralization was that of RC, which was moderately critical of "the devolution invoked by the rich regions of the North, governed by the right, which aims actually at breaking up the country" (RC 2001).

In 2006 and 2008 both the center-right and center-left coalitions confirmed their support for further reforms of the territorial structure of the state. In 2007 the nationalist AN merged with FI to form the PDL, finally abandoning its centralist tradition; meanwhile, the UDC began to express centralist tendencies, proposing some state constraints on decentralization (e.g., the "supremacy clause," according to which the state can prevail over regional law and the redistribution of legislative competencies) in its 2008 manifesto.

In the 2010s the financial crisis became the foremost political concern, even as federalist reform remained incomplete. According to the results of a survey conducted in 2011 by the LAPS[22] of the University of Siena, 43% of citizens were strongly or somewhat in favor of federalism, 35% were opposed, and 22% were undecided.[23] And even this support was not without its uncertainties:[24] one-third of Italians were afraid that it would threaten the unity of the nation (33%),[25] and a majority (52%) thought it could increase local taxation;[26] likewise, only 38% thought it would enhance the efficiency of the healthcare system.[27] In keeping with the ambivalence among the electorate, the new decade saw the LN start to devote less attention to its autonomist cause, instead spending its rhetorical energies on more national questions like immigration and Euroscepticism. The political discourse on decentralization became more a part of a broader debate on structural reforms than an issue on its own. Decentralization was therefore mostly framed as a process meant to simultaneously satisfy demands for enhanced autonomy and greater responsibility for local authorities and respect the need for a strong and effective central state to address the economic crisis. Accordingly, in 2013 elections both the center-right and the center-left proposed a project of federal reform within the structure of a unitary central state. The PDL outlined a program "for a federal and unitary Italy: North, Centre and South as protagonists" (PDL 2013); likewise, the *Partito Democratico* (PD) declared its commitment to "reformulate a responsible and well-ordered federalism, which would make the autonomies as a point of strength of the democratic and unitary system of the country" (PD 2013). It was only the new actor on the political scene, the M5S, that expressed criticism for the devolution, and specifically the devolution of the healthcare system, which can be seen as part of its overall "antisystem" approach.

The findings presented above show that, in line with hypothesis H1a, most parties over time have shared substantial reasons to support the process of decentralization. And this position could prove to be strategically rewarding as well, because public opinion since the 1960s has been increasingly favorable of the regionalizing process. This was particularly evident in the Second Republic: Until the 1980s, there was still little awareness of the regions among the electorate, and a share of conservative, nationalist voters was afraid of jeopardizing national unity. At the end of the First Republic and during the Second Republic, however, public opinion showed increasing support for a federal state, along with growing dissatisfaction with the current structure of the state. Accordingly, even when parties were skeptical about the benefits of surrendering competencies or had not yet developed a clear position on the issue, they often opted for accommodative, or at least ambiguous (blurring or contradictory), strategies rather than outright adversarial ones, as suggested by hypotheses H1c and H1a-*bis*. Adversarial approaches were almost exclusively adopted by those parties for which support for decentralization was neither plausible nor credible for ideological reasons, as in the cases of the nationalist MSI and the conservative PLI until the 1970s, in line with hypothesis H1b.

The Devil Is in the Details: Is There Conflict Behind the Surface Consensus?

As the reader may sense from the above account, Italian parties have mostly converged over time on accommodative strategies on decentralization. The topic has apparently not been a battlefield for political competition, as most political forces share a common blueprint for territorial restructuring.

But is this picture accurate? After all, if one conceptualizes parties as strategic actors, it would not seem to be electorally advantageous to campaign on an issue on which every actor shares the same view; voters would not be able to clearly identify the party that better represents their own preferences. As a result, those issues should cease to influence voting behavior, and parties should not want to waste their time and effort campaigning on a subject that does not attract more voters (Green-Pedersen 2007, 2012; Green-Pedersen and Krøgstrup 2008). Nevertheless, as seen in Chap. 3, decentralization has always been a salient issue in the political debate, albeit to varying degrees over time. How can one explain an issue that retains its political salience even as it ceases to be a matter of party competition?

As suggested with hypothesis H1a-*bis*, a possible clue to this dilemma comes from a closer inspection of the gray zone of ambiguous documents seen in the previous section. As previously noted, a not insignificant number of party documents have imbued the electoral rhetoric with a certain degree of ambiguity. In a few cases, this ambiguity seems to represent an intentionally vague approach. In most cases, however, directional certainty scores close to zero are due to contradictory preferences on specific subtopics within the category of decentralization. Extending this examination to the entire corpus of coded documents, it becomes evident that even those parties classified as strongly or mildly decentralist seldom reached scores of a full 1 on directional certainty denoting a clear-cut decentralist position; this was observed in only 19 documents. Apart from this small stronghold of sincere decentralists, in fact, even those parties that adopted straightforward accommodative stances (with scores of directional certainty between 0.5 and 1) expressed reservations on specific aspects of the process of territorial restructuring or in some other way added nuance to their preferences. Given the way in which directional certainty is measured (Chap. 1), the presence of even one critical statement on a single, specific aspect of the process of decentralization means a decrease of the decentralist score from its maximum of 1.

It is necessary at this point to explain how it is possible to hold contradictory preferences on the same issue. The answer lies in the peculiar nature of the topic of decentralization. As discussed in Chap. 1, the generic notions of "territorial issues" and decentralization include a plethora of policy areas involved in the process of redistributing powers downward, ranging from fiscal policy to health and education.[28] Parties might hold different preferences about whether or how to devolve each subtopic to subnational levels. Furthermore, the process of decentralization can take many forms and approaches: it can manifest as a mere redistribution of administrative powers to local authorities or extend to bestowing legislative competencies; it can be achieved by implementing the existing constitutional provision or necessitate a constitutional change. In other words, a party's support for decentralization in general has little meaning if considered outside the context of the political debate. Instead, to really understand the dynamics of party competition on this issue, we must consider what kind of decentralization political actors actually support and pursue.

It can therefore be expected that, as argued in hypothesis H1a-*bis*, while parties may generally agree on the purported advantages of a decentralized state structure, they actually disagree on the specific policy areas in which such reforms should take place. This argument is consistent with Keating and Wilson's (2010, 2) statement, according to which "below the surface consensus, each party interprets federalism differently … while the apparent federal consensus holds back the kind of concrete understanding reached through political contestation."

The coding scheme allows the inspection of party positioning on decentralization across different policy areas to see whether parties favor the redistribution of competencies in certain policy fields while supporting state control in others (Chap. 1). This analysis will shed light on the contradictory strategy (hypothesis H1a-*bis*) pursued by many Italian parties over time.

The Greater the Complexity, the Higher the Conflict

Before examining the nature of party conflict in specific policy areas involved in the process of decentralization, it makes sense to explore the complexity of this policy dimension over time. How many subtopics have been the subject of electoral debate? Have parties covered a wide range of policy areas, or have they tended to focus on only a few of them (e.g., fiscal federalism or constitutional reforms)?

The first question can be answered by simply counting the number of subtopics covered in each electoral campaign from 1948 onward. Figure 4.5 shows both the number of policy areas related to decentralization addressed in party documents and the entropy score (see below) for each electoral year. Looking at the data, it is clear that the number of territorial policy areas involved in electoral debate increased considerably after 1963. Indeed, until that point the main question was simply whether or not to implement the constitutional provisions envisaging the creation of the ordinary regions and limiting the range of related subtopics to agriculture, administrative decentralization, fiscal autonomy, and a few others. When the regional structure of the state began to become more concrete, however, political actors had to decide what these regions should concretely be required to do. Accordingly, the debate was expanded, and now included references to actual competencies and the kind of powers—either legislative or merely administrative—to be transferred to the new subnational authorities. As attention to decentralization declined in the 1980s, the richness of the debate also decreased. The revitalization of the issue's salience in the 1990s occurred simultaneously with an increase in the number of subtopics covered, and new fields were introduced to the political debate (see also below). The last decade has been characterized once again by a focus on a few subthemes.

Besides merely counting the policy areas covered in political debate, a more nuanced assessment can be achieved by considering the concentration, or spread, of party attention across all the possible subtopics. The distinction is a subtle but significant one: even if the political agenda deals with a variety of subtopics, most party attention might still focus on only

144 L. BASILE

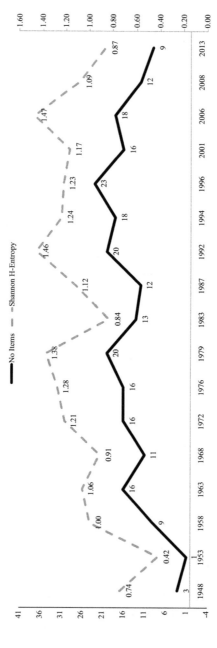

Fig. 4.5 Number of subtopics in the political discourse (left axis) and entropy score (right axis)

a few of them, or parties might devote attention to all the subtopics equally. For this reason, policy agenda literature has proposed indexes to measure *attention diversity*—that is, the degree to which the attention of political actors is distributed across items in the political agenda (Boydstun et al. 2014). By applying this methodology to the issue of decentralization (here considered a macro-category in the party agenda system) and the several subtopics related to it, it is possible to measure whether parties focused their attention on only one aspect of decentralization (complete concentration) in any given election or devoted almost equal attention to the entire range of policy areas that might be involved in the process of decentralization (complete diversity). Among the proposed indexes, the Shannon's H entropy formula has been increasingly popular in studies concerning agenda setting and policy attention (ibid.; John and Jennings 2010).

The Shannon's H entropy formula[29] is $-1 \cdot \sum_{i=1}^{n} p(x_i) \cdot \ln p(x_i)$ where x_i are the number of statements made in party manifestos on each individual policy area (e.g., health, education, fiscal federalism). It calculates the proportion of attention that each subtopic received in a given electoral campaign, multiplied by its natural log. These products are then summed up and multiplied by negative one. This formula was applied using the list of 25 subtopics plus a further category called "general" containing the remaining statements dealing with decentralization. Shannon's H has therefore been calculated by considering the share of statements mentioning each subtopic compared to the overall number of statements in the electoral documents *in each election*.

The result indicates a point on a spectrum between two hypothetical extremes. In the one extreme, all parties focus on a single aspect of decentralization, for instance generic aspects concerning the implementation of the subnational authorities. In this case, the proportion of attention would be 1 (i.e., 100% of attention) for this category and zero for the others; as the natural log of 1 is 0, the final index will be equal to 0 (complete concentration).[30] At the other extreme, all parties devote exactly the same amount of attention to all 25 subtopics plus the generic category, and the value of the index is 1.99.

As Fig. 4.5 shows, the entropy score generally follows the same pattern as the number of subtopics covered, but with a few significant deviations. In 1983, for example, though there were 13 policy subtopics addressed in the debate, the entropy score was relatively low (0.84). This was because that year the bulk of the political discourse focused exclusively on fiscal autonomy (28% of statements) and generic statements concerning decentralization (56% of statements). The entropy peaks in 1992 (1.46) and 2006 (1.47), on the contrary, reflect a political debate in which party attention was fairly evenly dispersed across, respectively, the 20 and 18 categories addressed in those electoral campaigns.

The "Yes, but..." Strategy on Decentralization

The entropy analysis reveals that, overall, the political debate on decentralization has been characterized by a certain degree of complexity; with a few exceptions, the parties have dedicated attention to the details of decentralization in addition to its broad appeal. But was there conflict among the parties on the concrete, specific aspects of decentralization? Or did parties tend to converge on similar positions on all of the facets of the territorial policy dimension?

A synoptic view of party positioning on each subtopic is presented in Fig. 4.6 and Table 4.3. The former uses a box plot to show the distribution of values for directional certainty for each policy subtopic. Like the directional certainty values on decentralization in general, values here can range between −1, or opposed to decentralization on that subtopic, and +1, or favorable to a transfer of competencies (Chap. 1). Accordingly, when the box covers all the options, this means that party documents, over time, featured opposing positions on the decentralization of competencies in that policy area. This is seen in many policy areas, including agriculture, domestic macroeconomic issues, education, energy, foreign policy, health, labor policy, law and order, legislative competencies, tourism, transportation, and welfare. In all these cases, content analysis revealed that party documents adopted positive, negative, and neutral stances on decentralization in these areas.

Table 4.3 provides further details on the number of documents featuring positive, neutral, and negative stances on each policy subtopic; documents are also classified according to their overall strategy on decentralization—namely, accommodative, neutral or adversarial. In other words, if a party document shows a directional certainty value above 0.5 on decentralization, it is considered accommodative; however, if there are critical statements on decentralization throughout the document on the health system, for example, this document is counted as negative on that policy area. Then, for each subtopic, a calculation is made to determine the consistency (in terms of percentage) of documents' positions on the subtopic with their

POSITION: SHARP CONFLICT OR SHARED CONSENSUS? 147

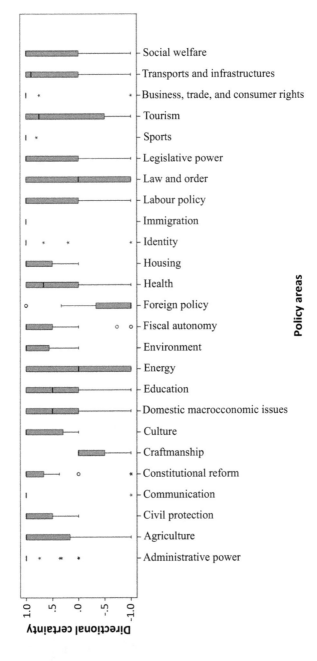

Fig. 4.6 Directional certainty on decentralization concerning specific policy areas (entire corpus of document; n = 120)

Table 4.3 Number of documents, and related positions, dealing with each policy subtopic, classified according to the party's overall strategy on decentralization (accommodative, ambiguous, adversarial)/consistency of party position on subtopics with overall strategy on decentralization (%)

	Accommodative			% Consistency	Ambiguous			% Consistency	Adversarial			% Consistency	n
	Positive	Neutral	Negative		Positive	Neutral	Negative		Positive	Neutral	Negative		
Craftsmanship	0	2	1	0	0	0	0	–	0	0	0	–	3
Energy	2	0	2	50	0	0	0	–	1	0	0	0	5
Trade	10	0	1	91	0	0	0	–	1	0	0	0	12
Tourism	7	2	2	64	0	0	0	–	0	0	1	100	12
Agriculture	19	3	0	86	0	2	0	100	0	1	2	67	27
Housing	14	4	0	78	0	1	0	100	0	0	0	–	19
Transports	9	3	1	69	0	0	0	–	0	0	1	100	14
Civil protection	3	1	0	75	0	0	0	–	0	0	0	–	4
Environment	10	2	0	83	0	0	0	–	0	0	0	–	12
Health	16	4	1	76	1	2	0	67	0	0	3	100	27
Welfare	18	6	3	67	0	2	0	100	0	0	1	100	30
Education	16	7	3	62	0	0	1	0	0	1	1	50	29
Culture	14	5	0	74	0	1	0	100	0	1	0	0	21
Communication	6	0	0	100	0	0	0	–	0	0	0	–	6
Sports	8	0	0	100	0	0	0	–	0	0	0	–	8
Immigration	2	0	0	100	0	0	0	–	0	0	0	–	2
Law and order	4	3	3	40	1	0	2	0	0	1	0	0	14
Legislative comp.	16	4	3	70	2	1	0	33	2	1	1	25	30
Admin. comp.	23	4	0	85	1	1	0	50	7	1	0	0	37
Const. reform	23	1	1	92	1	0	0	0	1	2	4	57	33
Identity	19	1	0	95	1	0	0	0	1	0	1	50	23
Fiscal autonomy	54	9	0	86	2	1	1	25	4	1	2	29	74
Labor policy	10	2	1	77	0	0	0	–	0	0	2	100	15
Foreign policy	2	1	6	22	0	0	2	0	0	0	0	–	11
Economy	17	4	6	63	0	1	1	50	0	1	1	50	31

overall position on decentralization. For example, if all documents considered accommodative on decentralization also contain positive statements on immigration, then it means that party positions on that subtopic tends to align with their overall positions on decentralization. The opposite would indicate that parties are taking contrasting positions in this area to differentiate their political discourse from that of their rivals—for example, criticizing the surrender of competencies in a specific area despite expressing overall support for the process of territorial restructuring.

At the aggregate level, it is clear that only a few policy areas are consistent in this sense, including the fields of communication, immigration, and sports, where positive statements on decentralization in general were found in all accommodative party documents. Likewise, the only negative statements on tourism, transportation, health, welfare, and labor policy were included in the documents of those parties that were adversarial toward the process of decentralization itself.

The other policy areas are characterized by nuanced and diversified positioning. In particular, while the "accommodative" parties represent the vast majority, as previously discussed, most of their documents present differentiated positions on specific subtopics, in line with the contradictory strategy hypothesis (H1a-*bis*), for instance opposing the surrender of state competencies in certain areas. A significant number of "accommodative" documents differentiated their political discourse by adopting negative or neutral stances when decentralization in policy fields like welfare, education, foreign policy, and law and order was at stake. To a certain extent these documents are all expressions of party strategies, drawing distinctions and adding nuances to their broad support for decentralization. They are all manifestations of a "yes but ..." strategy that conceals underlying conflicts behind the overall consensus, conflicts that kept the decentralist issue alive against all odds as a relevant issue for party competition, despite the (apparent) convergence.

The following subsections examine these patterns of party competition on the concrete aspects of decentralization more thoroughly. For explanatory purposes, the policy fields included in the coding scheme have been grouped into macro-areas.

Productive Activities
The first group of policy fields includes the productive activities, most of which were affected by the transfer of competencies to the regions with the presidential decrees of 1972 (Chap. 2).

Agriculture has been by far the most addressed area within the political discourse on decentralization over time. Decentralist parties have advocated transferring competencies to subnational authorities in this field, while the centralist parties opposed it, in keeping with their overall strategies on decentralization (e.g., PLI 1963 and RC 2001). In some cases, some ambiguity emerged, such as in the 1968 manifesto of the PSU, which called for effective decentralization "while, at the same time, setting a program of agricultural reconversion with a national and not regional vision" (PSU 1968).

Other sectors like tourism, trade, craftsmanship, and energy, on the other hand, were areas of party conflict and exposed internal inconsistencies between parties' positions on decentralization in general and the subtopic in particular. This was the case with the leftist pole in the Second Republic, for example; despite its accommodative strategy and its crucial role in the process of decentralization, the 1996 *Ulivo* coalition manifesto and 2006 *Unione* manifesto favored strengthening state control in these sectors. The *Ulivo* manifesto claimed that the central government should have been guaranteed the roles of coordination, programming, and monitoring in the area of tourism, leaving regions only implementation; moreover, in the area of craftsmanship it envisaged "the development of regional policies within a national legislative framework" (*Ulivo* 1996). Likewise, the 2006 *Unione* manifesto restated the need to retain the state's authority on tourism as well as on consumer protection, consumers' rights, and energy (*Unione* 2006). More recently, the 2013 manifesto of the decentralist SC offers another example of an "accommodative strategy with differences." It called for a "modification of Title V of the Constitution in order to return to the State the decisions concerning the energy infrastructures"[31] (SC 2013).

Land Management and the Environment
The second group is made up of policies like urban planning, transportation, civil protection, and the environment, which are traditionally considered areas where knowledge of the territory and its needs make subnational authorities the most appropriate level of governance. Parties consistently tended to converge toward support for decentralization in these areas, or at least adopt ambiguous stances. The latter was true of the accommodative PdL—for example, in its 1996 document it envisaged an urban law based on an enhanced role for local authorities, while at the same time calling for a state law on the matter to lay the framework for future regional legislation.

One interesting exception is the 1972 DC manifesto on transportation and infrastructure, which represents a clear example of a contradictory strategy. Despite the party's overall accommodative stance on decentralization, it opposed the surrender of powers downward in this sector, distinguishing its programmatic platform from that of its adversaries: "it is necessary to give coherence to the big infrastructural works that, albeit in the full implementation of the regional structure, must be kept on the national budget" (DC 1972).

Social Policies and Services to Citizens
Unlike the previous two areas, the group of social policies and services to citizens reveals interesting patterns of polarization and conflict among the parties. Policies like education, health, and welfare aim to provide adequate levels of assistance and support for social development while addressing potential disparities both between citizens and across poorer and richer areas. Accordingly, some political actors have been skeptical about bestowing such crucial competencies on local authorities and potentially jeopardizing equal access to services for all citizens nationwide. Debate on the decentralization of these competencies increased considerably during the Second Republic when the reform process began moving in a federalist direction.

Education is one of the main areas where political forces have expressed dissenting views, followed by welfare and health. Aside from those parties that opposed decentralization in general (e.g., PLI 1963), even firm decentralist actors like the *Ulivo* in 2001 have expressed criticism concerning the transfer of competencies in this area, as this quotation shows: "it would be … dangerous to integrally delegate to Regions the educational activities" (Ulivo 2001). In other cases, party programs have expressed somewhat ambiguous stances on this aspect of decentralization. For instance, the 1983 PCI manifesto, which expressed an overall accommodative strategy on decentralization, made a distinction between basic education, which should be "unitary … so to guarantee in the entire national territory the achievement of adequate formative levels" and "professional education, with the actual programming competencies of the Regions" (PCI 1983).

Similar patterns of dissent emerge in the field of welfare, mainly thanks to leftist actors, which have expressed concern for the need to ensure equality across the regions alongside their firm support for decentralization. This can be seen, for example, in the 2006 *Unione* manifesto, which claimed that "it should be up to the national government [to define] the basic levels of assistance to be guaranteed to all citizens in the entire national territory" (Unione 2006). Similar warnings also appeared in the documents published by other political forces, such as the DC in 1963: "the State ... has the duty to promote the related [welfare] services and to coordinate all the interventions at national, regional and local levels" (DC 1963).

Health policy has been deeply affected by the process of regionalization, in particular the reforms of the early 1990s,[32] the Bassanini reform of 1997, and the constitutional reform of 2001, with the latter including health among the concurrent competencies.[33] In light of evidence of disparities across the regional health systems (OECD 2014),[34] some dissent emerged about whether to delegate authority over this basic right to subnational levels. Opposition to the decentralization of the health system emerged not only among parties that expressed generally adversarial strategies (e.g., PLI in 1979; RC in 2001 and M5S in 2013); concerns about the potential for territorial gaps in this sector were also voiced by the traditionally decentralist PD in 2008, which called for a strengthening of the National Health Service "by correcting the territorial gaps that limit the right to health in some Regions of the country, especially in the Mezzogiorno" (PD 2008).

The other three policy areas included in this group (culture, communication, and sports) are less affected by these concerns for regional and local equality, and have received less attention in the political discourse. These topics are consistently characterized by broad convergence among the parties. Nonetheless, the parties have made a few fine distinctions in these sectors as well by pointing out the importance of a state role in monitoring and coordination. It is interesting that, in its 1994 manifesto, even the LN reined in its strong decentralist rhetoric and acknowledged the need for the central government to play a coordinating role in the field of culture.

Organization of the State, Home Affairs, and Citizens' Rights
The fourth group of policy subtopics is rather varied: on the one hand, it includes fields that are traditionally considered state competencies (law and order, immigration) and identity policies; on the other hand, this group also includes statements concerning the kind of decentralization being pursued by political parties, focusing in particular on aspects such as the transfer of administrative and legislative competencies as well as constitutional reforms.

The issue of decentralization of migration policy has been addressed only recently and with no significant pattern of conflict. Likewise, apart from a few references from the PCI and DEM.PROL. In 1976, matters concerning law and order and justice entered the political discourse in terms of decentralization only in the Second Republic. However, some conflict has emerged in this field, especially as a reaction to the autonomist political discourse. Since the 1990s, the LN has advanced the idea of a "devolution to the Regions of responsibilities ... for the defense of citizens from urban crime" (Lega Nord/Polo 2001). As a result, other parties, even those that are genuinely decentralist, have been compelled to reassure their voters that the federalist project would not affect these state competencies. It is interesting that these reassurances have come predominantly from the FI/PdL when it has not been in a coalition with the LN—for instance, in 1996 the PdL proposed a federal authority "holding the primary competence ... in the administration of justice" (PdL 1996), similar to something proposed in the 1994 FI document. Further criticism of decentralization of law and order can be found in the manifestos of RC, which was more ambiguous concerning its overall support for decentralization in general.

Concerning identity, it is interesting to note that the only significant distinction comes from a centralist party. While all the accommodative political actors have also been in favor of measures to protect minorities and local identities, in 1968 the centralist PLI addressed the protection of the German-speaking minority in Alto Adige "in the respect of the sovereignty, borders, and laws of the Italian state" (PLI 1968).

Shifting to the approach to decentralization, it is immediately clear that even the adversarial parties have expressed favorable attitudes toward the transfer of merely administrative powers to the regions, making it one of the largest areas of convergence among the parties. The MSI, for example, declared its support for "a serious administrative decentralization" in 1968, even while expressing its aversion to the implementation of the ordinary regions (MSI 1968). Similarly, the PLI reaffirmed its opposition to any regional reforms in 1953 while calling for "safer administrative decentralization" (PLI 1953). In other words, there has been a certain amount of convergence among the parties on at least a minimal approach to decentralization, the surrendering of administrative competencies to subnational levels.

The picture changes when the debate shifts to the transfer of legislative competencies (i.e., the regions' ability to legislate in specific policy areas).

In this area party positions are much more nuanced, with even decentralist parties drawing certain distinctions. For instance, in 1968 the DC displayed a certain amount of ambiguity on this aspect of decentralization, saying on the one hand that "Regions should carry out eminently a legislative function in those areas expressly attributed by the Constitution," but on the other calling for constraints on this competence: "Regions should legislate within a harmonic system, guaranteed by ... the framework laws adopted by the regional Parliament" (DC 1968). In 1976 the DC took an even more nuanced approach, claiming to strongly support the process of decentralization while also declaring that "the Parliament and the Government should be able to carry out, with authority and prestige, the fundamental tasks of ... the civil legislation" (DC 1976).

Finally, there is a large amount of convergence among the parties on the need to pursue decentralization through constitutional reform. Critical stances mostly emerged among the centralist parties, for instance the PLI, which in 1963 called for a revision to the Constitution to address "those parts that revealed to be defective in the light of the mediation and democratic experience. One of these points is the Regions" (PLI 1963). Even when this party shifted to a more accommodative strategy in the 1980s, it retained its skepticism toward constitutional reforms moving in a federalist direction, "refusing the hypothesis of transforming the Senate into a Chamber of the Regions, which would push towards the Federal State" (PLI 1983). This topic has been particularly salient in the Second Republic; three constitutional reforms have actually been approved by the Parliament, though two were rejected by popular vote (Chap. 2).

Foreign/Defense Policy and Economic/Fiscal Policy
The last group of subtopics includes economic issues and foreign and defense policy. The latter is traditionally considered a key feature of the nation-state according to Max Weber's definition. In the case of Italian decentralization, it actually represents an exceptional case of backward convergence: all parties but the LN in its early years (1992 and 1994) have agreed that even in a federalized system the central government should retain authority over defense and international affairs. Indeed, only the autonomist party broke the taboo on challenging the state's monopoly of the use of force, for instance envisaging the creation of "regional militias" rooted in their territory (LN 1994). The 2001 *Ulivo* manifesto, however, also scored positively on this topic, as it encouraged the southern regions to "engage in international relations with neighbors"

according to the powers envisaged by "the new constitutional law on federalism" (Ulivo 2001).

Moving to economics, fiscal autonomy, which has been present in every electoral campaign with the exception of 1953, reached a peak in terms of attention during the Second Republic. Parties have tended to cluster toward supporting this policy; however, some dissent emerged in the First Republic, mainly among the centralist (MSI 1983 and 1992) and ambiguous parties (PSDI 1983). Moreover, a significant number of parties have maintained ambiguous stances on fiscal autonomy. This is most common when the political discourse has turned to details concerning the division of tax revenues between the regions and the central state, as in PDL's 2013 program.

On macroeconomic issues, the picture is a bit more nuanced. During the First Republic, most parties sought to decentralize responsibility over so-called economic planning, allowing local authorities to use their familiarity with their territory to better address their areas' economic needs. Nonetheless, in that period there were also cases in which support for decentralization went along with more or less centralist economic positions, such as the DC manifesto of 1976, which reaffirmed the role of the central state in the "promotion and control of economic action" (DC 1976). In the Second Republic, consensus paved the way to a somewhat conflicting pattern: A number of manifestos, especially in the 1990s, expressed concern regarding the possibility that, in a federalized structure, the central state would renounce control over fundamental choices concerning the political economy. This concern was shared by both center-left and center-right actors. In 1996, for instance, the PdL reaffirmed that the central, federal authority should retain the primary competence on monetary policy; the same year, the *Ulivo* manifesto pointed out, among other things, the "essential role of state policy in the financing of investments," and it even entertained the possibility of suspending the autonomy of regions that breached the budget constraints (Ulivo 1996).

Finally, the topic of labor policy has received less attention, and most references have been generally supportive of further decentralization in that area, with the exception of those from adversarial parties; however, in 1996, even a generally accommodative manifesto like that of the PdL included criticism of the process of decentralizing labor policy, chastising the "inadequacy of the Regions' management of the vocational education" (PdL 1996).

A Reality Check for Parties: From Electoral Pledges to Parliamentary Behavior

Research on electoral party attitudes often claims that party pledges, as expressed in manifestos and other programmatic documents, should serve as a clue for understanding the path taken by reform on a given policy issue. This argument, however, implies that there is a convergence between what parties say in their programmatic platforms and how they eventually vote in Parliament, and this cannot be taken for granted. A closer examination is required to answer the following crucial question: do parties actually do what they promise once in Parliament?

The analyses carried out thus far have provided a detailed account of party electoral statements on decentralization. To address the problem of a possible gap between electoral rhetoric and institutional practice, this section compares party electoral rhetoric with parliamentary debate and party voting behavior on the occasion of major decentralist reforms adopted from 1948 onward. This will provide a test for hypotheses H2a–d, presented in section "Why Do Parties Vote as They Do? Party Competition in the Parliamentary Arena" in this chapter. In this case, party voting behavior on the occasion of territorial reform is the main dependent variable, while the independent variables include electoral party preferences, measured according to the salience and position of the issue in their manifestos; party role, either in government or in the opposition; and the country's political system, either consensual or majoritarian. The empirical analysis will be carried out first through a detailed reconstruction of party behaviors and dynamics over time based on official records and parliamentary debates and will be further substantiated by statistical analysis based on TERRISS data. The findings should help answer whether, as anticipated in the theoretical model, the determinants of party voting behavior are different from those that explain electoral positioning. The importance of a party's role in government and the party system in the determination of its voting choices will be given special attention.

Parties at the Proving Ground: The Approval of L. 62/1953

The first, albeit modest, step in the process of decentralization was the so-called Legge Scelba adopted in Legislature I (Chap. 2). The bill, a government initiative, was presented almost at the onset of the new legislature, on December 10, 1948. Most articles were discussed in the Committee for Home Affairs, while the rest were reserved for the Assembly, which eventually approved the law by secret ballot on November 22, 1951.[35] In the absence of a record of votes cast, party positions have to be determined from the explanations that followed the vote and other passages of parliamentary debate.

The leading party, the DC, was the main proponent of the law, though it had assumed a rather ambiguous position on decentralization during the electoral campaign. In keeping with its electoral strategy, it took an ambivalent position on territorial issues once in Parliament as well; it proposed and passionately supported this reform, which pursued a certain amount of decentralization while simultaneously introducing limits and constraints on the substance of regional autonomy. This ambivalence was primarily the result of divisions that emerged within the party on decentralization, as is clear from Giuseppe Bettiol's (DC) explanation of the vote: "within the party there were convinced supporters of the local autonomy and convinced but more moderate ones. Hence, since the Constituent Assembly, our group has chosen a median, … which would not jeopardize, through the regional autonomy, the unity of the State" (Camera dei Deputati, meeting n. 803 of November 22, 1951, 33393). The choice of the DC was nevertheless in line with the expectations of hypothesis H2b, which posited support for decentralist bills from a governing party, assuming that its policy preferences are not too distant from the final bill adopted (H2a).

The two main opposition parties, the PSI and the PCI, both took strongly decentralist positions in the electoral campaign, as previously discussed. When faced with a bill on decentralization, they had to choose between leaving the issue of regionalism to the DC by opposing the law or staying coherent with their regionalist stances and supporting it. They both chose the latter option, while at the same time pointing out the inherent limits of the reform (and blaming the Christian Democrats for them). In other words, the leftist opposition supported a government bill out of a sense of responsibility to the Constitution. In the words of Giulio Turchi (PCI): "our favorable vote does not mean that we appreciate the reform, neither that the Regions it envisages are those we wished, that the constituent fathers wished. … The consequences of the rejection of the law [would be] that Regions would not be set up …, the shadow of the centralist State … would take shape and everything would be like before, worse than before" (ibid., 33392). Likewise, Lucio Mario Luzzatto (PSI) conveyed the socialists' support while pointing out that "in several parts the law does not meet the needs. ... Our vote does not mean to renounce to denounce [the shortcomings of the law], but it is our duty to vote for the law that finally establishes the norms for the constitutions and functioning of regional bodies" (ibid., 33394). Both the PCI and the PSI proposed amendments in the Assembly to reduce the constraints to regional authority imposed by the bill, such as the state's control over the statutory autonomies and limits to the legislative competence of the regions. This behavior of the opposition forces in Parliament is in line with the hypothesis arguing that opposition parties are likely to vote coherently with their policy preferences (H2c), especially in consensual systems like the First Republic (H2d).

Among the centralists, both the MSI and PLI had ignored the issue during the electoral campaign. In parliamentary debate, the MSI which was in the opposition, reaffirmed its strong, "convinced and fierce antiregionalist position," while accusing the leftist parties of promoting the creation of the regions with the sole "purpose to gain the power in some regions," as stated by Giorgio Almirante (MSI) (Camera dei Deputati, meeting no. 369 of December 14, 1949, 14365–14369). The PLI was a member of the first government of Legislature I, which proposed the bill,[36] but it later became one of the bill's sharpest critics when shifted to the opposition; it even proposed that discussion be suspended concerning the creation of the regions, which was not considered an urgent issue, and expressed its fierce aversion to the regional structure (Camera dei Deputati, meeting no. 796 of November 14, 1951, 33094–33100). This behavior of the centralist forces further confirms the hypotheses on the role of party preferences (H2a) and their interaction with the party's role in government (H2c).

Among the minor parties, the PRI, which was in government with the DC throughout the Legislature, was coherent with its strongly decentralist electoral stance, as is clear from the debates in which the republicans urged the approval of a law to implement the Constitution. On the other hand, the PSLI (then renamed the PSDI), which participated in two of the three governments in this legislature, showed moderate support for the reform in parliamentary debate akin to the prudent gradualism of the DC.[37]

The Approval of Law 108/1968: Between Parallel Convergences and Harsh Obstructionism

As mentioned earlier, the essential L. 108/1968 concerning the election of the regional councils was approved at the very end of Legislature IV, which featured socialists in the governing coalition for the first time in Republican history.[38] In the speech delivered by appointed Prime Minister Aldo Moro to the Senate asking for their confidence, the first center-left government proposed to complete "among its first acts, the implementing law of the ordinary Regions" (Senato della Repubblica, 71st public meeting, December 12, 1963, 3768). It actually took four years before the government's bill concerning the election of the regional council was finally presented to Parliament in June 1967. After overcoming harsh obstructionism from the rightist parties, the law was finally approved thanks to the "parallel convergences"[39] between the center-left in government and the communists in the opposition. The decentralist PCI contributed to the creation of the regions by voting in favor of the law, while at the same time criticizing the "extreme hesitation" concerning the regions mentioned by Prime Minister Moro; as Pietro Ingrao (PCI) said, "it is necessary to go ahead with a strong groundbreaking audacity" (Camera dei Deputati, meeting no. 754 of October 17, 1967, 40207–40209). The majority supporting the government voted in favor of the reform, with the PSI expressing its satisfaction with the approval of this "essential step for the implementation of this democratic reform" (ibid., 40219–40222) and urging the completion of the process of decentralization. The PSDI and PRI also voted in favor of the law.

As mentioned previously, the rightist parties waged a brutal war against the law in Parliament. In keeping with the centralist stance they demonstrated in the electoral campaign, both the MSI and the PLI fiercely opposed its approval, denouncing the law as a concession to the communists. In the words of Arturo Michelini (MSI) (ibid., 40217–40218), the MSI blamed the ambivalence of the DC for the law's creation, criticizing the party's hesitation to create the regions and its sudden transformation into an outright supporter of decentralization in response to the center-left coalition. Similarly, the PLI explained its opposition by arguing that the creation of the regions would increase the inefficiency and costs of the Italian bureaucracy and furthermore would have paved the way to power for the communists, as is evident from statements made by Giovanni Malagodi (PLI) (ibid., 40209–40212). In this case as well, the expectations of hypotheses H2a through H2d are largely confirmed.

Emerging Patterns of Dissent: Regionalist Reforms in the 1970s

The parallel convergences diverged in Legislature V, which saw the approval of L. 281/1970 and L. 775/1970. As argued in Chap. 2, these two laws charted a minimalist course to decentralization, envisaging limited administrative and financial autonomy for the regions, which largely left the regionalists unsatisfied (Putnam et al. 1985 and Chap. 2). The communists opted to abstain from both laws, citing the fact that these provisions lagged behind the expectations of genuine decentralization supporters. In his explanation of his vote on L. 281/1970, Alberto Malagugini (PCI) stated that it represented "a controlled autonomy, a reaffirmed willingness to aberrantly consider Regions as subordinated to the State, to the executive, to the bureaucracy" (Camera dei Deputati, meeting no. 252 of January 26, 1970, 15687). The *Partito Socialista Italiano di Unità Proletaria* (PSIUP) which had adopted a decentralist profile during the elections, abstained as well, citing similar motivations. The opposition's abstention,[40] however, did not mean outright opposition, thus partially supporting the expectations of H2c.

On the other hand, the governing parties, including the DC and the PSI, supported the laws. It is interesting that the PRI, which was a firm supporter of decentralization and a member of the governing coalition, expressed profound dissatisfaction with L. 281/1970 and also opted to abstain, quoting the same reasoning as the PCI. The Republican position, meanwhile, was expressed well by Michele Pinto (PRI): "for us, the problem is not whether or not to make the Regions, but how to make them well. ... We do not vote in favor of this law in order to fulfill our duty to express our dissent for a [regional] structure that we accept in principle but not in the ways of implementation. We are confident that our critical position ... will contribute to keep a lively and extant debate on the regional structure" (Senato della Repubblica, meeting no. 284 of May 15, 1970, 14925–14926). However, the PRI voted in favor of the subsequent L. 775/1970, though it expressed reservations about the content of the reform.

On the centralist front, the right-wing MSI remained coherent with its centralist attitude, opposing L. 281/1970 for reasons similar to those it expressed two years before—namely inefficiency, the increase of state costs that would result from the creation of the regions, the threat they posed to the unity of the nation, and the argument that: "who takes advantage [from the Regions] is the communist party, which intends to make concrete—and does not hide it—its goal to gain power," as is made clear in Cristoforo Filetti's (MSI) statement on the subject (ibid. 14932–14933). The MSI moderated its opposition slightly on the occasion of the vote on L. 775/1970, when it opted for abstention. The other centralist party, the PLI, strongly opposed both laws. It is interesting that in explaining his party's contrary vote on L. 281/1970, Benedetto Cottone (PLI) used an argument related to the European Union (see also Chap. 5) to oppose regionalism: "which is the sense of splitting Italy in Regions, within the framework of a united Europe, in which Italy is itself a region?" (Camera dei Deputati, meeting no. 252 of January 26, 1970, 15681).

The consensual reform climate, however, returned on the occasion of the vote on L. 382/1975. The communists, though they criticized the minimalist approach the government had adopted on the autonomy of the regions and the limits of the reform under discussion, voted in favor, along with the main governing parties (DC and PSI). Once again, opposition came from the antiregionalist forces—namely, the MSI and PLI. Overall, even the party behavior observed on the occasion of the vote for the two laws adopted in the 1970s confirms the scenarios formulated in the hypotheses.

The Polarized Way to Reform in the Second Republic

As the previous section shows, the main decentralist reforms of the First Republic often succeeded thanks to a convergence among the main decentralist parties; the main line of polarization was along the centralist-decentralist divide. Thus it was possible to consider party electoral support for decentralization a reliable indication of institutional behavior and a party's role in the actual process of reform. As previously argued, however, the emergence of "parallel convergences" on specific reforms was also made possible by the basically consensual system on which the First Republic was based. A bipolar system emerged in the Second Republic and laid the basis for the further polarization of the party system, which increased the likelihood of highly contested partisan reforms. Few, if any, parties have explicitly expressed centralist positions in their electoral campaigns from 1994 onward. More than two decades after the creation of the ordinary regions, there were no more political actors arguing for the need for a unitary, centralized state; even the right-wing AN, the successor to the MSI and a frequent coalition partner of the LN, shifted toward decentralist positions. Nonetheless, while this surface consensus could paper over dissent on specific topics, it did not lead to consensual reforms.

The first test of the sincerity of parties' decentralist attitudes was the vote on L. 59/1997 (*Leggi Bassanini*), proposed by the center-left government. The governing coalition unanimously voted in favor, as did RC, which was then externally supporting the government. On the other hand, the center-right pole in opposition, along with the LN, voted against the law counter to overall decentralist preferences, as it pursued "federalism at unvaried constitution." Parties of the center-right pole justified their apparently inconsistent behavior in various ways. The LN blamed the limits and the inadequacy of the reform in addressing autonomist needs. In parliamentary debate, it defined the reform as an "insipid soup of federalism ..." and claimed that it would have pursued the path of "independence and self-determination," according to Francesco Tirelli (LN) (Senato della Repubblica, meeting no. 147 of March 11, 1997). Meanwhile, both FI and AN pointed out inconsistencies and inherent drawbacks of the reform, though they expressed a certain appreciation for the decentralist direction adopted by the government.

Polarization became even more evident on the occasion of the vote on the watershed reform of Title V of the Constitution in 2001, and the divide between the government and opposition, which then included RC, accurately predicted the outcome of vote. The opposition employed different arguments to support the apparent inconsistency of its institutional behavior with its electoral rhetoric, ranging from direct political attacks against the governing majority (which it accused of having pursued a reform without the consent of the opposition) to criticism concerning the lack of solidarity and the inherent limits of the reform. The LN, for instance, evoked gloomy authoritarian scenarios that would presumably result from mechanisms hidden within the reform that would strengthen central control, and Roberto Castelli (LN) even referred to a "surrender of the country's sovereignty to the technocrats of Brussels, pursuant to the first paragraph of article 117"[41] (Senato della Repubblica, meeting no. 1052 of March 8, 2001).[42] The CdL, on the other hand, defined the reform as "a fake federalism a federalism without solidarity, not cooperative, not competitive, not feasible ... a fraud law against the Italian citizens," as harshly described by Enrico La Loggia (FI) (ibid.). The opposition of the far-left RC was more in line with its ambiguity on decentralization during the electoral campaign. Giovanni Russo Spena (RC) explained that his party criticized the reform for lacking solidarity, calling it "the federalism of the rich and privileged territories" as envisaged by the LN, a liberalist project that would jeopardize the conditions of the working class (ibid.).

As discussed in Chap. 2, the opposition parties' strident resistance resulted in the center-right pole's calling for a confirmative constitutional referendum, in which a large majority of voters approved the reform (though admittedly with a low turnout). This was nevertheless only the first act of the "battle over the reforms" between the center-left and the center-right, which featured prominently in the 2000s. The two reforms of 1997 and 2001 confirm the expectations of H2d, which posited a government opposition divide in an eminently majoritarian system; indeed, this would also lead to the rejection of H2c under specific systemic conditions.

Failed Reforms and Fiscal Federalism

In 10 years, from 2006 to 2016, Italy underwent two failed attempts at decentralist reform embedded within a wider project to reform the structure of the state, which was eventually rejected by constitutional referendum (Chap. 2). The two episodes are perfect mirrors of each other: they were proposed, respectively, by a center-right and center-left majority, and each was strongly opposed by the opposition. The 2006 reform was approved by Parliament despite the opposing votes of *Ulivo* and RC, and it was the center-right's turn to stand accused of having pursued federalism without solidarity—exactly the same accusation made by the center-right in 2001. The Senate of the Regions envisaged by the reform and mentioned in most party manifestos, including *Ulivo*'s in 2001, was defined as a "dead Chamber, which on occasion, including the discussion of the State budget, becomes an Arabic *suk*, where Regions bargain and split up the State budget," in the words of Gavino Angius (DS) (Senato della Repubblica, meeting no. 573 of March, 25 2004). Moreover, the opposition parties blamed LN blackmail for the approval of a "law that would break up the unity of the nation to obey Lega Nord" (ibid.). RC, on the other hand, displayed a certain coherence with the centralist, albeit moderate, attitudes it expressed in the electoral campaign, especially by pointing out the risk that the reform would widen the gap between the north and the south. Aside from critical notes on the federalist elements included in the reform, the opposition's strong dissent focused on what it considered to be the excessive strengthening of the powers of the prime minister included in the bill.

Within the governing coalition, the LN claimed credit for the reform, which it called a "devolution." The UDC, which had neglected the topic of decentralization in its 2001 manifesto and would express somewhat centralist attitudes in the 2008 elections, actually voted in favor of the reform, but unlike the LN, it emphasized the balance between state and regional powers included in the reform, such as the supremacy clause.

In fact, despite the overall cohesion within the CdL in defense of the reform, it proved to be divisive for the coalition. There were some dissenting voices within the AN delegation,[43] who expressed their disapproval of a decentralist law advocated by the secessionist LN that they believed would detract from the unity of the nation, as expressed by Renato Meduri (AN): "today, a minister of the Republic [Umberto Bossi], who should manage this reform, intends instead to burn [the Italian flag] and refers to Rome as robber Rome" (ibid.). Likewise, a few members of the UDC[44] refused to support the reform in the Chamber of Deputies, pointing out problems such as those related to strengthening the premiership, and abstained from the vote. At the end of the legislative process the law was finally approved, though it was eventually rejected by popular vote in the constitutional referendum in 2006 (Chap. 2).

To tell the story of the second failed constitutional reform 10 years later it would be sufficient to invert the names of the main protagonists, albeit with a few new entries. This time the reform was strongly supported by a governing center-left coalition. It is debatable whether the changes to Title V should be interpreted as a sign of the PD's coherence with its own decentralist profile; as was discussed in Chap. 2, the Renzi-Boschi constitutional reform envisaged a recentralization of some competencies, and the new Senate was designed more to address the problem of perfect bicameralism than federalist ambitions. Among the other parties, SC (which was then called *Alleanza Popolare*), at the time part of the Renzi government, voted in favor of the reform, in line with the decentralist direction it displayed in the electoral campaign.

Legislature XVII, however, was characterized by several splits and changes within the majority coalition, which exacerbated tensions surrounding the approval of the reform. The *Sinistra and Libertà* (SEL) group, which had shared a party manifesto titled *"Italia. Bene Comune"* with the PD in 2013 elections, did not join either the Enrico Letta government or the Matteo Renzi government, and voted against the Renzi-Boschi bill while in the opposition. On the other hand, the *Nuovo Centro Destra* (NCD), which emerged from a split in the PDL after the latter party decided to revive *Forza Italia*, became a member of the governments' coalitions throughout Legislature XVII and voted in favor of the reform. The bill was opposed by two decentralist parties in the opposition, the FI-PDL and the LN. The latter criticized the reduced autonomy of the regions envisaged by the new constitution.

However, most of the harshest parliamentary debate focused on the methods used to draft the reform, the lack of consensus among the main political forces, and several other changes that the reform would have implied for the structure of the state. The M5S expressed its criticism of the decentralization reform in its electoral manifesto, though it devoted only a few references to the subject. In Parliament, the M5S voted against the reform, although mostly to demonstrate its disagreement with the main governing party, the PD. Unlike in the constitutional reforms of 2001 and 2005, in 2016 the topic of decentralism remained in the background during the political debate over reform.

This account of the pattern of party parliamentary competition in the 2000s should conclude with the vote on L. 42/2009 on fiscal federalism, proposed by the center-right governing coalition. Following the usual pattern of party polarization that characterized the Second Republic, this law was approved with the support of LN and PdL from the governing coalition, in keeping with their support for decentralization. On the other hand, despite electoral claims for fiscal federalism in its 2008 manifesto, the PD decided to abstain.[45] Such a choice was a purely political one based on criticism of the government in general and has little to do with the merits of the reform itself, which were mostly acceptable. As Anna Finocchiaro (PD) declared in explaining her vote, the final text of the law included several proposals from the PD, the result of a "political cooperation, a political convergence ..." that produced "a useful text, not only for the rich Regions, but also for those in difficulty" (Senato della Repubblica, no. 197 of April 29, 2009). Likewise, Antonello Soro (PD) stated: "our abstention marks the acknowledgment of a path that has been virtuous in the method ... and brings our ideas and our vision of Italy. ... But our abstention also marks our reservations regarding the tasks that the Government should carry out in the next stage" (Camera dei Deputati, meeting no. 151 of March 24, 2009). The other opposition parties adopted different strategies. *Italia dei Valori*, which had ignored the issue of decentralization in its manifesto, voted in favor of the reform. The UDC, on the other hand, presented an electoral manifesto in 2008 that leaned toward centralist positions, although it was favorable to fiscal federalism. Once in Parliament, the party cast a contrary vote against a law that it said would lead to the "disappearance of the juridical and economic unity of the country. … A fiscal federalism that is not necessary to anyone" (Senato della Repubblica, meeting no. 197 of April, 29 2009). It is interesting that, as argued in Chap. 2, the law approved in 2009 had to take into account the nationalist positions of AN, which had joined the governing coalition of PdL. It bridged this gap by crafting a compromise between the drive for autonomy, accountability, and responsiveness at the subnational levels (addressed by L. 42/2009) and a need for territorial solidarity. Although AN shared the (mildly) decentralist PdL manifesto, it kept its centralist background, which also emerged in the dissent expressed on the occasion of the reform of 2006. This resulted in the introduction of compromises to preserve national unity and solidarity, thus providing some support to the expectations of hypothesis H2b-*bis* concerning the voting behavior of centralist parties in government.

Do Parties Walk the Walk?

The narrative account of party voting behavior presented thus far reveals a substantial difference between the strategies pursued by Italian parties in the First Republic and those pursued in the Second. Indeed, until 1992 most of the crucial reforms on decentralization were adopted with the agreement of the major political forces from both the governing majority and the opposition, nearly all of which supported decentralization in their programmatic platforms. When these parties were critical of a reform proposed by the government, they opted to abstain rather than cast an outright contrary vote. Centralist parties from the right adopted parliamentary behavior that was consistent with their ideology, expressing their fierce opposition to all decentralist reforms throughout the First Republic.

The scenario changed dramatically in the Second Republic. Under the new bipolar system, the pattern of conflict on territorial reforms in Parliament tracked the government/opposition divide, with the latter voting against or abstaining even when this stance stood in apparent contrast with its decentralist rhetoric. This polarization, paradoxically, occurred just when outright opposition to decentralization had nearly disappeared from the electoral discourse. Admittedly, when current centralist parties like the RC, M5S, and UDC coherently vote against bills on decentralization, it is difficult to ascertain whether their behavior should be explained by their ideological platforms or their roles in the opposition.

This narrative account can be also expressed with numbers. Table 4.4 shows the cross tabulations of the party vote (in favor, against, and abstain) on decentralist reforms in relation to the predictors of voting behavior, as suggested by hypotheses H2a–d.[46]

Table 4.4 Parties' voting behavior cross tabulated with electoral position on decentralization, role in government, and left-right ideological positioning (%)

			Oppose	Favor	Abstain	N	Total
Parties' electoral position on decentralization	First Republic ($n = 33$)	Neglecting	67	0	33	6	100
		Centralist	83	0	17	6	100
		Ambiguous	0	100	0	2	100
		Decentralist	0	84	16	19	100
	Second Republic ($n = 21$)	Neglecting	0	100	0	1	100
		Centralist	100	0	0	3	100
		Ambiguous	–	–	–	–	–
		Decentralist	41	53	6	17	100
Parties' role in government	First Republic ($n = 33$)	Government	0	100	0	11	100
		Some government role	17	67	17	6	100
		Some support	100	0	0	3	100
		Opposition	38	23	38	13	100
	Second Republic ($n = 21$)	Government	0	100	0	7	100
		Some government role	0	100	0	2	100
		Some support	67	0	33	3	100
		Opposition	89	11	0	9	100
Parties' ideological position	First Republic ($n = 33$)	Left	0	43	57	7	100
		Center-left	0	91	9	11	100
		Center	0	100	0	5	100
		Center-right	100	0	0	5	100
		Right	80	0	20	5	100
	Second Republic ($n = 21$)	Left	60	20	20	5	100
		Center-left	25	75	0	4	100
		Center	–	–	–	–	100
		Center-right	50	50	0	12	100
		Right	0	0	0	0	100

The first element to examine is parties' electoral stances on decentralization. In the First Republic, 67% of neglecting parties and 83% of centralist voted against reforms; the majority of decentralist parties (84%) and all ambiguous ones (100%) cast a favorable vote, while abstention was chosen by an almost equal number of decentralist (16%) and centralist (17%) parties, with neglecting parties prevailing here (33%). In the Second Republic 41% of decentralist parties voted against reforms, while centralist parties have kept perfect consistency with their policy preference (100%); favorable votes were cast by 53% of decentralist parties and by a neglecting party; abstention was chosen by a minority of decentralist parties (6%).

Moving to the governing role, it should be noted at the outset that during a Legislature there is usually more than one government; this is especially true during the First Republic, when majorities were even less stable. In some cases, parties did not join a government but abstained or expressed external support during the vote of confidence. These variations can be expressed with values identifying the role each party played in each government during each legislature, ranging from 1 (government) to 4 (opposition), through 2 (external support) and 3 (abstention). These values are then summed up and reduced by the number of governments that were formed in each legislature. This index of a party's governing roles has been split into four categories to classify parties according to whether they played some governing role during the legislature or not: the government group includes those parties that remained somewhat stable in government throughout the entire legislature (values of the index between 1 and 2, with 2 excluded), for instance the PSI during Legislature IV, when it joined all the legislature's governments but Leone I in 1963, when it abstained from the vote of confidence. "Some government role" is made up of parties that during the same legislature alternated between governing roles and opposition roles, external support or abstention, although it their governing role was predominant (values of the index between 2 and 3, with 3 excluded). Once again PSI offers an example in Legislature VI, when the party shifted from opposition to participation in government, and then abstention and external support. When a party falls under the "some support" category, it means that during the legislature it gave some external support to the government or abstained from the vote of confidence on some occasion and never clearly assumed a governing role (values of the index between 3 and 4, with 4 excluded); this was the case of RC in Legislature XIII, when it remained in the opposition for the entire legislature except for the Prodi

I government, when it gave external support. Finally, the "opposition" group includes those parties that remained in the opposition throughout the entire legislature (value of 4 in the index).

It emerges that during the First Republic 38% of the opposition parties (mainly the MSI and PLI) and 100% of those parties included in the "some support" group voted against the reform; on the contrary, 23% of opposition parties voted in favor of decentralist reforms, with support mainly coming from the PCI, followed by the forces playing a prevailing (67%) or complete (100%) governing role during the legislature. The support of the opposition for decentralist reforms decreased in the Second Republic (11%), except for the case of the small IDV in 2008; on the other hand, 89% of opposition parties, followed by 67% of parties giving some support, voted against the territorial reforms. On the contrary, the totality of the parties holding a role in government voted in favor of reforms. Abstention was chosen by 33% of parties assuming some supporting role in a legislature. This was the case with PD in 2008, whose score in the index is explained by the fact that it had supported the technical government in the same legislature and, as mentioned earlier, chose to abstain from voting on L. 59/2009.

Besides the variables mentioned in the hypotheses, Table 4.4. also accounts for left-right[47] ideology to assess whether ideological background has some impact on voting behavior. This variable seems to be a good predictor of parliamentary votes in the First Republic because the right, as seen earlier when discussing the determinants of party preferences, represented the anti-regionalist front (80% voted against decentralization and 20% abstained); leftist parties generally voted for decentralist reforms. In the Second Republic, the right ceased to be a front of anti-decentralization, splitting its votes evenly between voting for and against decentralist reforms, while the center-left has sometimes opted to vote against.

To confirm these findings, a robust logistic regression (Table 4.5) was run to ascertain the effects of governing role and political discourse on decentralization in the preceding election on a party's likelihood to vote in favor of bills concerning reforms on decentralization, controlling for left-right orientation. The dependent variable is measured with a dichotomic variable in which 1 means that the party voted in favor and 0 that the party voted otherwise. Accordingly, it is not possible to observe nuanced party behaviors—for example, the use of a vote of abstention. A party's role in government is measured according to the index explained above, which ranges from 1 (government) to 4 (opposition). Party

Table 4.5 Logistic regression of party voting behavior on decentralist reforms

	Model 1	Model 2	Model 3	Model 4
Role in government	−2.391*			−0.990
	(0.967)			(1.456)
First Republic	−1.456	−1.231	2.632	26.70**
	(2.736)	(0.965)	(1.643)	(8.759)
First Republic* Role in government	0.654			−14.38**
	(1.065)			(4.924)
Party electoral preference on decentralization		0.0623		3.207
		(0.0511)		(2.314)
First Republic* Party electoral preference on decentralization		1.061**		−8.846**
		(0.332)		(2.913)
Role in government* Party electoral preference on decentralization				−1.137
				(0.653)
Left-right position			0.156	0.235
			(0.194)	(0.445)
First Republic* Left-right			−0.451	
			(0.276)	
First Republic* Party electoral preference on decentralization* Role in government				4.787***
				(1.331)
Constant term	6.663**	−0.38	−0.932	0.999
	(2.419)	(0.522)	(1.100)	(5.772)
n	54	54	54	54
Pseudo R^2	0.521	0.348	0.058	0.810
Log lik	−17.92	−24.39	−35.23	−7.099
Chi-squared	21.26	13.54	2.922	33.22

*p < 0.1; **p < 0.05; ***p < 0.01.

electoral preferences are measured using the value of directional intensity from the TERRISS Dataset. To measure the features of party and political systems, a dichotomic variable has been created accounting for the period in which the reform was voted, either the First (1) or Second Republic (0). Finally, the models used a control variable accounting for the left-right orientation ranging from 0 (extreme left) to 10 (extreme right). Four models have been run, three to test the impact of each predictor (role in government, party preferences, and left-right orientation) individually and a fourth one to include all the variables and their interactions.

The analyses reveal that being in the opposition during the legislature reduces the likelihood of voting in favor of a reform, as is shown by the statistically significant and negative coefficient of the role in government variable in Model 1. In the full model, however, it is statistically significant only in interaction with the dichotomic variable of party system. This result suggests that opposition parties tended to be against the government's reforms in the First Republic, although this apparently contrasts with H2c and H2d and the finding that emerged in the previous section, showing that the main opposition party, the PCI, voted in favor of some decentralist reforms. This might be explained by the fact that the dependent variable does not differentiate between a contrary vote and abstention, although the PCI has also opted for this latter choice.

Ideology, which has been introduced as control variable, is not a strong predictor of voting in favor of decentralist reform, either in Model 3 or in Model 4; as argued before, decentralization has been a largely transversal issue that has crosscut the left-right divide, and over time laws on territorial restructuring have been crafted by both sides of the political spectrum.

Instead of left-right ideology, a good predictor of voting behavior is party electoral position on decentralization. The coefficient is positive in both Models 2 and 4, meaning a higher likelihood of a favorable vote as the value of directional intensity increases, although the coefficient is not statistically significant; it becomes significant in Model 2 when put in interaction with the variable measuring the features of the party system. This finding thereby confirms a higher tendency to adopt behavior consistent with electoral claims in the First Republic than in the Second (hypothesis H2d). It is interesting that the coefficient of the same interaction term becomes negative in the full model. This apparently contradictory result might be explained by the introduction of a further interaction term in Model 4 that includes the three main predictors. In this case, the coefficient is positive and statistically significant, meaning that the likelihood of a favorable vote depends on the interaction of the following conditions: governing role, decentralist preferences, and the presence of a consensual/majoritarian system. Finally, the positive, statistically significant coefficient in the dichotomic variable measuring party system in Model 4 suggests a higher likelihood of shared consensus in the First rather than in the Second Republic.

To better interpret the changes in terms of the significance of each predictor between the First and the Second Republic, the predictive margins are also shown. As Fig. 4.7 reveals, although being in the opposition increases the likelihood of voting against reforms, this effect was much more marked in the Second than in the First Republic. On the other hand,

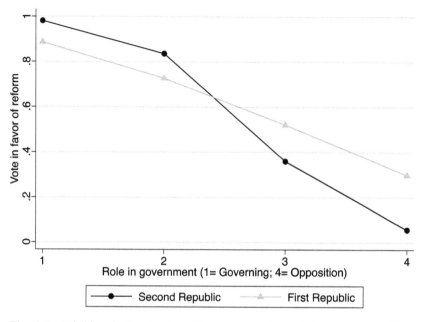

Fig. 4.7 Likelihood of voting for reforms compared to role in government: First and Second Republic

Fig. 4.8 shows that in the First Republic there was a stronghold of centralist parties voting coherently against the reforms; at the time, favorable votes were almost evenly distributed among both the ambiguous supporters of decentralization and its more ardent fans. In the Second Republic, although the decentralist direction of party positioning suggests a higher likelihood of a favorable vote, the effect of this determinant is somewhat limited.

Concluding Remarks

This chapter helped illustrate the pattern of party competition on decentralization by pointing out the key distinction between electoral strategies and voting positions.

The findings presented here reveal a substantial convergence among most parties in the decentralist direction of the territorial continuum, which partially confirms the expectations formulated in the theoretical

POSITION: SHARP CONFLICT OR SHARED CONSENSUS? 173

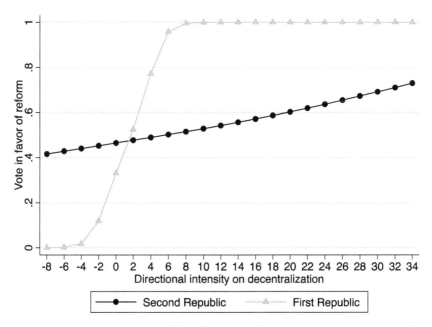

Fig. 4.8 Likelihood of voting for reforms and directional intensity on decentralization: First and Second Republic

model. In particular, it confirms that at least three factors matter in the definition of an electoral strategy: substantial agreement with the purposes and benefits of decentralization, ideological plausibility of this position, and strategic considerations. The accommodative strategy that currently prevails was established for both substantial and strategic reasons. During the First Republic, many actors saw strategic convenience in the possibility that decentralization might create new opportunities for gaining power at the subnational level. This, along with increasing if still somewhat weak public support, encouraged a convergence among most of the parties toward decentralist positions. In the Second Republic, increased popular support for a federal state along with the electoral threat posed by the LN made strategic considerations even more crucial for the definition of party strategies. As a result, most parties converged on support for decentralization. Thus, over time, most parties, even those for whom decentralism holds no direct, strategic interest, have opted for accommodative strategies to avoid losing votes to the "proponent" parties.

Such consensus, however, does not mean that there has not been party conflict on this issue. Rather, parties have often sought to differentiate their political proposals by presenting their own views and approaches to decentralization, distinguishing their support for decentralization in different policy areas and thus differentiating their proposals from those of their adversaries. Indeed, behind the surface consensus, a closer inspection of the manifestos reveals contradictions and nuanced party positions. Despite general agreement with the need to decentralize the state's structure, parties have also expressed support for decentralization in some policy areas but not in others. This strategy has allowed parties to differentiate their accommodative strategies from those of their adversaries and make decentralization a dimension of party competition, leaving aside the overall convergence on the broader goal.

The main constraints to an accommodative strategy are ideological plausibility and credibility, which explains the adversarial strategy adopted by the nationalist MSI, for example, and the PLI until the 1970s. Those parties that did not develop clear positions on decentralization often opted for ambiguous stances rather than outright adversarial strategies when strategic considerations made adversarial strategies risky.

When in Parliament, the strategic considerations in play during the electoral campaign are further complicated by other factors, such as a party's governing role and the party system. During the First Republic, parties were often coherent with their electoral pledges, even when in the opposition, apart from a few exceptions. This consensual style of policy making was a byproduct of the polarized multiparty system, which made compromise between the main forces necessary to adopt reforms. With the advent of a bipolar system after 1992, winning coalitions could rely on their own majorities to approve reforms. As a result, the approval of laws has often been characterized by a clear government-opposition divide.

At this point, there is still the question of whether the consensual approach that developed throughout the First Republic, when the regions were approved thanks to the parallel convergences between the DC and the PCI, was more effective than the divisive, partisan reforms adopted since the 1990s or whether, on the contrary, a "majoritarian" approach has been advantageous, to the extent that it has allowed the approval of innovative and daring reforms that would be impossible to achieve if a great deal of compromise and bargaining were needed. Indeed, this analysis suggests further avenues of research on the trade-offs between the quantity and the quality of reforms as well as the crucial influence that the state's basic rules (e.g., electoral law, party system, and government) have on the path (and quality) of reforms. As already argued, however, the answer to this question would go beyond the goals of this book, which more modestly aims to provide a full-fledged account of party strategies on decentralization.

There is still a piece missing from this account, one that is complementary to questions on "whether," "to what extent," and in "which direction" parties talk about decentralization—namely, "how" parties frame their discourse on this policy dimension.

Notes

1. Franco Bassanini, "Le regole del gioco si (ri)scrivono insieme" [The rules of the game are to be (re)drafted all together—author's translation], *Il Sole 24 Ore*, March 24, 2004.
2. In a tweet on electoral law, then-Prime Minister Matteo Renzi (@matteorenzi) said: "Electoral law. The rules are to be drafted all together. Make them based on majority voting is a style that we have always contested," Twitter, January 15, 2014. See also a similar declaration expressed at a convention in Cagliari on February 8, 2014, www.rainews.it/dl/rainews/articoli/renzi-ventennio-da-superare-riforme-colloqui-centrodestra-90d8acb8-853b-4187-8226-207ea09d0c3e.html?.
3. The distinction between substantial and ideological support is a subtle but necessary one. The two mostly tend to overlap, although there might be cases in which a party might share at least some of the reasons in favor of decentralization but they are inconsistent with its overall ideological background. For clarity's sake, however, the two aspects are considered together, under the implicit assumption that a substantial support (or opposition) to decentralization is often grounded on broader, ideological premises or that at least, as the reported examples reveal, parties tend to reconcile ideology and substantial reasons through the manipulation of frames.
4. Although it might be an oversimplification, for explanatory purposes it can be assumed that these two are intrinsically related to each other and tend to coexist. Indeed, if decentralization is quite popular among the electorate, it is reasonable to assume that proponent parties would have electoral advantages from this.
5. To be precise, it is not the party but the parliamentarians, who belong to parliamentary groups generally corresponding to political parties, who

carry out their duties (including voting bills) "without a binding mandate" (Article 67 of the Constitution). This means that deputies and senators might vote differently from what is officially indicated by their political party. This has occurred in a few relevant cases, and episodes of lack of party discipline on the issue of territorial reforms is reported in the empirical sections. Nonetheless, for simplification purposes, this chapter assumes political parties are groups of parliamentarians expressing a cohesive behavior on territorial reforms, based on their party's overall stance on the issue.

6. Party decisions are further constrained by veto players, the result of intraparty divisions and the emergence of internal dissent, which is likely to occur when crucial reforms are at stake (Farinelli and Massetti 2011). The analysis of these aspects, however, goes beyond the aims of the book.
7. It should be also noted that in Italy governments have been the promoters of most of the laws adopted by Parliament (Cotta and Marangoni 2015, 201).
8. Legge December 21, 2005, n. 270, declared partially unconstitutional by the Constitutional Court in 2013.
9. To discourage smaller parties, the voting threshold to be seated in Parliament was set at 4% for parties running alone and 2% for parties included in coalitions.
10. This calculation includes both the coalition documents and those of their members, unless otherwise specified. Although this system can count the same actor twice—such as in the case of the 1996 election, where it would count *Democratico della Sinistra* as one and Ulivo as another—this information allows a sense of the overall tone of attitudes on decentralization in the PSA, as expressed in their programmatic documents.
11. The survey question was: "Do you think that the setting up of the Regions would be more to the benefit or more to the detriment of this country?" The survey was conducted by the DOXA. Raw data are not available; the authors do not report information on the sample size.
12. The remaining 10% were divided between "Neither benefit nor detriment" (6%) and "Both benefit and detriment" (4%).
13. The other two neutral options remained almost unchanged: "Neither benefit nor detriment" (11%) and "Both benefit and detriment" (6%).
14. The text of the question was: "Have you ever heard of the regional government?" Answer options were "Very much," "Somewhat," "A Little," and "Not at all." Here too no information on the sample size was available.
15. As mentioned earlier, the survey question was: "Do you think that the setting up of the Regions would be more to the benefit or more to the detriment of this country?" Answers options were "More to the benefit," "More to the detriment," "Neither benefit nor detriment," and "Both

benefit and detriment." This question was part of a panel survey conducted in 1960, 1963, 1976, 1979, 1981, 1982, and 1987.
16. It is interesting that the documents from 1987 and 1992 are almost identical in their statements concerning decentralization.
17. Actually, the structure of the state envisaged by the MSI was basically unitary, with administrative decentralization based on an enhanced role for provinces and municipalities.
18. The author is referring to a panel survey conducted by Ispo/Cra-Nielsen and published by the newspaper *Corriere della Sera* on June 3, 1996. The survey interviewed 2792, 2899, and 4510 people, respectively, in September 1995, January 1996, and May 1996. The survey question was, "With which of the following proposals of State reform do you agree the most?" Answer options were "The current structure is good," "More powers to municipalities," "More powers to regions," "Federal state with current regions," "Federal state with macro-regions," and "Confederation of macro-regions."
19. Author's elaboration on data from ITANES 2001, postelectoral survey conducted on the occasion of the general elections on May 13, 2001; conducted between May 18 and June 20, 2001, with Computer-Assisted Personal Interviewing (CAPI) methodology, using a sample of 3209 people (unweighted data).
20. "Can you tell me how important each of the following problems is for Italy …?"; Item 9: "The Federal Reform of Italy."
21. Survey question was, "To what extent do you agree with the following …?"; Item 6: "More autonomy should be given to Regions"; Item 7: "Tax money should be given to Regions which will administrate these funds on their own." Data differentiated by geographical area reveal that support for such statements was particularly high in the north, with almost 10 percentage points difference from the south.
22. Laboratorio Analisi Politiche e Sociali (LAPS). The survey was commissioned by the municipality of Siena on the occasion of the 150th anniversary of Italy's unification. The survey was carried out on a representative sample of 803 individuals, aged 18 or over, between January 24 and February 7, 2011. Interviews were conducted over the telephone using Computer-Assisted Telephone Interviewing (CATI) methodology.
23. Survey question was: "Overall, would you say you are favorable or contrary to the introduction of federalism in Italy?"
24. The following survey items were part of an experimental set of questions. The sample was divided into two halves, and each received a different introduction to the set of items. Sample A: "There are different opinions about the effects that the federal reform currently under discussion in Parliament can have *on our country*. Please tell me how much you agree or

disagree with each of the following statements. ..." Sample B: "There are different opinions about the effects that the federal reform currently under discussion in Parliament can have *on the national unity*. Please tell me how much you agree or disagree with each of the following statements. ..." Because the experiment did not have a significant impact on answers, responses were merged.
25. Item text: "The federal reform will threaten the national unity."
26. Item text: "The federal reform will increase local taxation."
27. Item text: "The federal reform will enhance the health system."
28. For a list of the 25 policy areas involved in the debate on decentralization, see Table 1.1 (Chap. 1).
29. This index was originally developed using the information theory by Claude Shannon (1948).
30. If attention devoted to other subtopics actually drops to zero, the natural log cannot be calculated, because the natural log of zero is undefined. Some authors assume that in these cases it is 0 (e.g., John and Jennings 2010, 579), while others replace it with a small number like 0.0000001 (Boydstun et al. 2014, 183). This analysis has opted for another solution—namely, calculating the log of x_i plus a constant term of 0.1. As a consequence, the lowest possible score of H is not 0 but 0.1.
31. Production, transportation, and distribution of energy are among the concurrent legislative competences pursuant to Article 117 of the Constitutions, as modified in 2001.
32. Decreto legislativo December 30, 1992, no. 502 "Reorganization of the discipline concerning health, pursuant to article 1 of the Legge 23 October 1992, n.421," also known as Reform Amato-De Lorenzo.
33. After the 2001 reform, however, health became one of the areas featuring the highest levels of uncertainty in the division of competencies between the state and the regions.
34. "OECD Reviews of Health Care Quality: —Italy 2014," available at www.keepeek.com/Digital-Asset-Management/oecd/social-issues-migration-health/oecd-reviews-of-health-care-quality-italy-2014_9789264225428-en.
35. Chamber of Deputies, meeting number 803. The definitive approval of the Senate was dated January 22, 1953.
36. PLI was in the De Gasperi V government (May 24, 1948 to January 28, 1950).
37. This ambivalence can be deducted from the PSLI's rejection of the amendment proposed by Renzo Laconi (PCI), which aimed to reduce state control over regional statutes (meeting November 14, 1951, 33106–33107).
38. The three governments led by DC Prime Minister Aldo Moro from December 1963 to June 1968.

39. This expression is historically attributed to Aldo Moro, although the circumstances have never been verified. It nevertheless indicates an approach typical of Moro's political attitude, which was based on the constant pursuit of agreement between the DC and the PCI.
40. At the Chamber of Deputies, a bill is approved with the votes of the majority of those present (Article 48 of the Rules of the Chamber), and regulations define *present* as voting for or against a measure. Accordingly, abstention does not affect the calculation of the majority. On the other hand, in the Senate approval requires the majority of the senators to participate in a vote, thus accounting for those who abstained (Article 107 of the Regulation of the Senate). Abstention in the Senate means a vote against something, but its political meaning is different.
41. The intervention referred to "compliance with the Constitution and with the constraints deriving from EU legislation and international obligations" mentioned by the new Article 117 of the Constitution. It was also an example of the Eurosceptic positions the LN began adopting in the early 2000s.
42. Senato Della Repubblica, www.senato.it/japp/bgt/showdoc/frame.jsp?tipodoc=Resaula&leg=13&id=7399
43. Renato Meduri and Domenico Fisichella (AN) voted against the reform, and the latter left the party after this vote. Some newspapers reported that many AN deputies were not actually in favor of the reform, but voted for it anyway, not out of party discipline but because they were sure that the reform would be defeated by the referendum (declaration of Michele Bonatesta, AN, reported by La Repubblica, June 23, 2006, http://ricerca.repubblica.it/repubblica/archivio/repubblica/2006/06/23/cresce-la-fronda-nella-cdl-siamo-noi.html?ref=search).
44. They were two notable members of the UDC: Bruno Tabacci and Marco Follini.
45. Although some members of the PD decided to vote against.
46. For these analyses, a subset of data has been considered that includes only those electoral years that were followed by the adoption of decentralist reforms. For 2013 elections, parties that split during the legislature (NCD, SEL) were considered separately from the parties they left (respectively, PdL and PD). Although these parties had shared the same party platform, they adopted different voting behaviors when it came time to vote on the constitutional reform of 2016. Furthermore, as discussed in Chap. 3, these analyses consider only party-official positions as expressed in coalition manifestos for the years 1996 and 2001.
47. Left-right positioning is based on data drawn from the ParlGov Database based on expert surveys. Scores range from 0 (left) to 10 (right).

References

Barlucchi, M. Chiara. 1997. Quale Secessione in Italia? *Rivista Italiana Di Scienza Politica*, No. 2/1997: 345–372.

Basile, Linda. 2015. A Dwarf Among Giants? Party Competition Between Ethno-Regionalist and State-Wide Parties on the Territorial Dimension: The Case of Italy (1963–2013). *Party Politics* 21 (6): 887–899.

———. 2016. Measuring Party Strategies on the Territorial Dimension: A Method Based on Content Analysis. *Regional & Federal Studies* 26 (1): 1–23.

Borghetto, Enrico, Marcello Carammia, and Francesco Zucchini. 2014. The Impact of Party Policy Priorities on Italian Lawmaking from the First to the Second Republic, 1983–2006. In *Agenda Setting, Policies, and Political Systems: A Comparative Approach*, ed. Christoffer Green-Pedersen and Stefaan Walgrave, 164–182. Chicago: University of Chicago Press.

Boydstun, Amber E., Shaun Bevan, and F. Herschel Thomas III. 2014. The Importance of Attention Diversity and How to Measure It. *Policy Studies Journal* 42 (2): 173–196.

Budge, Ian, and Richard I. Hofferbert. 1990. Mandates and Policy Outputs: U.S. Party Platforms and Federal Expenditures. *The American Political Science Review* 84 (1): 111–131.

Bull, Martin, and Gianfranco Pasquino. 2007. A Long Quest in Vain: Institutional Reforms in Italy. *West European Politics* 30 (4): 670–691.

Cotta, Maurizio. 1996. La crisi del governo di partito all'italiana. In *Il gigante dai piedi d'argilla*, ed. Maurizio Cotta and Pierangelo Isernia, 11–52. Bologna: Il Mulino.

Cotta, Maurizio, and Francesco Marangoni. 2015. *Il Governo*. Bologna: Il Mulino.

Cotta, Maurizio, and Luca Verzichelli. 2016. *Il sistema politico italiano*. 2 edizione ed. Bologna: Il Mulino.

De Giorgi, Elisabetta. 2017. *L'opposizione parlamentare in Italia. Dall'antiberlusconismo all'antipolitica*. Roma: Carocci.

Democrazia Cristiana. 1948[1968]. Appello della Democrazia Cristiana al Paese, 4 Marzo 1948. In *Atti e Documenti della DC 1943-1967*, 377–378. Roma: Cinque Lune.

———. 1958[1968]. Programma della Democrazia Cristiana per il quinquennio 1958–1963: per garantire al popolo italiano 'progresso senza avventura'. In *Atti e Documenti della DC 1943-1967*, 928–937. Roma: Cinque Lune. April 12, 1958.

———. 1963[1968]. Programma elettorale della DC per la IV Legislatura. In *Atti e Documenti della DC 1943-1967*, 1473–1519. Roma: Cinque Lune.

———. 1968. Il programma della DC al servizio del paese. *Il Popolo*, April 19, 1968.

———. 1972. Gli impegni programmatici. *Il Popolo*, April 1, 1972.

———. 1976. Il programma elettorale della DC. *Biblioteca della Libertà* Anno XIII (61/62): 85–127.

———. 1979. Il programma elettorale della DC. *Il Popolo*, May 12, 1979.
———. 1987. Libertas: un programma per l'Italia. Elezioni politiche 14–15 giugno 1987.
Fabbrini, Sergio. 2009. The Transformation of Italian Democracy. *Bulletin of Italian Politics* 1 (1): 29–47.
———. 2013. Political and Institutional Constraints on Structural Reforms: Interpreting the Italian Experience. *Modern Italy* 18 (4): 423–436.
Farinelli, Arianna, and Emanuele Massetti. 2011. Eppur Non Si Muove? Prospects for Constitutional Reforms in Italy After the 2009 European and 2010 Regional Elections. *Journal of Modern Italian Studies* 16 (5): 685–704.
Fortunato, David. 2017. The Electoral Implications of Coalition Policy Making. *British Journal of Political Science*: 1–22.
Froio, Caterina, Shaun Bevan, and Will Jennings. 2017. Party Mandates and the Politics of Attention: Party Platforms, Public Priorities and the Policy Agenda in Britain. *Party Politics* 23 (6): 692–703.
Fusaro, Carlo. 1998. The Politics of Constitutional Reform in Italy: A Framework for Analysis. *South European Society and Politics* 3 (2): 45–74.
Gargano, Rodolfo. 1999. Luigi Sturzo Tra Autonomismo e Federalismo. *Il Federalista* Anno XLI (1): 9–25.
Giuliani, Marco. 2008. Patterns of Consensual Law-Making in the Italian Parliament. *South European Society and Politics* 13 (1): 61–85.
Green-Pedersen, Christoffer. 2007. The Conflict of Conflicts in Comparative Perspective. Euthanasia as a Political Issue in Denmark, Belgium, and the Netherlands. *Comparative Politics* 39 (3): 273–291.
———. 2012. A Giant Fast Asleep? Party Incentives and the Politicisation of European Integration. *Political Studies* 60 (1): 115–130.
Green-Pedersen, Christoffer, and Jesper Krøgstrup. 2008. Immigration as a Political Issue in Denmark and Sweden. *European Journal of Political Research* 47 (5): 610–634.
Harmel, Robert, and Kenneth Janda. 1994. An Integrated Theory of Party Goals and Party Change. *Journal of Theoretical Politics* 6 (3): 259–286.
John, Peter, and Will Jennings. 2010. Punctuations and Turning Points in British Politics: The Policy Agenda of the Queen's Speech, 1940–2005. *British Journal of Political Science* 40 (3): 561–586.
Keating, Michael, and Alex Wilson. 2010. *Federalism and Decentralisation in Italy*. PSA Annual Conference, Edinburgh, March 2010.
Lega Nord. 1992. Programma elettorale. Politiche 1992. Milano.
———. 1994. Sintesi Programma. In Lehmann, Pola, Theres Matthieß, Nicolas Merz, Sven Regel, and Annika Werner. 2017. *Manifesto Corpus*. Version: 2017-2. Berlin: WZB Berlin Social Science Center.
Lega Nord-Casa delle Libertà. 2001. Documento Patto Lega-Polo. April 5, 2001.
L'Ulivo. 1996. Tesi per la definizione della piattaforma programmatica de L'Ulivo. 6 dicembre 1995. Retrieved from http://www.perlulivo.it/radici/vittorieelettorali/programma/tesi/. Accessed 10 Apr 2018.

———. 2001. *Rinnoviamo l'Italia, Insieme. Il programma dell'Ulivo per il governo 2001/2006 presentato da Francesco Rutelli*. Roma: Newton & Compton Editori.
L' Unione. 2006. Per il bene dell'Italia. Programma di Governo 2006–2011 (Originally retrieved from the website of the coalition). Official party manifesto, according to art. 1 paragraph 5 of L. 260/2005.
Massetti, Emanuele, and Simon Toubeau. 2013. Sailing with Northern Winds: Party Politics and Federal Reforms in Italy. *West European Politics* 36 (2): 359–381.
Mazzoleni, Martino. 2009. The Italian Regionalisation: A Story of Partisan Logics. *Modern Italy* 14 (2): 135–150.
Meguid, Bonnie M. 2008. *Party Competition Between Unequals: Strategies and Electoral Fortunes in Western Europe*. Cambridge: Cambridge University Press.
Movimento Sociale Italiano. 1953. *MSI. Programma per le Elezioni Politiche 1953*. Roma: Tambone.
———. 1968. Manifesto del Movimento Sociale. Per non svegliarsi comunisti. *Secolo d'Italia*, May 7, 1968.
———. 1983. Il messaggio degli anni '80. Roma, May 1983.
———. 1992. E' giunto il tempo del cambiamento. *Secolo d'Italia*, March 10, 1992.
OECD. 2014. *OECD Reviews of Health Care Quality: Italy 2014: Raising Standards*. Paris: OECD Publishing.
Palermo, Francesco, and Alex Wilson. 2013. *The Dynamics of Decentralization in Italy: Towards a Federal Solution?* European Diversity and Autonomy Papers (EDAP), No. 04.
Paolazzi, Luca, and Mauro Sylos Labini. 2012. L'Italia Alla Sfida Del Cambiamento: Le Lezioni per le Riforme e I Benefici Di Un Cammino Appena Iniziato. Policy Paper. Cambia Italia: Riforme per Crescere.
Partito Comunista Italiano. 1958. *Progetto di Programma Elettorale che i Comunisti Presentano agli Italiani*. Roma: Partito Comunista Italiano.
———. 1963. Battere la DC. Rafforzare il PCI. Il Programma elettorale del PCI. *L'Unità*, March 3, 1963.
———. 1972. Il programma dei comunisti: per un governo di svolta democratica. *L'Unità* (Special issue), March 26, 1972.
———. 1983. Un programma per cambiare. Sintesi delle proposte programmatiche del PCI. *L'Unità*.
———. 1987. Il PCI per la decima legislatura. Gli impegni programmatici fondamentali. *L'Unità*, May 30, 1987.
Partito Democratico. 2008. Il Programma di governo del PD. Elezioni 2008. February 25, 2008. Retrieved from https://www.partitodemocratico.it/archivio/programma-governo-del-pd/. Accessed 11 Apr 2018. Official party manifesto, according to art. 1 paragraph 5 of L. 260/2005.
———. 2013. L'Italia. Bene Comune. Retrieved from https://www.partitodemocratico.it/archivio/italia-bene-comune/. Accessed 11 Apr 2018. Official party manifesto, according to art. 1 paragraph 5 of L. 260/2005.
Partito Democratico della Sinistra. 1992. Costruiamo una nuova Italia. PDS opposizione che costruisce. *L'Unità* (supplemento).

———. 1994. *Per ricostruire un' Italia più giusta, più unita, più moderna. Dieci grandi opzioni programmatiche.* Roma: l'Unità.
Partito Liberale Italiano. 1953. Punti Programmatici Fissati dal Partito Liberale Italiano nel VI Congresso di Firenze. *Firenze,* January 23, 1953.
———. 1963. *Sulla linea di una tradizione sicura.* Novara: Segreteria del PLI.
———. 1968. Il programma elettorale del Partito Liberale Italiano. In Lehmann, Pola, Theres Matthieß, Nicolas Merz, Sven Regel, and Annika Werner. 2017. *Manifesto Corpus.* Version: 2017-2. Berlin: WZB Berlin Social Science Center.
———. 1976. Il programma elettorale del PLI. *Biblioteca della Libertà* Anno XIII (61/62): 197–226.
———. 1983. Manifesto liberale per le elezioni del 26 giugno 1983. In Lehmann, Pola, Theres Matthieß, Nicolas Merz, Sven Regel, and Annika Werner. 2017. *Manifesto Corpus.* Version: 2017-2. Berlin: WZB Berlin Social Science Center.
———. 1992. Elezioni 1992. Dateci la forza per cambiare le cose. In Lehmann, Pola, Theres Matthieß, Nicolas Merz, Sven Regel, and Annika Werner. 2017. *Manifesto Corpus.* Version: 2017-2. Berlin: WZB Berlin Social Science Center.
Partito Popolare Italiano. 1994. Un programma per gli italiani. In Lehmann, Pola, Theres Matthieß, Nicolas Merz, Sven Regel, and Annika Werner. 2017. *Manifesto Corpus.* Version: 2017-2. Berlin: WZB Berlin Social Science Center.
Partito Repubblicano Italiano. 1948. Il Programma del partito repubblicano per le elezioni del 18 aprile 1948. In Lehmann, Pola, Theres Matthieß, Nicolas Merz, Sven Regel, and Annika Werner. 2017. *Manifesto Corpus.* Version: 2017-2. Berlin: WZB Berlin Social Science Center.
———. 1968. Il programma elettorale del Partito Repubblicano Italiano. *Mondo Economico* 19: 25–27.
———. 1972. Il documento programmatico approvato dal Consiglio Nazionale repubblicano. *La Voce Repubblicana,* March 10, 1963.
———. 1983. *Trenta punti per una legislatura. Il Programma repubblicano.* Roma: PRI.
Partito Socialista Democratico Italiano. 1979. Programma del Partito Socialista Democratico Italiano. Piattaforma politica. *L'Umanità,* 3–5.
———. 1983. Il PSDI agli elettori: indicazioni per un programma di governo. *L'Umanità,* n. 127.
Partito Socialista Italiano. 1958. *Per una politica di alternativa democratica.* Roma: Seti.
———. 1963. *Il Programma del PSI.* Roma: Seti.
———. 1976. La proposta politica del PSI. *Biblioteca della Libertà* Anno XIII (61/62): 299–314.
———. 1983. Rigore, equità, sviluppo: Il senso della proposta socialista. In Lehmann, Pola, Theres Matthieß, Nicolas Merz, Sven Regel, and Annika Werner. 2017. *Manifesto Corpus.* Version: 2017-2. Berlin: WZB Berlin Social Science Center.
Partito Socialista Unificato. 1968. *Una risposta ai problemi della nostra epoca. Programma elettorale del PSI e PSDI unificati.* Roma: Seti.

Patto per l'Italia. 1994. Le Idee, il Progetto, Il Programma. La grande sfida riformista per costruire l'Italia liberal-democratica. Roma, February 5, 1994.

Polo delle Libertà. 1996. *100 impegni per cambiare l'Italia: programma del Polo per le Libertà*. S. Donato Milanese: Centro grafico Linate.

Popolo delle Libertà. 2013. Programma elezioni politiche 25 25 febbraio (Originally retrieved from the website of the party). Official party manifesto, according to art.1 paragraph 5 of L. 260/2005.

Putnam, Robert D., Robert Leonardi, Raffaella Nanetti, and Istituto Carlo Cattaneo. 1985. *La pianta e le radici: il radicamento dell'istituto regionale nel sistema politico italiano*. Bologna: Il Mulino.

Putnam, Robert D., Robert Leonardi, and Raffaella Y. Nanetti. 1993. *Making Democracy Work: Civic Traditions in Modern Italy*. Princeton: Princeton University Press.

Rifondazione Comunista. 1996. Ricominciare da sinistra per l'alternativa. In Lehmann, Pola, Theres Matthieß, Nicolas Merz, Sven Regel, and Annika Werner. 2017. *Manifesto Corpus*. Version: 2017-2. Berlin: WZB Berlin Social Science Center.

———. 2001. *Un voto utile per il paese per costruire una sinistra di alternativa e una sinistra plurale*. Roma: Rifondazione Comunista.

Rovny, Jan. 2013. Where Do Radical Right Parties Stand? Position Blurring in Multidimensional Competition. *European Political Science Review* 5 (1): 1–26.

Sartori, Giovanni. 1976. *Parties and Party Systems: A Framework for Analysis*. Cambridge: Cambridge University Press.

Scelta Civica. 2013. Cambiare l'Italia, Riformare l'Europa. Un'Agenda per un Impegno Comune. Primo Contributo ad una Riflessione Aperta. Official party manifesto, according to art. 1 paragraph 5 of L. 260/2005.

Shannon, Claude. 1948. A Mathematical Theory of Communication. *The Bell System Technical Journal* 27 (3): 379–423.

Somer–Topcu, Zeynep. 2015. Everything to Everyone: The Electoral Consequences of the Broad-Appeal Strategy in Europe. *American Journal of Political Science* 59 (4): 841–854.

Sorens, Jason. 2009. The Partisan Logic of Decentralization in Europe. *Regional & Federal Studies* 19 (2): 255–272.

Taviani, Ermanno. 2004. Il primo centro-sinistra e le riforme 1962–1968. *Annali della facoltà di Scienze della formazione Università degli studi di Catania* 3: 323–368.

Toubeau, Simon, and Emanuele Massetti. 2013. The Party Politics of Territorial Reforms in Europe. *West European Politics* 36 (2): 297–316.

Toubeau, Simon, and Markus Wagner. 2015. Explaining Party Positions on Decentralization. *British Journal of Political Science* 45 (1): 97–119.

Unione di Centro. 2008. Programma elettorale. In Lehmann, Pola, Theres Matthieß, Nicolas Merz, Sven Regel, and Annika Werner. 2017. *Manifesto Corpus*. Version: 2017-2. Berlin: WZB Berlin Social Science Center.

CHAPTER 5

Frames: The Art of Justifying Preferences

ISSUE FRAMING AND THE PARTY SYSTEM AGENDA

The previous chapters have explored the role of party competition in triggering and shaping the process of decentralization. As previously observed, an increase in the amount of attention paid to this issue in the party system agenda (PSA) is one key driver of reform, emphasizing the importance of the manipulation of the issue's *salience* in party strategies (Chap. 3). Besides party attention, however, reform also needs the consensus of at least the majority of the political actors, which makes party *positioning* another crucial variable for understanding the path of reform and its development (Chap. 4).

Something is still missing from the picture, however. When confronted with a policy issue, parties have to make a decision not only concerning the amount of attention to pay to it and the direction to adopt but also justifying their decision and explaining the rationale behind their strategic choice to contextualize their stance within their broader worldview, ideas, and values. In other words, they have to *frame* the issue.

Issue framing is in no way a secondary aspect of the dynamics of party competition; it is an extremely important element of party competition in its own right, for several reasons. First, parties use frames to connect their attitude on an issue with their attitudes on other issues. Second, when one political actor is able to define an issue first, it "not only sets the term of the debate, it also seizes the high ground" (Dean in Lakoff 2004, ix). Third, defining an issue ultimately allows a party to set the agenda and shape policy.

Based on these premises, this chapter examines issue framing on decentralization in the Italian political discourse. Contrary to the analyses presented thus far, this chapter does not look at the impact of party strategies on reforms. Instead, it takes a step back to focus on party strategies themselves, examining whether and how this third complementary tool contributes to shaping party competition.

In particular, this chapter seeks to address the following questions: How have Italian parties framed decentralization? Have they used definitions that fit with their own worldviews and values? Which political party, if any, was able to define decentralization first by setting the terms of the debate? And how did other political actors react? Did they ignore, modify (reframe), or imitate the frames introduced by their adversaries? Last, and related to the latter question, did the breakthrough of the *Lega Nord* (LN) onto the political scene affect the framing of decentralization? If so, how?

To answer these questions, the next section presents theoretical insights on which the analysis of frames can be grounded. The following sections examine the use of a set of frames in party manifestos over time through a qualitative account of party discourse, which is further substantiated by descriptive quantitative evidence.

Don't Think of a Region![1]

The Importance of Issue Framing for Party Competition

Classic models of party competition traditionally limit the array of strategic tools available to parties for manipulating salience and positioning (Meguid 2008). Nonetheless, attitudes toward issues are further shaped by the manipulation of the arguments used to justify party decisions on salience and position—namely, the framing.

The notion of framing has been developed mostly for media analysis and social movements as an attempt to understand the impact of a particular representation of an issue on public opinion (Chong and Druckman 2007; Helbling et al. 2010). However, as Slothuus and de Vreese (2010, 630) point out, framing research has neglected the role of political parties as a source of issue frames, with a few noteworthy exceptions (e.g., Helbling et al. 2010). Moreover, extant studies focus on frames' potential to sway public opinion (ibid.; Druckman 2001), while little attention has been paid thus far to issue framing as a strategic tool of party competition per se.

But what are frames, and why they are so important in party competition? Cognitive linguist George Lakoff (2004, xv) defines frames as "mental structures that shape the way we see the world. ... In politics, our frames shape our social policies and the institutions we form to carry out policies." Frames are part of our "cognitive unconscious": when we "hear a word, its frame (or collection of frames) is activated in our brain." The author provides an example of issue framing that helps clarify what we are talking about: imagine a political debate on taxes. In the rhetoric of conservative parties, any discussion concerning *taxes* is associated with the notion of *relief*. Talking frequently about tax *relief* primes an (unconscious) cognitive mechanism that associates the notion of taxes with affliction and pain, portraying the party that reduces taxes as a sort of hero. When the party does so, it invokes those ideas and values that are also part of its own worldview. Regarding the use of frames in the dynamics of party competition, two scenarios are likely, which are easier to explain using examples explicitly referring to the territorial dimension. In the first scenario, political actors agree on the same policy goal but use diametrically opposed arguments to justify their positions—for example, decentralizing reforms might be supported by either reminding voters of the need to ensure territorial solidarity among the subnational units or citing the "federalist" principle that resources should be left where they originate. In the second scenario, the same argument is used to support contrasting perspectives on decentralization. For instance, the need to strengthen the efficiency of state machinery can justify either the redistribution of competencies downward or, on the contrary, a further centralization of state powers. Against this backdrop, it is possible to identify at least three main goals that parties pursue through the manipulation of rhetorical frames.

First, parties use frames to justify their attitudes. As Helbling et al. (2010, 496–497) argue: "in addition to simply analyzing the positions of political actors, we must also consider how they *problematize* [a policy issue] and *why* they are against or in favor of it. ... [W]e scrutinize which arguments they mobilize to justify positions. ... In general, knowing how parties conceive and represent [a policy issue] will allow us to understand better their positions towards it."

Second, frames allow parties to tie their position on a given issue to their broader worldview. Parties express their positions on a vast array of different policy issues, and some issues, like decentralization, represent secondary dimensions of party competition outside the traditional socioeconomic ones (Elias et al. 2015). Through the manipulation of frames, parties are able to integrate this secondary dimension into their broader socioeconomic ideologies. An example might be useful to clarify this point: A progressive, leftist party's set of values might include anti-authoritarianism and the development of political and civil freedoms and equality for all citizens. If this party also favors further decentralization, it can justify this attitude by using arguments that fit within its anti-authoritarian and egalitarian worldview. The party would therefore frame decentralization in terms of greater democracy, accountability, and protection for minority rights. On the other hand, a conservative party advocating free markets and the reduction of state economic regulation might frame its support for decentralization as a matter of enhanced efficiency and a less interventionist state.

Third, frames are instruments of party competition. When a party is able to define an issue according to its own worldview before any other party has an opportunity to do so, it basically sets the terms of the debate, and compels the other parties to either discuss the issue using the same language or attempt to reframe the issue according to their own sets of values.[2]

Framing Decentralization in Italy

The three main purposes of issue framing outlined above suggest two theoretical expectations concerning issue framing in the Italian party debate on decentralization. Although they are not full-fledged hypotheses, they nevertheless contribute to developing a theoretical framework for issue framing analysis in party competition dynamics.

The first expectation is that each party family would tend to frame decentralization differently according to its own worldview. This is related to the first two goals of issue framing—namely, justifying attitudes and integrating issues into a party's broader worldview. Due to its high level of party fragmentation, the Italian party system does not feature completely distinct and competing worldviews in the way that, for example, the progressives and conservatives in the United States do (Lakoff 2004); nevertheless, it is possible to identify at least some very broad sets of values that are typical of parties at various points along the left-right continuum, both in the First and Second Republics. On the left, the communist parties (e.g., the *Partito Comunista Italiano* [PCI] in the First Republic and the *Rifondazione Comunista* [RC] in the Second Republic), socialist parties (e.g., the *Partito Socialista Italiano* [PSI] and the *Partito Socialista Democratico Italiano* [PSDI], both in the First Republic), and social democratic parties (e.g., the *Partito Democratico della Sinistra* [PDS/DS], later renamed the *Partito Democratico* [PD]) diverge historically and ideologically and take different approaches to capitalism, but they still share a common set of values, including equality, solidarity, social justice, the promotion of civil and political rights, the protection of minority rights, and support for state regulatory interventions. The center has historically been dominated by the Christian Democrat parties like the *Democrazia Cristiana* (DC) in the First Republic, which feature some social democratic values (such as social justice, equality, and solidarity), some conservative values (e.g., the promotion of traditional moral values and the rejection of Communism), and a few unique values (like subsidiarity). Moving to the right, the conservative parties (e.g., the *Partito Liberale Italiano* [PLI] in the first Republic and *Forza Italia* [FI] and the *Popolo delle Libertà* [PDL] in the Second Republic) emphasize free trade, property rights, individual initiative, tradition, morality, authority, and limited state intervention in the economy. Likewise, nationalist parties like the *Movimento Sociale Italiano* (MSI) in the First Republic, later the *Alleanza Nazionale* (AN), have emphasized the promotion of tradition, morality, and authority alongside their nationalist rhetoric.

Although the above-mentioned sets of values do not accurately reflect the ideological idiosyncrasies of each party, this is a useful framework for discussing how parties have sought to frame decentralization by using arguments that fit within their own worldviews. Accordingly, one would expect leftist parties to emphasize the democracy or identity frames, while the efficiency or economic liberalization arguments would be more consistent with the conservative mind-set.

The second expectation is that new dynamics of party competition, such as the emergence of an electorally relevant autonomist party in the political arena, are likely to introduce new frames to the political discourse and revitalize the terms of political debate. This expectation is related to the third goal of issue framing. Following Baumgartner et al. (2008, 100–101 and 137), although there is not one single event or factor that can explain why old issues are sometimes revitalized by the introduction of new arguments, issue reframing is usually accompanied by the emergence of proponent movements in the political system. The rhetoric on territorial issues used by the LN in Italy after 1992 offers a typical example of how an emerging movement can introduce new language to old debates. According to Giordano (2000, 446), although "political regionalism is not a new phenomenon in Italy," Bossi's movement brought at least three dominant themes to the Italian political debate: resentment of "wasteful" southern Italy; the inefficiency of the central state, epitomized by the slogan "robber Rome" (*Roma ladrona*); and the autonomy of the allegedly historical geographical entity called "Padania." Although some of these frames were not totally new, the LN articulated them in terms of a new and more politically contentious northern question. Consequently, mainstream parties were forced to change the ways they conceptualized and discussed territorial issues, linking them to different socioeconomic and cultural arguments (Basile 2015, 893–894).

Based on these premises, the following sections provide an account of the main Italian parties' use of frames on decentralization over time. In particular, they focus on two aspects already outlined—namely, framing as a part of a subsuming strategy, through which parties connect a secondary dimension of competition to their broader worldview, and framing as a tool of party competition, with particular emphasis on the impact of the reframing promoted by LN on the niche-mainstream dialectic.

A List of Frames

Before proceeding with the analysis, some attention should be paid to what kind of images the issue of decentralization evokes.

As previously argued, frames have to do with language, ideas, and the unconscious associations they are likely to activate; in particular, frames might imply the cause of a problem and of the potential effects of specific policy solutions and may contextualize the actors related to the issue. Accordingly, a list of frames related to decentralization can be deductively developed by drawing on the main literature on territorial politics, which includes the main reasons and rationales used to explain decentralization processes. For the content analysis performed using the TERRISS Dataset, the list was generated by looking at the main decentralizing pressures and actors present in decentralizing countries in western Europe as well as some drivers specific to the Italian context. These frames can be classified into three broader groups, each referring to different arguments related to decentralization—namely, functional pressures, identity pressures, and structures of political opportunity (see also Table 1.2 in Chap. 1 for the full list of frames used in the content analysis).

Based on this classification, the following sections examine frames in light of the theoretical expectations already outlined.

Functional Pressures and Frames

The first group comprises the *functional pressures* pushing for decentralization, including the following frames: efficiency, democracy, liberalism, and territorial solidarity. They all answer the hypothetical question, Why is decentralization useful or beneficial for the functioning of the state? (or, on the centralist front, Why would it would be harmful?) or What advantages—or drawbacks—might decentralization mean for the political system? Within this framework, parties might frame decentralization as a way to ensure (or hinder) the flexibility and efficiency of public administration and government machinery (the efficiency frame). Another argument deals with decentralization's potential to strengthen (or weaken) the accountability of political actors and increase (or decrease) citizens' participation in political processes by bringing citizens closer to the decision-making loci (the democracy frame). Furthermore, territorial restructuring can be defined as a way to develop (or jeopardize) a liberal state by limiting the authority of the central government (the liberalist frame). Finally, decentralization can be associated with efforts to redistribute economic resources between richer and poorer areas of the country to bridge socio-economic gaps (the territorial solidarity frame).

As Fig. 5.1 shows, the efficiency and democracy frames were extremely popular both before and after the advent of the LN in 1992 and were among the most common arguments employed in the political debate on decentralization. The average salience of these arguments actually tracks the relevance of the issue of decentralization in general. On the other hand, the liberalist argument has played a somewhat minor role over time. The territorial solidarity frame, meanwhile, saw little use until the 1990s, when it gained popularity following the emergence of the LN.

Decentralization: A Panacea for the State Public Sector's Malaise?

Italy's public sector has often been considered rather inefficient, thanks in part to its cumbersome bureaucracy, widespread clientelism, corruption,

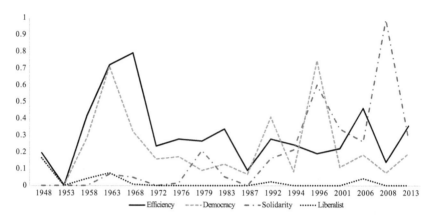

Fig. 5.1 Mean salience of frames related to functional pressures for each electoral year (1948–2013)

and lack of adequate training and administrative modernization, in addition to its elaborate system of regulations, norms, and procedures. All these drawbacks negatively affect the delivery of public services and lead to the waste of public resources. The above-mentioned weaknesses are in part the result of a "centralized political culture and party system" (Tarrow 1979, 180), which dates back to at least the Piedmontese centralized bureaucracy of post-unification Italy (Foot 2003, 98).

In light of such deeply rooted gridlock and the country's stubborn bureaucracy, regional reform has been seen since the early 1960s as a sort of "panacea for Italy's many ills" (Tarrow 1979, 179): it was considered a tool for relieving central governments of the responsibility for delivering a number of public services, which would be transferred to the local authorities, allowing the central state to concentrate on key issues like the economy and foreign policy. Moreover, because local governments are closer to citizens, they should theoretically be more attuned to local conditions and needs, increasing the quality of the public goods delivered to people. Those opposed to decentralization, however, have pointed out some potential disadvantages: diseconomies of scale, with higher costs for locally provided services (Giordano and Tommasino 2011), scant control over local resources, and weak technical and administrative capacities at the local level. All these shortcomings, the centralists argue, would further enhance the inefficiency of the system rather than reduce it.

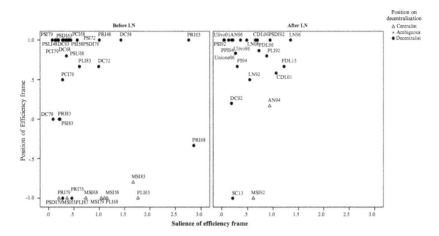

Fig. 5.2 Position and salience of the efficiency frame, before and after the emergence of LN (1992): parties are classified according to their overall attitude toward decentralization (i.e. centralist, ambiguous, or decentralist)

During the First Republic, the efficiency argument was evoked by most political parties that supported decentralization, which pointed out the purported advantages of surrendering competencies downward (Fig. 5.2). In particular, the DC, the primary force in government, constantly used the efficiency frame during the reforming period from the late 1950s through the 1970s. In this way, it could justify its support for the creation of the regions with the need to simplify and "make more efficient the action of the Government" (DC 1972). In its 1963 manifesto, for instance, the DC stated that it wanted "to reaffirm that we are in favor … of the local autonomies, [which] guarantee freedom and an efficient restraint to the centralization of the state, and allow [local authorities] to select useful energies and competencies …" (DC 1963). To a certain extent, this was a way to reassure those voters who were still skeptical (or unaware) of decentralization, especially the most conservative voters, that regions would not hinder the traditional state structure.

From the left, the socialists also framed their support for decentralization by referring to the purported beneficial effect it would have on the efficiency of the state. These parties used criticism of the country's bureaucratic sclerosis as a way to convince the electorate that decentralizing the state was the right choice, as the following quotation shows:

"the creation of an ... efficient administration is not possible if not grounded in the regions, as an opportunity to unify and modernize the whole, state apparatus" (*Partito Socialista Unitario* [PSU] 1968). At the same time, as references to a less centralized state machinery did not fit well with the communists' worldview, the PCI scarcely used this frame to justify its support for decentralization. Few references to efficiency were found in the PCI manifestos of 1968, 1976, 1979, or 1987, and when efficiency was mentioned, it was mostly cited in generic statements on the need to pursue decentralization while reforming public administration (PCI 1968) or statements criticizing the shortcomings of the regionalizing process rather than outright justifications of decentralization as a means to enhance efficiency.

It should be noted that the decentralist parties only rarely used this frame in a negative way, and mostly to address shortcomings in the actual outcomes of the reforming process, which had in many respects lagged behind regionalist expectations. This was the case with the PSDI in 1979—for example, it pointed out the risk of further inefficiency created by the limits and drawbacks of the way in which the process of reform had been carried out. Likewise, in 1968 the *Partito Repubblicano Italiano* (PRI) expressed wariness about the risks of overlapping competencies and structures: "... in the current state of public structures, with their tendency to increase their costs and bureaucracy, it would be a serious and dangerous mistake to add the regional structure to other public facilities that already exist ..." (PRI 1968).

However, the adversarial, centralist parties—namely, the PLI and the MSI—often used this frame negatively. Consistent with their conservative, centralist values, they regularly warned that a decentralized system would jeopardize state efficiency. The PLI, for instance, explained its opposition to the creation of the regions by stressing its potential costs, defined as "a huge and useless cost ... a huge mountain of Lire spent without a real benefit for the citizens" (PLI 1963); it also pointed out the risks of further confusion and corruption that would be created by the multiplication of the layers of authority. The MSI likewise warned that "the institutions of the regions ... would stop economic growth. Regions and local authorities would be troubled by budgetary problems, and would be unable to serve as agents of development and rebirth, becoming instead unbalanced companies" (MSI 1963).

There was a turning point in 1992 that changed the way the efficiency frame was used in the debate on decentralization. That year the Italian political system was in political turmoil due to the so-called *Tangentopoli* (Bribesville) corruption scandals. The LN exploited the rhetoric of the inefficiency of the central state and its crisis of legitimacy in all its electoral campaigns, especially in the 1990s. Under the combative slogan robber Rome, it criticized the inefficiency of the central institutions, which when combined were often described as a heavy bureaucratic machine characterized by corruption and the waste of resources at the expense of taxpayers in the north and proposed federalist solutions to tackle the deep-seated inefficiencies of the system (Basile 2015). In other words, the LN *reframed* the efficiency argument, emphasizing the contrast between local authorities and the wasteful central government; it also blamed the parasitism of certain areas of the country (i.e., the south) for the system's inefficiency, claiming it would be more efficient if resources were used by those who produced them. LN's 1996 manifesto provides many paradigmatic examples of this rhetoric: "[with federalism] there will be no need any more to go to Rome hat in hand to gain some scant Lira to build a street ..., but we could use the money of the Municipality, the Province, the Region, which will be surely sufficient, without the greedy hand of Rome's government to take them away in a strange place of waste"; "the public debt ... for which we should 'thank' the subsidy mentality and irresponsible politics hitherto pursued by the Borbonic and centralist State"; "the central Parliament has wasted and dilapidated the richness, bringing Italy to its knees"; and, referring to the productive people in the north: "those who work and produce will be not anymore penalized by lazybones and parasites." Federalism was also presented as an instrument that would improve the functionality of state machinery: "federalism is inevitably translated into simplification and rationalization of the overall system" (LN 1996).

In the face of such rhetoric, which appealed to an increasingly discontent electorate, statements opposing territorial reforms in the name of state efficiency almost disappeared from the political discourse, with MSI being the last party to use the frame against decentralization in the early 1990s. More recently, *Scelta Civica* (SC) advanced a proposal in 2013 to further recentralize the energy sector to simplify and streamline governance, while adopting a generally accommodative, although ambiguous, strategy on decentralization.

The main parties of both the center-right and the center-left coalitions have sought to appease public discontent with the state's performance by pointing out the potential benefits of territorial reforms. Despite these similarities, however, some differences emerge in the ways the two coalitions use the efficiency frame, as they are contextualizing decentralization within different sets of values. The most interesting examples come once again from the electoral campaign of 1996. From the center-left, the *Ulivo* stressed the aspects of enhanced responsibility in the use of public resources, which would improve the delivery of public services in line with the social democratic welfare state model: "by transferring to the subnational levels the functions of fiscal levy … decentralization and federalism bring together autonomy of the decision making and a more direct responsibility for the management and the choices of use of resources for the citizens, who are the recipients of the supply of public goods and services" (Ulivo 1996). From the center-right, the coalition *Polo delle Libertà* (PdL) emphasized the advantages of decentralization by referring to potential reductions in public spending and resource usage, in keeping with its conservative, liberal platform: "[through federalism] it will be achieved a reduction of the public spending and a concrete possibility of fiscal consolidation of the state accounts"; and: "[we should] eliminate the duplication of costs without coordination, through the regionalization of the local public transportation" (PdL 1996).

Bringing Democracy Closer to the Citizens

By bringing decision making closer to citizens and giving local communities greater control over their own affairs, decentralization could constitute a means to strengthen democracy and enhance the stability of the country. Unlike the efficiency frame, there has been widespread convergence on the positive use of the democracy argument among many decentralist parties (Fig. 5.3).

It is interesting that before 1992 this frame was always present in the manifestos of the PCI, as it perfectly fit the communists' set of values, which stressed the importance of popular participation in decision making; in 1972, for instance, the PCI manifesto stated that: "by implementing a large decentralization of their powers to the Municipalities and their associations, and to the Provinces, working together with the trade unions, mass organizations, both social and cultural, the Regions and local autonomies have to introduce in the political and administrative life of the country a democratic method of management of the public life, by fostering and promoting in several forms, the widest participation of the workers" (PCI 1972).

FRAMES: THE ART OF JUSTIFYING PREFERENCES   197

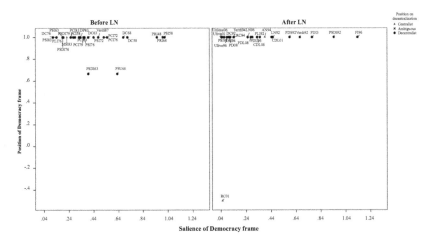

Fig. 5.3 Position and salience of the democracy frame, before and after the emergence of LN (1992): parties classified according to their overall attitude towards decentralization (Note: To improve the readability, party manifestos showing a salience on the democracy frame higher than 2 were excluded. They were PRI 1963 [decentralist], PDS 1996 [decentralist], and RI 1996 [decentralist].)

Likewise, the democracy frame fit well with socialist values: "Regions represent the historical outcome of a successful fight against the authoritarian and centralized view of the state. ... Regions should be the central engines of initiatives to promote the citizens' participation to the planning policies" (PSI 1963). However, the democracy frame apparently fit just as well into very different worldviews, like that of the DC. The latter often stressed the importance of local authorities in increasing both citizens' participation in public life and the accountability of decision makers, as this statement shows: "Regions will bring the public action to a more direct contact with the citizen that increases his possibilities of participation ..." (DC 1968). This frame was entirely outside the worldviews of the centralist parties, relying as it did on conservative values; this might explain why parties like the PLI and MSI did not use it, even in a negative way. Instead, the MSI suggested an alternative to the regional structure in 1983, which "puts communities and citizens at the center of institutional reform, through popular participation and control" (MSI 1983).

Moving to the post-1992 period, it should be noted that the democracy frame was not among the main issues in LN's autonomist repertoire. The party nevertheless managed to partially use it, pointing out the widespread corruption in Rome, which could be overcome only if the citizens exerted greater control over decision making through federalism.

Parties from both sides of the left-right continuum have continued to use this frame to justify decentralization as a means to get people closer to the governing authorities, thus increasing the accountability of decision makers. In this sense, the claims made by the *Ulivo* coalition in its promotion of a decentralized fiscal system—"closer to everyone, in order to better evaluate the actions of those who manage the taxes" (Ulivo 1996)—do not differ much from those employed by the PdL in favor of fiscal federalism: it is described as a way to "increase citizens' control over the use of public money and goods," and "bring politics closer to people" (Pdl 1996).

The 2001 RC manifesto represents a notable exception in the use of the democracy frame. In that period, the party had further strengthened its antiglobalization rhetoric, which became a reaffirmation of national sovereignty. In line with this set of values, RC adopted a critical stance against "localism and regionalism that, far from being a democratic process of getting citizens closer to the institutions, is an outcome of globalization, which brings together the stronger areas of business at the expenses of the poorer ones. Within this framework the national policies are weakened, especially for what concerns the political economy. ... This process implies a loss of sovereignty, in favor of an a-democratic order and system with an international scope" (RC 2001).

Decentralized State, Less State

The liberalism frame basically refers to the idea that powers should not be concentrated within a central authority and there should be limitations on the intervention capacities of the state. Decentralization is then seen as a way to break up and distribute state powers to different levels of authority to avoid authoritarian and oppressive tendencies. Although it has been a minor factor in the political debate, it is interesting to look at how this frame has fit in with the values of those parties that have used it.

Both the PCI and the DC, for instance, hold to antifascist and antitotalitarian values. Accordingly, in 1958 the PCI used this frame to explain its aversion to an "oppressive and centralizing state," which could be overcome only with the implementation of the regions. Likewise, the DC considered the local autonomies as "guarantees of liberty, effective constrain to the centralizing tendencies of the State" (DC 1963).

In 1992 the LN reinterpreted this frame in economic terms,[3] saying that "federalist liberalism, as opposed to an absolute liberalism, [which is entirely] grounded on money and consumption ... implies the harmonization of the economic activities with the needs of the society and of its moral and material values." The 2006 manifesto of the *Unione*, however, returned to the original use of the liberal frame, evoking the need to limit the central authority. For instance, in this statement the center-left coalition criticizes the legislative activity of the central state, which exceeded the limits imposed by the reform of 2001, by defining it as "behavior of oppressive and invasive centralism" (Unione 2006).

Decentralization Will Not Tear Us Apart

The territorial solidarity frame is used by parties to link decentralization to the problem of socioeconomic disparities between poorer and richer areas of the country. A positive sign ascribed to this frame means that the party supports "extreme" federalism, meaning resources should be kept where they are produced; on the contrary, a negative sign indicates that the party supports forms of territorial solidarity, which generally means a redistribution of resources managed by the central state (Basile 2015, 894).

Before the emergence of the LN, this frame, though scarcely present in electoral manifestos, was used by both decentralist and centralist parties to emphasize the need for further territorial solidarity between the north and the south (Fig. 5.4). No party dared to deny the importance of redistributing wealth to bridge the north-south gap. The anti-regionalist front led by the MSI and the PLI, however, warned about the risks of decentralization for territorial cohesion. Discussing the regionalization of the health system, for instance, the PLI stated that it would have had "as immediate consequence a disparity of treatment from one place to another, which will hinder the principle of equality among citizens" (PLI 1979). Likewise, the MSI said: "The groups of MSI-DN in the Chamber of Deputies and Senate will present ... a group of bills, also on constitutional reform, in order to include the administration of local authorities, municipalities, provinces, regions, within the life of the central state, in order to avoid ... the sharpening of the gap at the expenses of the center-southern regions" (MSI 1979). The few decentralist parties that used this frame before 1992 have sought

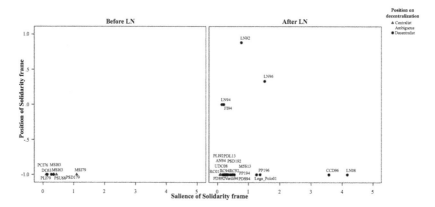

Fig. 5.4 Position and salience of the territorial solidarity frame, before and after the emergence of LN (1992): parties classified according to their overall attitude toward decentralization

to reassure voters that the process of decentralization would take into account "the peculiar problems of each regions, by ensuring to them, in an effort of distributive justice, the necessary financing" (DC 1963).

After the electoral debut of the LN, however, this frame appeared in 30 out of 49 manifestos collected over the 1992–2013 period. This dramatic increase in the use of the solidarity frame can be explained by the fact that the LN reframed it, adopting an anti-southern and anti-solidarity perspective. While claiming more autonomy for the north (the so-called Padania) from the south, the autonomist party expressed hostility toward the wasteful south, which it often portrayed as "an area in which people have no real desire to work and are only interested in claiming state benefits" (Giordano 2000, 459). Accordingly, in the 1990s the LN achieved a positive score on this frame. An example of its harsh rhetoric can be found in this quotation from 1996: "the People of the North would be able to reduce the public debt to sustainable limits by itself, but it obviously cannot carry the burden of all the debt created to accommodate the needs of a politics managed in a wasteful way, in favor of parasites living off state aid" (LN 1996). This reframing compelled many statewide decentralist parties to reassure their voters, especially the southern Italian ones, that the proposed decentralization was not merely the selfish autonomy proposed by the LN, and that it would not call into question the solidarity among Italy's regions (Basile 2015, 895). There was broad, cross-party agreement on this use of the territorial solidarity frame, which overcame any differences in worldview. It was used by parties on both the center-left and center-right; the center-left stated that: "It is still necessary to ensure forms and instruments of state and/or interregional solidarity, enabling the less prosperous regions to ensure adequate services and to promote the development of their communities" (Ulivo 2001). Meanwhile, the center-right coalition released manifestos with similar language: "the institutions of the new [federal] system should be able to remove, within a framework of national solidarity, the multiple causes of inequality in the initial conditions among the different Regions" (PdL 1996).[4] A few parties, however, did use the territorial solidarity frame to express centralist positions. The RC, for instance, used it in 2001 to express opposition to the LN's rhetoric and its project of devolution, which it defined as a policy that would lead to the "separation, the secession of the stronger regions from those in greater difficulty" (RC 2001).

It should be noted that since the 2000s the LN has moderated its political discourse compared to the 1990s, turning to stances more amenable to greater solidarity: "[on fiscal federalism] there might be a vertical redistribution, from the central state to Regions, to reduce the wealth gap; it might be also a horizontal one, between Regions" (LN 2008). Decentralist parties have continued to refer to territorial solidarity as a fundamental, unquestionable principle on which any decentralizing reform must be grounded, as in this sentence from the manifesto of the *Unione* 2006: "our idea is that of a solidarity federalism [*federalismo solidale*], aiming above all to overcome the gap in the weakest areas and in the Mezzogiorno" (Unione 2006). Centralist parties, meanwhile, have continued to use this same frame to point out the negative impact decentralization would have on interregional cohesion, as expressed by *Movimento Cinque Stelle* (M5S) in 2013, which warned about the factors that: "are undermining the universality and homogeneity of the National Health System," among which was "devolution, which delegates health assistance to regions and sharpens territorial differences and the private health systems" (M5S 2013).

Identity Pressures and Frames

The second group of frames relates to the *identity pressures* pushing for decentralization. It includes arguments related to whether and how decentralization would address the state's cultural heterogeneity. This is the frame being used when decentralization is discussed as a way to promote, or centralization as a way to reduce, the variety of regional and local traditions, cultures, and symbols within a country (identity frame). Another identity-related argument refers to the unity of the nation, seen either as a value to protect or an obsolete principle that should be abandoned (national unity frame).

The unity frame was already somewhat popular in the First Republic and regained popularity after the emergence of the LN. The identity frame, however, has been generally neglected over time, although its salience briefly increased in the early 1990s (Fig. 5.5).

Cultural Heterogeneity in a Decentralizing Country

Decentralization is often conceived as a means to deal with the cultural heterogeneity of a country. By empowering local communities, nation states seek to accommodate different needs and claims in culturally heterogeneous societies. Italy has a long tradition of cultural diversity indeed, and since the beginning of the Italian unification the nation has pursued a policy of assimilation and integration, well expressed in the famous quote by Massimo D'Azeglio: "We have made Italy, now must make the Italians."

Nonetheless, contrary to expectations, the processes of modernization, globalization, and supranational integration that occurred over the second half of the twentieth century have revitalized local identities and territorial distinctions, instead of undermining them. Today Italy's several identities

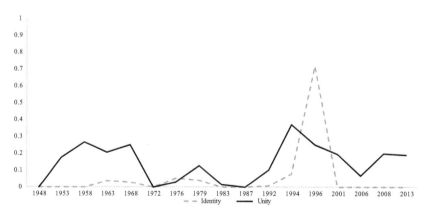

Fig. 5.5 Mean salience of frames related to identity pressures for each electoral year (1948–2013)

are still alive in the many dialects spoken across the peninsula, the local traditions, and even common stereotypes. Moreover, the country has several ethnic minorities, like the Trentino Alto Adige, featuring unique cultural attributes that also contribute to ethnic unrest.

Despite the relevance of cultural diversity for the country, the identity frame has not often been used to justify support for decentralization. Before 1992, it was cited occasionally by the DC and the smaller socialist PSDI—for example, in its 1968 joint manifesto with the PSI, the PSDI invoked this frame by making specific reference to the autonomy and cultural identity of the Alto Adige, and in 1976 it explicitly mentioned the need for regional institutions "without constraining traditions, culture, local needs that should live as visible past" (PSDI 1976). Likewise, the 1963 DC manifesto explicitly referred to the need to address the identity issues of the Alto Adige and apply "the constitutional principle of the minorities' protection" (DC 1963). No adversarial party mentioned this frame negatively, which would presumably have meant identifying cultural diversity as a potential threat to national identity. The identity frame was used only to oppose decentralization in the Second Republic, when the centralist AN explicitly criticized the tendency toward regional exceptions and cultural fragmentation: "[Europe] does not need a mere collection of Venetians or Lombards, Romans or Umbrian, Tuscans or Sicilians, tenacious in splitting the spoils of Italy" (MSI 1994). It should be noted that in those years Italy was experiencing a revival of local identities, fostered by the rhetoric of the LN, which sought to build its secessionist claims around a myth of an alleged historical territorial entity called Padania. In light of this propaganda, some parties, like the *Centro Cristiano Democratico* (CCD), adopted mixed approaches to cultural diversity. While the CCD promoted the protection of the "minor national identities" and the "recovery of the deep sense of regional and provincial culture," it also advanced a proposal for a federalism that "put the building of the national Italian identity as the goal of our new season of identity" and called for "intransigent defense of the Italian language"; it further said that it was "the pride of the *Italianness* that we must revalue and fill with the proper contents of the several local cultures" (CCD 1996).

Aside from this manifesto, the few decentralist parties to mention identity in their political discourse adopted statements in favor of the promotion and development of the local cultures and traditions, using the same language regardless of any ideological divide; even the PDS manifesto of 1994 and the PdL manifesto of 1996 used very similar statements. In other words, it seems that most parties are aware of the cultural diversity of the country and see it as a value and a source of richness. This frame is likely to overcome any form of party competition.

Is the Italian Republic Really One and Indivisible?

Article 5 of the Italian Constitution states that "the Republic is one and indivisible." The national unity frame captures those statements that refer to the need to preserve the integrity of the state within the framework of a decentralizing process. A positive score on this frame refers to radical arguments that question national unity in the name of the highest level of independence for the local authorities. A negative score means a party fully supports the principle of the indivisibility of the nation and believes it should be preserved even in a highly decentralized system.

Before 1992 no party questioned the principle of the unity of the nation. Although this frame is present in a few documents (15 out of 71), every statement received a negative score. The frame was used to justify both adversarial and accommodative strategies on decentralization; indeed, the national unity frame represents an intriguing example of how the same argument can be used to support diametrically opposed perspectives (Fig. 5.6). The centralist MSI, for example, often invoked this frame to oppose territorial restructuring projects, arguing that they jeopardized

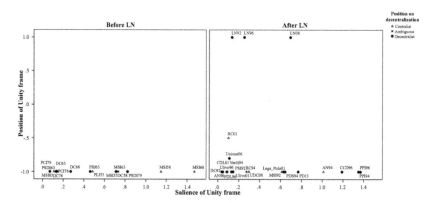

Fig. 5.6 Position and salience of the national unity frame, before and after the emergence of LN (1992): parties classified according to their overall attitude toward decentralization

the integrity of the country: "regionalism is an instrument of dissolution of the political unity of the Nation" (MSI 1963). On the other hand, decentralist parties like the DC and to a lesser extent the PCI, PSDI, and PRI showed genuine support for the value of national unity, notwithstanding their principled support for decentralization, as the following statement shows: "[the DC will propose measures to ensure] the gradual implementation of the regional structure, in the full respect of the unitary integrity of the State" (DC 1958).

When the LN entered the political arena, it broke the taboo regarding the inviolability of national unity, seeking to achieve the autonomy of northern Italy. The movement claimed a fragment of the peninsula and called into question the ideals of the Risorgimento. In fact, in three of LN's manifestos this frame is scored positively (Fig. 5.6), due to statements like the following: "[the project of reconstruction of the Italian state, based on federalism] implies moving on from a constrained and fictitious unity with the bestowing to the communities of the people the powers of self-government within the framework of a more articulated federal system …" (LN 1992) and "the supposed unitary 'national' state represents a system that belongs to the past" (LN 1996).

Such extreme autonomist claims, which went as far as invoking the ghost of secession, forced competing statewide parties to recognize that national unity was no longer an unquestioned value, at least not for a significant share of the northern electorate. As a result, they felt compelled to defend the integrity of the state in their documents. The use of this frame to justify a decentralist position became much more common among mainstream actors than it had been in the past, featuring in half of the documents analyzed from 1992 through 2013. Decentralist parties in particular, on both the left and right, had to reassure their own voters that supporting decentralization did not mean jeopardizing the traditional nation-state and its values. A clear example of this use of the national unity frame with the explicit aim of creating clear distance from the secessionist demands of the LN can be observed in the 1994 manifesto of the PDS: "[We aim at rebuilding the State, based on] the regional self-government, with a strong federalist inspiration, a clearer and more transparent national solidarity, in order to refrain the disaggregating processes and strengthening the unity of the country" (PDS 1994). Similarly, in 1996 the PdL invoked "a large decentralization of the powers, going so far to change our form of State in a federalist way, with solutions that will not put under question the unity and indivisibility of the Republic" (PdL 1996). Aside from this use of the national unity frame to reassure voters, adversarial parties like the MSI/AN and RC used it to point out the inherent risks decentralization entailed for the integrity of the state, which were exacerbated only by the secessionist claims of the LN. This frame has been used in different ways depending on the party's worldview. The nationalist AN, for example, emphasized national identity and the unitary tradition of the state: "to break up the State means to sentence it to death. ... A federalist proposal, valid for other countries with different traditions and cultures and secular unitary national experiences, does not rebuild the state but destroys it definitely" (MSI 1994). On the other hand, the leftist RC reaffirmed the importance of national unity in the context of ensuring social rights for the entire national territory: "we will ask the center-left and the center-right to acknowledge the right to social assistance as a concrete right in the entire national territory, not subject to the limits of the local budgets, by reaffirming, consistently with the constitution, the unity of the Republic, although articulated in regional and local autonomies" (RC 2001).

Political Opportunity Structures and Frames

The third group includes those frames referring to the structures of opportunity that are likely to support or hinder the process of decentralization. This group includes those frames that cast political adversaries as either obstacles to or promoters of decentralist reform (the political foe frame) and similar frames that refer to those parties demanding greater autonomy for ethno-territorial minorities as dividing forces (autonomist frame).

A second set of frames within this group concerns the role of the European Union in supporting processes of territorial restructuring (EU frame); it also includes those arguments that evoke the principle of subsidiarity, as defined by Article 5 of the Treaty of the European Union, which commits member states to pursuing further decentralization (subsidiarity frame).

During the First Republic, the political foe frame was commonly used, but was mostly replaced after 1992 with the autonomist party argument. The frames related to the role of the EU and the subsidiarity principle were present in early debates, but really became popular only in the aftermath of the Maastricht Treaty of 1992 (Fig. 5.7).

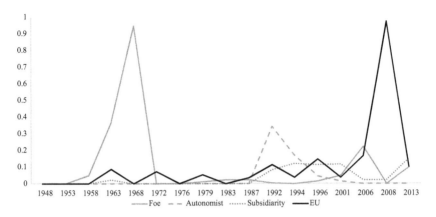

Fig. 5.7 Mean salience of frames related to political opportunity structures for each electoral year (1948–2013)

Whose Fault Is It?

A typical party strategy is blaming political adversaries for failures to effectively address problems. Some parties, especially during the First Republic, have sought to use the political foe frame to blame their opponents for the shortcomings in the process of decentralist reform (Fig. 5.8).

It is interesting that the use of the political foe argument communicated more about a party's political role—either in government or in the opposition—than its sets of values. Among the decentralist parties, the main governing party, the DC, used it to criticize both the anti-regionalist movements (which it described as obstacles to reform) and the leftist approach to decentralization (which it felts was too hasty and adventurous): "this decided inclination towards the regional reform … distinguishes us from the anti-regionalist parties. … The prudence, the awareness and the anti-mythic seriousness, with which we want to proceed in this path, thus ensuring the right conditions and adequate timing for the reform, distinguish us from those parties that are less sensitive or do not feel at all the implicit risks of a hasty, disordered and untimely implementation of the reform" (DC 1963). But opposition parties used this frame as well to accuse the DC of not carrying out the process of reform effectively. The PSI, for instance, used this frame in 1963 before entering into government, rebuking the DC for "the non-fulfillment of the programmatic commitment with the center-left concerning the approval of the laws to

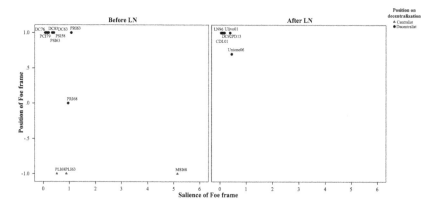

Fig. 5.8 Position and salience of the foe frame, before and after the emergence of LN (1992): parties classified according to their overall attitude toward decentralization

implement the regions by the end of the legislature" (PSI 1963). Once in government, the PSI used this argument against the political forces it deemed responsible for the government's crisis and the early termination of the legislature, blaming them for having "put an end to the reform of the local autonomies" (PSI 1987).

On the centralist front, MSI and PLI used this argument in their political discourse to criticize adversaries' support for territorial reforms. These attacks were directed against the leftist parties in particular, which it accused of pushing for the creation of the regions just to "gain economic and political power" (PLI 1963). And in this somewhat paternalistic and old-fashioned passage from its 1963 manifesto, the liberals addressed the female electorate, saying: "Madam, do you know what … center-left mean[s]? … That, rather than spending public money for your children's school, they think to spend billions to split the State in several regions, in order to give Marxists the pleasure to create their autonomous governments in several regions" (ibid.). Similarly, the 1968 manifesto of the MSI reaffirmed its fight against "the goals that the left, especially the communists, pursues with the servile acquiescence of the DC." The regions were defined as an instrument for the "pursuit of subversive goals"—namely, the strengthening of communist power among local authorities and "threatening seeds of antinationalist and pro-communist policies" (MSI 1968).

The political foe frame was also present in several manifestos from the Second Republic, where it was used by decentralist parties to blame their adversaries for the shortcomings of the process of reform. One example was the electoral campaign of 2001, which took place after the vote on the constitutional reform and on the eve of the referendum. The center-left rebuked the center-right for not having voted to reform Title V, while differentiating its approach to autonomy from those of its adversaries, who it accused of trying to "practice a sort of new local centralism, which constrain the autonomies and delays the decentralizing process" (Ulivo 2001). At the same time, the center-right coalition *Casa delle Libertà* (CdL) criticized the "state-centric and interventionist left," which it accused of being reluctant to bestow responsibilities on the regions, specifically those concerning the environmental policies (CdL 2001).

Following the 1992 elections, however, the political foe frame was mostly replaced by the autonomist one. Indeed, in those years most political actors converged in their opposition to the harsh autonomist rhetoric of the LN (Fig. 5.9). They increasingly identified Bossi's movement as the political foe, while distancing themselves from the LN's divisive statements. This hostility toward the LN brought together pro- and

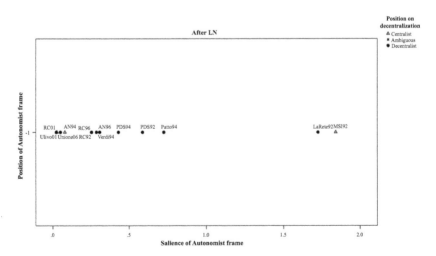

Fig. 5.9 Position and salience of the autonomist frame, after the emergence of LN (1992): parties classified according to their overall attitude toward decentralization

anti-decentralist actors and parties on the left and right, rendering the LN a common enemy for most statewide parties. From the centralist front, for instance, the leftist RC stated that: "any reference to a federal model should be abandoned, which are the result, in our country, of a debate marked by separatist movements" (RC 2001). Similar voices emerged within the rightist adversarial front, which in 1992 warned about "the success of the separatist tendencies that result in the phenomenon of the *Leghe*. ... This tendency manifests itself with particular seriousness in the case of the Lega Lombarda, which contests the elections with a program of open secession from the Nation" (MSI 1992). Among the supporters of decentralization, the manifestos of the center-left parties, such as the PDS and the *Unione*, were the most likely to contain critical references to the LN, such as "[the state's crisis] has opened a hole, which feeds dividing forces and opposing *leghismi*" (PDS 1994).

This frame was obviously absent from the political discourse of the LN's main ally—namely, the center-right pole; although the rightist AN expressed a somewhat critical stance toward its autonomist coalition partner, holding it responsible for the spread of "autonomist stances pushed to the limits of federalism" (MSI 1994). When in 1996 AN found itself untethered from Bossi's party, it did not hesitate to sharply attack it once again: "the Lega Nord has represented this process of dissolution of the old political divides and aggregation in new territorial dichotomies." The AN called the LN the "party-Homeland which denies the concept of Italy" (AN 1996).

The Europe of the Peoples

Although seldom used, the Europe of the Peoples argument—according to which the EU represents an opportunity to provide structure for assisting in decentralizing efforts—was represented in the earliest debates on the territorial dimension, which coincided with the early phases of the European integration project. It is interesting to note the strongly Europeanist statement included in the republican manifesto of 1963, which anticipated many of the arguments of the so-called Europe of the Peoples: "Contrary to what was affirmed by the anti-regionalists, the creation of the European Community and the starting of a federal integration not only are not in contradiction with the regionalist restructuring of the state, but rather they require it" (PRI 1963).

It was only after the Maastricht Treaty of 1992 that the EU began to significantly and concretely support the development of subnational levels, setting up multiple points of access for subnational actors, including the Committee of the Regions. This shift prompted parties to support their decentralist stances by invoking European support for subnational levels. This frame went beyond ideological divides and center–periphery cleavages; it was used extensively, for example, by the LN in its 1996 manifesto, which evoked the "Europe of the Peoples, of the Regional and Local communities" and even a "Senate of the Regions as a second chamber of the European Parliament" (LN 1996). The same year, the center-right pole also promoted the development of "the new European role of the Regions" (PdL 1996), and references to the "Europe of the Peoples" were included in all center-rights manifestos until 2013. The center-left also included references to the EU in its discourse on decentralization, promoting the strengthening of "the presence of the Regions in the EU, with autonomous forms of representation in the EU institutions" (Ulivo 1996). The centralist AN, however, expressed its criticism of the idea of a Europe of the Peoples: "It is absurd the idea of grounding Europe, which is our destiny, upon the breaking up of the Nations and the decay of the States; and it is utopian to conceive of [the EU] as a great federation of several regional entities" (MSI 1994).

The Maastricht Treaty further fostered decentralizing processes in Europe with the introduction of the principle of subsidiarity, which precludes the EU from claiming competencies in areas that can be sufficiently managed by the member states, either at the regional or local level. This decentralizing principle encouraged the further distribution of powers among different layers of authority, establishing that higher levels of authority should not interfere with lower ones in those areas where the latter can effectively take responsibility for the decision-making process.

Although mentioned by the PRI in 1963, the subsidiarity argument became popular only in 1992, when it began to be used by parties from all points of the continuum to justify the need to redistribute competencies across territorial levels. The PdL manifesto of 1996, for example, included several statements concerning the "rigorous application of the subsidiarity principle, that is to say the definition of competencies of the EU, Member States, Regions and local authorities," pointing out that the aim "according to which decisions should be taken as close as possible to the citizen" should be respected (PdL 1996). Indeed, similar wording was used in the *Ulivo* manifesto of the same year, which affirmed the goal of the "implementation of the subsidiarity principle ..." and the idea that "political problems should be addressed by the level of government closest to citizens" (Ulivo 1996).

Concluding Remarks

A comprehensive, full-fledged analysis of party strategies on decentralization would not be complete without mentioning the role and use of frames. In the Italian political discourse on decentralization, parties have sought to advance their positions with a wide array of arguments, ranging from functional justifications to the structures of political opportunity through identity-related frames. As shown above, they have used these arguments to both tie their issue preferences into broader political discourses and gain positional advantage over their opponents.

The analysis conducted in this chapter has shown the role of frames as instruments parties use to justify their attitudes on specific issues and connect them to a broader worldview.

In some cases, these frames have been explicitly and strongly related to a party's set of values; the efficiency, democracy, liberal, and unity frames in particular have been used by different parties to emphasize their ideological narratives. Social-democratic, leftist values, for example, have been used to define decentralization as a way to effectively manage state resources for redistributive purposes (the efficiency frame), enhance citizen participation in decision making as well as increase the accountability of politicians (the democracy frame), and create a less oppressive state (the liberalism frame). On the other hand, conservative values have been expressed with references to less wasteful state machinery (the efficiency frame) and a less interventionist state (the liberalism frame).

In other cases, frames like the unitary and efficiency frames have been used differently by decentralist and centralist parties. They are prominent examples that demonstrate how the same argument can be employed in the political discourse to pursue opposing goals.

The analysis also showed that some frames, like the identity, autonomist, EU, and subsidiarity frames, have been characterized by widespread consensus among the decentralist parties, which reveals the presence of shared values concerning the issue of decentralization among otherwise ideologically diverging parties.

Regarding the use of frames to gain political advantage, this analysis highlighted the importance of those arguments (efficiency, national unity, and territorial solidarity) that have undergone processes of reframing, especially as carried out by the LN since 1992, for the dynamics of party competition. The harsh rhetoric against Rome and the south employed by the autonomist party forced most statewide parties, despite their ideological differences, to emphasize aspects like territorial solidarity and national unity while criticizing the autonomist actor. These frames were manipulated as instruments of party competition between autonomist and statewide parties. The political foe frame was also used in government-opposition dynamics of party competition.

To conclude this account, the examples and evidence presented in this chapter point to the role of frames as alternative yet complementary tools of party strategy that define and shape party ideology and the dynamics of party competition. They are part of a wider cognitive process through which parties connect specific issues, like decentralization, to their broader set of values; in this way, they make their strategies plausible and credible in the eyes of the electorate, and are able to differentiate their positions from those of their adversaries, fostering dynamics of issue competition. Given their importance in explaining party strategies, it is thus impossible not to think of frames.

Notes

1. The title of section "Don't Think of a Region!" is a paraphrased quote from George Lakoff's essay "Don't think of an elephant!" (2004). The title refers to the idea that when something such as an elephant (or a region!) is mentioned, it will inevitably cause the listener to think about it because words evoke frames (i.e., images, knowledge, memories) that people associate with them. Mentioning regions, for example, might evoke frames such as one's region of origin, the map of the country, and different dialects and foods but also the differences between the rich and the poor regions along with many other images.
2. Lakoff (2004) argues that it can be risky for a party to use the same language as its adversary because this can draw it into the competitor's worldview. His advice, which is mostly addressed to the US Democrats, is to reframe issues by using arguments based on a party's own worldview to activate the ideas and values of its own electorate while simultaneously attempting to activate the ideas of people in the middle.
3. The Italian language distinguishes political liberalism (*liberalismo*, based on freedom and the constitutional limitation of state powers) with economic liberalism (*liberismo*, the laissez faire, which opposes state intervention in

economy). This distinction was at the center of a philosophical debate between Luigi Einaudi, who maintained that the two concepts intersect where they both oppose an interventionist state, and Benedetto Croce, who distinguished between the two.

4. It is interesting that this document put great emphasis on the word *solidarity* when referring to federalism; the word is found in four sentences.

REFERENCES

Alleanza Nazionale. 1996. Pensiamo l'Italia: il domani c'è già. Valori, idee e progetti per l'Alleanza Nazionale. Tesi Politiche Approvate dal Congresso di Fiuggi – Gennaio 1995. *Secolo d'Italia*, December 7, 1994.

Basile, Linda. 2015. A Dwarf Among Giants? Party Competition Between Ethno-Regionalist and State-Wide Parties on the Territorial Dimension: The Case of Italy (1963–2013). *Party Politics* 21 (6): 887–899.

Baumgartner, Frank R., Suzanna L. De Boef, and Amber E. Boydstun. 2008. *The Decline of the e Death Penalty and the Discovery of Innocence*. Cambridge: Cambridge University Press.

Casa delle Libertà. 2001. Piano di governo per un'intera legislatura. In Lehmann, Pola, Theres Matthieß, Nicolas Merz, Sven Regel, and Annika Werner. 2017. *Manifesto Corpus*. Version: 2017-2. Berlin: WZB Berlin Social Science Center.

Centro Cristiano Democratico. 1996. Punti di Programma del Centro Cristiano Democratico. In Lehmann, Pola, Theres Matthieß, Nicolas Merz, Sven Regel, and Annika Werner. 2017. *Manifesto Corpus*. Version: 2017-2. Berlin: WZB Berlin Social Science Center.

Chong, Dennis, and James N. Druckman. 2007. Framing Theory. *Annual Review of Political Science* 10 (1): 103–126.

Democrazia Cristiana. 1958 [1968]. Programma della Democrazia Cristiana per il quinquennio 1958–1963: per garantire al popolo italiano 'progresso senza avventura'. In *Atti e Documenti della DC 1943–1967*, 928–937. Roma: Cinque Lune. April 12, 1958.

———. 1963[1968]. Programma elettorale della DC per la IV Legislatura. In *Atti e Documenti della DC 1943–1967*, 1473–1519. Roma: Cinque Lune.

———. 1968. Il programma della DC al servizio del paese. *Il Popolo*, April 19, 1968.

———. 1972. Gli impegni programmatici. *Il Popolo*. April 1, 1972.

Druckman, James N. 2001. On the Limits of Framing Effects: Who Can Frame? *Journal of Politics* 63 (4): 1041–1066.

Elias, Anwen, Edina Szöcsik, and Christina Isabel Zuber. 2015. Position, Selective Emphasis and Framing: How Parties Deal with a Second Dimension in Competition. *Party Politics* 21 (6): 839–850.

Foot, John. 2003. *Modern Italy*. Houndmills: Palgrave Macmillan.

Giordano, Benito. 2000. Italian Regionalism or 'Padanian' Nationalism—The Political Project of the Lega Nord in Italian Politics. *Political Geography* 19 (4): 445–471.

Giordano, Raffaela, and Tommasino. 2011. Public Sector Efficiency and Political Culture. Bank of Italy Temi di Discussione. Working Paper, No. 786.

Helbling, Marc, Dominic Hoegliner, and Bruno Wüest. 2010. How Political Parties Frame European Integration. *European Journal of Political Research* 49 (4): 495–521.

Lakoff, George. 2004. *Don't Think of an Elephant! Know Your Values and Frame the Debate-The Essential Guide for Progressives*. 1st ed. White River Junction: Chelsea Green Publishing.

Lega Nord. 1992. Programma elettorale. Politiche 1992. Milano.

———. 1996. *Programma elettorale per la Padania. Elezioni politiche del 21 aprile 1996*. Milano: Lega Nord.

———. 2008. Parlamento del Nord. *Risoluzione federalismo*. Vicenza, March 2, 2008.

L'Ulivo. 1996. Tesi per la definizione della piattaforma programmatica de L'Ulivo. 6 dicembre 1995. Retrieved from http://www.perlulivo.it/radici/vittorieelettorali/programma/tesi/. Accessed 10 Apr 2018.

———. 2001. *Rinnoviamo l'Italia, Insieme. Il programma dell'Ulivo per il governo 2001/2006 presentato da Francesco Rutelli*. Roma: Newton & Compton Editori.

L' Unione. 2006. Per il bene dell'Italia. Programma di Governo 2006–2011 (Originally retrieved from the website of the coalition). Official party manifesto, according to art. 1 paragraph 5 of L. 260/2005.

Meguid, Bonnie M. 2008. *Party Competition Between Unequals: Strategies and Electoral Fortunes in Western Europe*. Cambridge: Cambridge University Press.

Movimento 5 Stelle. 2013. Programma. Stato e cittadini. Energia Informazione Economia Trasporti Salute Istruzione (Originally retrieved from the website of the coalition). Official party manifesto, according to art. 1 paragraph 5 of L. 260/2005.

Movimento Sociale Italiano. 1963. Il MSI agli italiani. Cyclostated.

———. 1968. Manifesto del Movimento Sociale. Per non svegliarsi comunisti. *Secolo d'Italia*, May 7, 1968.

———. 1979. Elezioni 1979 Il programma del MSI-DN. *Secolo d'Italia*, May 10, 1979.

———. 1983. Il Messaggio degli Anni '80. *Secolo d'Italia*, January 23, 1983.

———. 1992. E' giunto il tempo del cambiamento. *Secolo d'Italia*, March 10, 1992.

Movimento Sociale Italiano. 1994. Il programma della Destra di governo. In Lehmann, Pola, Theres Matthieß, Nicolas Merz, Sven Regel, and Annika

Werner. 2017. *Manifesto Corpus*. Version: 2017–2. Berlin: WZB Berlin Social Science Center.
Partito Comunista Italiano. 1972. Il programma dei comunisti: per un governo di svolta democratica. *L'Unità* (Special issue), March 26, 1972.
———. 1968. E ora di cambiare, si può cambiare: appello programma del PCI. *L'Unità*, May 12, 1968.
Partito Democratico della Sinistra. 1994. *Per ricostruire un' Italia più giusta, più unita, più moderna. Dieci grandi opzioni programmatiche*. Roma: l'Unità.
Partito Liberale Italiano. 1963. *Sulla linea di una tradizione sicura*. Novara: Segreteria del PLI.
———. 1979. *Appello Politico e programma elettorale. L'Italia dei liberali nell'Europa democratica*. Roma: cyclostated.
Partito Repubblicano Italiano. 1963. Programma elettorale del PRI. *La Voce repubblicana*, March 10, 1963.
———. 1968. Il programma elettorale del Partito Repubblicano Italiano. *Mondo Economico* 19: 25–27.
Partito Socialista Italiano. 1963. *Il Programma del PSI*. Roma: Seti.
———.1987. Programma socialista per la decima legislatura. In Lehmann, Pola, Theres Matthieß, Nicolas Merz, Sven Regel, and Annika Werner. 2017. *Manifesto Corpus*. Version: 2017–2. Berlin: WZB Berlin Social Science Center.
Partito Socialista Democratico Italiano. 1976. Il programma elettorale del PSDI. *Biblioteca della Libertà* Anno XIII (61/62): 267–298.
Partito Socialista Unificato. 1968. *Una risposta ai problemi della nostra epoca. Programma elettorale del PSI e PSDI unificati*. Roma: Seti.
Polo delle Libertà. 1996. *100 impegni per cambiare l'Italia: programma del Polo per le Libertà*. S. Donato Milanese: Centro grafico Linate.
Rifondazione Comunista. 2001. *Un voto utile per il paese per costruire una sinistra di alternativa e una sinistra plurale*. Roma: Rifondazione Comunista.
Slothuus, Rune, and Claes H. de Vreese. 2010. Political Parties, Motivated Reasoning, and Issue Framing Effects. *The Journal of Politics* 72 (3): 630–636.
Tarrow, Sidney. 1979. Italy: Crisis, Crises or Transition? *West European Politics* 2 (3): 166–186.

Concluding Remarks

So What?

This book opened with a question: Why do territorial politics matter? Recent events in contemporary politics, along with the continuing transformation of the territorial structures of postwar European states, provide a concrete answer to the question. The management of center–periphery relations within democratic political systems, the redistribution of competencies across different levels of authority in increasingly complex societies, the political accommodation of autonomist demands from ethnic and linguistic minorities; these are all key issues of the political debate and, as a result, the terrain of political competition. This point inspired the core research question of this volume. In western European political systems, in which political parties play the dominant role in policy making, what is the role of political parties in territorial politics?

In Chap. 1, the territorial dimension of politics was defined as the set of issues related to the organization of local authorities and the relationships between them. Under the "territorial" label there is a plethora of further issues, which can be pragmatically clustered around the two dichotomies of decentralization versus centralization and cultural differentiation versus homogenization. This study has mainly focused on the first group, which includes issues concerning the redistribution of powers and competencies across territorial authorities, and the territorial architecture of the state.

Hence, as the title highlights, this book explored "the party politics of decentralization"—namely, whether, to what extent, in which direction, and how political parties have dealt with the policy changes concerning the process of decentralization.

Italy, a country in a permanent quest for a definition of its territorial state structure—and one in which political parties play a prominent role in policy making—represented an ideal laboratory in which to test this research question. Case studies may have their limits, but they can also contribute to scientific knowledge. This book offered a detailed account of Italian parties' political discourse on decentralization, their party strategies, and their impact on policy change, supported by empirical evidence provided by an original coding scheme used to analyze the content of party manifestos.

At the end of this journey into the party politics of decentralization over the 70 years of Italian Republic history, it is time now to sum up our findings. Although the heading of this section, for the sake of convention, suggests that this part of the book will offer a conclusive answer to the research question, these remarks are not intended to be the final say; rather, they should provide insight and perspective for future research on this field.

Putting the Pieces of the Puzzle Together

Each chapter of this volume addressed the core research question by looking at it from a different angle and perspective. This section puts the pieces of the research puzzle together, connecting the analyses and findings to the broader theoretical framework.

The starting point of this study was a definition of party competition as one among several activities usually included in the notion of party politics, activities aimed at achieving a wide range of goals. In the political arena, parties need to develop appropriate *strategies*, which include *making decisions on policy issues* (Elias et al. 2015). This strategy is conceptualized here as the sum of the manipulation of three tools—namely salience, position, and frame. Parties take stances on issues by simultaneously deciding whether and to what extent they will pay attention to a policy dimension (i.e., the manipulation of salience), the direction to pursue it (i.e., the manipulation of position), and the way in which their positions will be justified (i.e., the manipulation of frames) (Chap. 1). Accordingly, Chaps. 3, 4, and 5 addressed each of these three decisional processes to provide a full account of party strategies on the territorial dimension in the Italian political debate, with a special focus on the aspect of decentralization, as previously mentioned. This account of party strategies has been framed within the context of the Italian process of decentralization, whose main reforms, both those that were implemented and those that failed, were outlined in Chap. 2.

Chapter 3 focused on salience. Using theoretical insights provided by agenda-setting literature, the analysis conducted in this chapter revealed that the salience of decentralization (here considered the independent variable) in parties' political discourse affects the process and, in particular, the timing of policy change and reform (the dependent variable). Specifically, the empirical analysis showed that reforms have occurred only after most of the parties have begun to pay more attention to decentralization and its salience has increased at the party system level. This finding underlines the importance of the (party) politics of attention in explaining the process of policy change.

Because party attention represents a key factor for understanding when reforms will actually occur in a political system, it is crucial to understand the factors and dynamics that can be expected to determine this attention. Accordingly, in the second part of the chapter, the strategies of party competition (i.e., salience) become the main dependent variable to be explained by the dynamics of party competition. The empirical analyses supported the oft-cited argument that leftist parties, especially before 1992, and autonomist parties, especially after the debut of the *Lega Nord* (LN), played prominent roles in influencing the party system and bringing attention to decentralist reform. The main implication of this finding is that parties, in their role as policy entrepreneurs, play a potentially crucial role in party competition on issues, which can effectively trigger the process of policy change.

Nonetheless, the attention of political parties is a necessary but not sufficient condition for reform to occur. Once an issue gets the attention of the party system, the majority of the political forces represented in Parliament have to converge on a specific policy solution, which can ultimately be shaped into a full-fledged reform. The analysis presented in Chap. 4 concerned patterns of party consensus (or disagreement) on policy solutions on decentralization, focusing on the strategic tool of position. Party strategies on whether to support or oppose processes of decentralization constitute the main variable under analysis, with results broken down between the positions expressed in party manifestos during electoral campaigns and the actual voting positions parties adopted on major decentralist reforms in Parliament. The data showed that several factors are likely to affect *electoral position*, including sincere support for the process of decentralization and the strategic convenience of backing these reforms; at the same time, concerns about ideological plausibility and credibility can limit a party's options.

The analysis also revealed that when there is broad support for the process of decentralization parties tend to distinguish their political discourse from those of the others by adopting different positions on each concrete aspect of decentralization. This strategy of differentiation keeps a certain degree of party competition on the territorial dimension alive, despite the broad support the process of decentralization already enjoys: even as the parties have converged in their general positions on the policy dimension, they have continued battling over the nuances, keeping the topic prominent in public discourse.

When parties move to the parliamentary arena, however, they have to consider factors behind the attitudes and positions they campaigned on. In particular, parties' governing or opposition role has been crucial in explaining voting behavior on decentralist reforms, especially since the radical changes to the party system in 1994. The significance for the process of policy change is that party consensus on a policy dimension (a necessary precursor to reform) is shaped by strategic, substantial, and ideological considerations; furthermore, the reform process is deeply affected by government-opposition dynamics, as well as by the features of the party system. Polarized, multiparty systems tend to reduce the importance of the government-opposition divide, while increasing the likelihood of consensual reforms based on compromise among the main political forces; meanwhile, bipolar systems are more affected by government-opposition dynamics, forcing the winning coalition to pass reforms itself without the consent of the opposition. Whether consensual or majority reforms are more effective, especially when it comes to a structural issue like decentralization, remains an open question.

Chapters 3 and 4 addressed the process of policy change, either directly or indirectly. Even when the dependent variable was party strategies rather than actual policy change, the underlying reasoning is that parties' strategic decisions concerning the amount of attention to devote to decentralization and the policy directions they support will ultimately affect the process of reform.

Chapter 5 focused on party strategies themselves, and in particular on the rationales behind these strategies. The analysis of frames conducted in the last empirical chapter revealed that parties have used different frames to connect the secondary policy dimension of decentralization to their broader worldviews; moreover, especially since the emergence of the LN in the political arena, frames have become an increasingly common tool of party competition, used by each party to differentiate its platform on decentralist issues from those of its adversaries. This last part of the analysis, though seemingly not connected to the rest of the account of the reforming process in Italy, actually demonstrates the value of examining frames as a complementary element of party strategies, one that is indispensable to a full account of party competition on issues.

THE PARTY POLITICS OF DECENTRALIZATION … À LA CARTE

As mentioned in the preface, this book was intended to provide insights and food for thought for different research areas and address a variety of audiences. As though offered a restaurant's menu, readers are presented with several areas of interest to choose from; ideally, everyone can find something to focus on and make use of in further research.

This section therefore sums up what might be of interest to different audiences.

Scholars and specialists in Italian history and those broadly interested in processes of territorial restructuring in contemporary nation-states. This group will find a detailed account of the evolution of the process of decentralization in Italy, especially in Chap. 2. In particular, this book questions the current direction the Italian territorial structure is taking, asking whether it is merely decentralizing or in fact leaning toward federalism; it also seeks to explain the intermittent nature of its development. At the time of this writing, Italy seems to be swaying between centralist traditions and federalist ambitions. The process of decentralization that was initiated almost 50 years ago now seems irreversible; nonetheless, federalist thrusts have been constrained by veto players in the past as well as by fears regarding threats to national unity. Moreover, the financial crisis laid bare the weaknesses of a decentralized system, sparking centripetal backlash and recentralization.

This book's focus on the role of political parties could also suggests useful insights for territorial studies. Indeed, the Italian case represents an interesting example of how the tensions between the center and peripheries in a divided society can be effectively channeled by the dynamics of party competition. When the party system incorporates autonomist demands within its political discourse, the likelihood of these demands being accommodated within the institutional, democratic systems increases, and the level of conflict within the society simultaneously decreases.

Scholars and researchers interested in party politics. Leaving aside the specifics of the territorial dimension, this book offers a new perspective on the analysis of party competition on issues, here defined as one of several activities included in party politics. Based on a definition of party strategies as the result of the manipulation of three tools—salience, position, and frame—this book introduces a coding scheme designed for the content analysis of party manifestos focusing on a single policy dimension. While the coding scheme builds on existing scholarly efforts concerning party evaluation, it adds a few innovative concepts as well and further theoretical insights.

First, the coding framework distinguishes between purposefully vague and blurred positioning and contradictory but clear and nuanced strategies. This distinction is particularly important in cases like decentralization in Italy, where there is broad general consensus but competition over subtopics. Moreover, both the analysis and the underlying coding scheme reveal that party competition on policy dimensions also manifests in different ways of framing the political discourse. As this short overview shows, the intrinsic interest of this coding scheme and the analyses conducted using it should be assessed beyond their use in studying the territorial dimension. The underlying theoretical assumptions, and the empirical application of the method, should in fact be well suited with due adaptation to measuring party strategies on other policy dimensions as well.

Scholars and researchers interested in agenda-setting dynamics and policy change. As argued in the preface to this book, by focusing on a single policy issue it is possible to investigate the actors, processes, and interactions that underlie the agenda setting and policy change processes in a given political system in general. Reviving the metaphor used in that section, it is like sending a scout out to explore the "black box" of policy making and getting back a detailed report of all the actors and mechanisms observed, to be used as a template to explain other processes of policy change. While keeping in mind that decentralization is "not just another policy output tailored to win votes" (Sorens 2009, 268), the theoretical models used to explain the party politics of decentralization should be applicable to other policy areas with appropriate adaptations.

To this end, the analyses conducted in Chaps. 3 and 4 reveal that, in parliamentary systems, political parties play a key role in agenda-setting and policy-making dynamics. Shifts in their attention, when they rise to the party system level, increase the likelihood of an issue being included in the policy agenda, and therefore being the subject of policy change. Furthermore, this research reveals that the dynamics of party competition, as well as the features of the party system, influence party strategies on policy issues, which, in their turn, affect the process of policy change; as a result, it is necessary to look at these dynamics in order to fully understand how reforms occur.

This volume, however, has fully achieved its purpose only if the findings, perspectives, and suggestions that emerged from these chapters "have sown doubts, rather than gathering certainties." In line with the premises mentioned in the preface, the goal of this book was to raise interest in territorial party politics as well as in its varied interrelated theoretical implications for other fields of investigation. The aim has been to shed some light on these topics while paving the way for further research.

If this book provides some inspiration for future studies, then the efforts put into its realization will not have been in vain.

References

Elias, Anwen, Edina Szöcsik, and Christina Isabel Zuber. 2015. Position, Selective Emphasis and Framing: How Parties Deal with a Second Dimension in Competition. *Party Politics* 21 (6): 839–850.

Sorens, Jason. 2009. The Partisan Logic of Decentralization in Europe. *Regional & Federal Studies* 19 (2): 255–272.

Appendix

Table A.1 List of parties, number of seats in Parliament, elected deputies of the parties whose manifestos have been coded (%), salience, directional certainty, directional intensity, and party typology on decentralization (Chap. 4)

Year legislature	Party acronym	Coded manifesto	Seats in the Chamber of Deputies (n)	Elected deputies of coded parties (%)	Salience	Directional certainty	Directional intensity	Typology
1948 Legislature I	DC	*Appello della Democrazia Cristiana al Paese, 4 marzo 1948.*	305		2.9	0.0	0.0	Reluctant ambiguous
	FDP[a]	*Il programma del Fronte Democratico Popolare.*	183		3.9	1.0	3.9	Strong decentralist
	MSI	*Noi e gli Altri.*	6		0.0	.	.	Neglecting
	PLI[b]	*Vota Blocco nazionale. I programmi concreti.*	19		0.0	.	.	Neglecting
	PRI	*Il programma del partito repubblicano per le elezioni del 18 aprile 1948.*	9		4.0	1.0	4.0	Strong decentralist
	PSLI[c]	*Il Nostro Programma d'Azione. Critica Sociale.*	33		2.9	0.7	2.0	Mild decentralist
	Not coded parties Südtiroler Volkspartei (SVP), Partito Nazionale Monarchico (PNM), Partito dei Contadini, Partito Sardo d'Azione (PSd'A)		19					
		Total seats:	574	96.7				

1953 Legislature II						
	DC	*Appello della Direzione DC al Paese per le elezioni politiche.*	263	0.0	.	Neglecting
	MSI	*Movimento Sociale Italiano. Programma per le Elezioni Politiche 1953.*	29	1.5	0.0	Reluctant ambiguous
	PCI	*Per la pace, la libertà, il lavoro, la concordia sociale. Il Programma dei Comunisti.*	143	0.0	.	Neglecting
	PLI	*Punti programmatici fissati dal Partito Liberale Italiano nel VI Congresso di Firenze.*	13	1.0	−0.5	Reluctant centralist
	PRI	*Partito Repubblicano Italiano.* (Electoral leaflet)	5	0.0	.	Neglecting
	PSDI	*Programma Politico del PSDI.*	19	0.0	.	Neglecting
	PSI	*Il PSI agli elettori. Vota alternativa socialista garanzia di progresso e di pace.*	75	2.2	1.0	Mild decentralist
	Not coded parties Südtiroler Volkspartei (SVP), Partito Nazionale Monarchico (PNM)		43			
	Total seats:		590	92.7		

(continued)

Table A.1 (continued)

Year legislature	Party acronym	Coded manifesto	Seats in the Chamber of Deputies (n)	Elected deputies of coded parties (%)	Salience	Directional certainty	Directional intensity	Typology
1958 Legislature III	DC	*Programma della Democrazia Cristiana per il quinquennio 1958-1963.*	273		3.6	1.0	3.6	Strong decentralist
	MSI	*Movimento Sociale Italiano. Lineamenti del Programma elettorale del MSI.*	24		2.3	−1.0	−2.3	Mild centralist
	PCI	*Progetto di programma elettorale che i comunisti presentano agli italiani.*	140		2.6	1.0	2.6	Mild decentralist
	PLI	*Il Partito liberale di fronte agli elettori: Lineamenti di un programma.*	17		0.0	.	.	Neglecting
	PRI[d]	*Per uno stato moderno e democratico. Una politica per la terza legislatura*	6		3.9	1.0	3.9	Strong decentralist
	PSDI	*Programma del Partito Socialista Democratico Italiano per le elezioni politiche del 1958 e la prossima legislatura.*	22		0.0	.	.	Neglecting
	PSI	*Per una politica di alternativa democratica.*	84		6.8	1.0	6.8	Strong decentralist

	Not coded parties Südtiroler Volkspartei (SVP), Partito Nazionale Monarchico (PNM), Partito Monarchico Popolare (PMP), Comunità, Union Valdôtaine (UV)		30			
	Total seats:		*596*	*95.0*		
1963 Legislature IV	DC	*Programma elettorale della DC per la IV Legislatura.*	260	6.7	0.5	3.0	Empty talker decentralist
	MSI	*Il MSI agli italiani.*	27	7.1	−0.1	−0.4	Empty talker centralist
	PCI	*Battere la DC. Rafforzare il PCI. Il Programma elettorale del PCI.*	166	6.1	0.8	5.1	Strong decentralist
	PLI	*Sulla linea di una tradizione sicura.*	39	4.7	−1.0	−4.7	Strong centralist
	PRI	*Programma elettorale del PRI.*	6	17.6	1.0	17.0	Strong decentralist
	PSDI	*Un più forte PSDI per uno stato efficiente e per il benessere del popolo italiano*	33	5.7	0.6	3.3	Strong decentralist
	PSI	*Il programma del PSI.*	87	8.2	0.8	6.8	Strong decentralist
	Not coded parties Südtiroler Volkspartei (SVP), Partito Democratico Italiano di Unità Monarchica (PDIUM), Union Valdôtaine (UV)		12			
	Total seats:		*630*	*98.1*		

(continued)

Table A.1 (continued)

Year legislature	Party acronym	Coded manifesto	Seats in the Chamber of Deputies (n)	Elected deputies of coded parties (%)	Salience	Directional certainty	Directional intensity	Typology
1968 Legislature V	DC	Il programma della DC al servizio del paese.	266		5.3	0.8	4.2	Strong decentralist
	MSI	Manifesto del Movimento Sociale. Per non svegliarsi comunisti.	24		10.3	-0.9	-8.8	Strong centralist
	PCI	E' ora di cambiare, si può cambiare: appello programma del PCI.	177		1.8	1.0	1.8	Mild decentralist
	PLI	Il programma elettorale del Partito Liberale Italiano.	31		6.2	-0.2	-1.0	Empty talker centralist
	PRI	Il programma elettorale del Partito Repubblicano Italiano.	9		9.5	0.3	2.9	Empty talker decentralist
	PSIUP	Il programma elettorale del PSIUP.	23		0.0	.	.	Neglecting
	PSU[e]	Una risposta ai problemi della nostra epoca. Programma elettorale del PSI e PSDI unificati.	91		5.2	0.4	2.2	Empty talker decentralist
	Not coded parties Südtiroler Volkspartei (SVP), Partito Democratico Italiano di Unità Monarchica (PDIUM)		9					
	Total seats:		630	98.6				

1972 Legislature VI	DC	Gli impegni programmatici.	266	7.6	0.6	4.6	Strong decentralist
	MSI	Un voto intelligente, un voto coraggioso per l'avvenire.	56	0.0	.	.	Neglecting
	PCI	Il programma dei comunisti: per un governo di svolta democratica.	179	7.6	0.9	6.9	Strong decentralist
	PLI	Il PLI agli elettori. Un voto al PLI per correggere il passato, per costruire l'avvenire con i liberali al governo.	20	0.0	.	.	Neglecting
	PRI	Il documento programmatico approvato dal Consiglio Nazionale repubblicano.	15	1.7	0.0	0.0	Reluctant ambiguous
	PSI	La proposta politica del PSI.	61	5.7	1.0	5.7	Strong decentralist
	Not coded parties Partito Socialista Democratico Italiano (PSDI), Südtiroler Volkspartei (SVP), Union Valdôtaine and other allies (DC-UV-RV-PSDI),		33				
	Total seats:		*630*	*94.8*			

(*continued*)

Table A.1 (continued)

Year legislature	Party acronym	Coded manifesto	Seats in the Chamber of Deputies (n)	Elected deputies of coded parties (%)	Salience	Directional certainty	Directional intensity	Typology
1976 Legislature VII	DC	Il programma della Democrazia Cristiana.	262		10.1	0.3	3.2	Empty talker decentralist
	DEM.PROL.	Democrazia Proletaria.	6		0.5	0.0	0.0	Reluctant ambiguous
	MSI-DN	Movimento Sociale Italiano—Destra Nazionale.	35		0.0	.	.	Neglecting
	PCI	Partito Comunista Italiano. E' necessaria una nuova guida politica e morale.	228		6.4	0.8	5.2	Strong decentralist
	PLI	Il programma elettorale del PLI.	5		1.3	0.7	0.9	Mild decentralist
	PRAD	Poteri dello Stato e libertà del cittadino.	4		2.2	1.0	2.2	Mild decentralist
	PRI	Il programma elettorale del PRI.	14		6.3	0.0	0.0	Empty talker neutral
	PSDI	Il programma elettorale del PSDI.	15		3.0	0.8	2.3	Mild decentralist
	PSI	La proposta politica del PSI.	57		8.4	0.7	5.5	Strong decentralist
	Not coded parties Südtiroler Volkspartei (SVP), Cartel DC-PSI-PdUP in the Aosta Valley		4					
	Total seats:		**630**	**99.4**				

1979 Legislature VIII							
	DC	Il programma elettorale della DC.	262	4.1	0.4	1.7	Empty talker decentralist
	MSI-DN	Elezioni 1979: il Programma del MSI-DN	30	3.3	-1.0	-3.3	Mild centralist
	PCI	46 Schede di governo. Il programma dei comunisti per l'VIII legislatura	201	4.7	0.7	3.5	Strong decentralist
	PLI	Appello Politico e programma elettorale. L'Italia dei liberali nell'Europa democratica.	9	1.5	-0.1	-0.2	Reluctant centralist
	PRI	I repubblicani verso gli anni ottanta. Il programma.	16	1.1	-0.3	-0.4	Reluctant centralist
	PSDI	Programma del Partito Socialista Democratico Italiano. Piattaforma politica.	20	4.9	0.2	1.1	Empty talker decentralist
	PSI	Idee per un programma.	62	2.1	0.9	2.0	Mild decentralist
	Not coded parties Südtiroler Volkspartei (SVP), Associazione per Trieste, Union Valdotaine-DEM-PROL.-PLI, Partito Radicale (PRAD), Partito di Unità Proletaria per il Communismo (PdUP)		30				
	Total seats:		630	95.2			

(continued)

Table A.1 (continued)

Year legislature	Party acronym	Coded manifesto	Seats in the Chamber of Deputies (n)	Elected deputies of coded parties (%)	Salience	Directional certainty	Directional intensity	Typology
1983 Legislature IX	DC	*Un programma per garantire lo sviluppo.*	225		2.7	0.6	1.6	Mild decentralist
	DEM.PROL.	*Il quadro dei problemi del paese.*	7		1.7	1.0	1.7	Mild decentralist
	MSI-DN	*Il messaggio degli anni '80.*	42		7.9	−0.3	−2.1	Empty talker centralist
	PCI	*Un programma per cambiare. Sintesi delle proposte programmatiche del PCI.*	198		3.6	0.4	1.3	Empty talker decentralist
	PLI	*Manifesto liberale per le elezioni del 26 giugno 1983.*	16		3.9	0.2	0.8	Empty talker decentralist
	PRI	*Trenta punti per una legislatura. Il Programma repubblicano.*	29		3.0	0.1	0.3	Reluctant decentralist
	PSDI	*Il PSDI agli elettori: indicazioni per un programma di governo.*	23		1.0	0.0	0.0	Reluctant ambiguous
	PSI	*Rigore, equità, sviluppo: Il senso della proposta socialista.*	73		2.0	0.5	1.0	Reluctant decentralist
	Not coded parties Südtiroler Volkspartei (SVP), Liga Veneta, Partito Sardo d'Azione (PSd'Az), Union Valdôtaine (UV) and other allies, Partito Radicale (PRAD)		17					
		Total seats:	630	97.3				

Year/Legislature	Party	Manifesto					Classification
1987 Legislature X	DC	*Libertas. un programma per l'Italia. Elezioni politiche 14–15 giugno 1987.*	234	3.2	0.5	1.5	Reluctant decentralist
	MSI-DN	*Stato, Nazione, Lavoro, libertà per la nuova repubblica degli italiani. La piattaforma elettorale*	35	0.0	.	.	Neglecting
	PCI	*Il PCI per la decima legislatura. Gli impegni programmatici fondamentali.*	177	1.5	1.0	1.5	Mild decentralist
	PLI	*Il manifesto 1987.*	11	4.6	0.3	1.1	Empty talker decentralist
	PSDI	*Una alternativa riformista per governare il cambiamento.*	17	0.0	.	.	Neglecting
	PSI	*Programma socialista per la decima legislatura.*	94	1.1	0.7	0.8	Mild decentralist
	Verdi	*Perche' una Lista Verde Nazionale.*	13	1.4	1.0	1.4	Mild decentralist

Not coded parties Partito Repubblicano Italiano (PRI), Südtiroler Volkspartei (SVP), Lega Lombarda, Partito Sardo d'Azione (PSd'Az), Democrazia Proletaria (DEM. PROL), Partito Radicale (PRAD), Union Valdotain and other allies

(*continued*)

Table A.1 (continued)

Year legislature	Party acronym	Coded manifesto	Seats in the Chamber of Deputies (n)	Elected deputies of coded parties (%)	Salience	Directional certainty	Directional intensity	Typology
1992 Legislature XI	DC	Un programma per l'Italia verso l'Europa. Prima l'Italia. Libertas, fai vincere il tuo futuro.	206		2.5	0.6	1.4	Mild decentralist
	LARETE-MOV.DEM	La Rete – Movimento per la democrazia. Il programma, le candidate, i candidati per le elezioni del 5–6 aprile 1992.	12		6.0	0.7	4.3	Strong decentralist
	LN	Programma elettorale. Politiche 1992.	55		10.8	0.8	9.1	Strong decentralist
	Verdi	Gli altri ti promettono la luna. Noi ti garantiamo la terra.	16		3.4	1.0	3.4	Strong decentralist
	MSI-DN	E' giunto il tempo del cambiamento.	34		8.6	−0.4	−3.7	Empty talker centralist
	PDS	Costruiamo una nuova Italia. PDS opposizione che costruisce.	107		4.4	0.5	2.1	Empty talker decentralist

PLI	*Elezioni 1992. Datecì la forza per cambiare le cose. Lista Marco Pannella*	17	5.6	0.9	4.9	Strong decentralist
PRAD		7	0.0	.	.	Neglecting
PRI	*Elezioni politiche 1992. Per un'Italia nuova*	27	3.4	1.0	3.4	Strong decentralist
PSDI	*Programma elettorale 1992. Piu' forza al PSDI per un domani sicuro*	16	5.7	0.8	4.7	Strong decentralist
PSI	*PSI. Un governo per la ripresa. Argomenti socialisti*	92	2.4	0.9	2.1	Mild decentralist
RC	*Programma elettorale. Dall'opposizione per l'alternativa*	35	2.0	0.8	1.5	Mild decentralist
Not coded parties Südtiroler Volkspartei (SVP), Federalismo-Pensionati-UV, Lega autonomista veneta, Lega Valle d'Aosta		6				
Total seats:		630	99.0			

(*continued*)

Table A.1 (continued)

Year legislature	Party acronym	Coded manifesto	Seats in the Chamber of Deputies (n)	Elected deputies of coded parties (%)	Salience	Directional certainty	Directional intensity	Typology
1994 Legislature XII	*Polo delle Libertà (PdL)*[f]		366					
	MSI-DN	*Il programma della destra di governo.*			4.1	−0.1	−0.2	Empty talker centralist
	FI	*Cinque obiettivi per quarantacinque proposte.*			3.2	0.4	1.3	Reluctant decentralist
	LN	*Sintesi programma.*			6.7	0.9	5.7	Strong decentralist
	Alleanza dei Progressisti[g]		213					
	LaRete	*La Rete. Le ragioni di un voto.*			0.0	.	.	Neglecting
	PDS	*Per ricostruire un'Italia più giusta, più unita, più moderna. Dieci grandi opzioni programmatiche.*			4.9	0.6	3.0	Strong decentralist
	RC	*La forza dell'alternativa. Difendi il lavoro: Cambia l'Italia con la sinistra.*			3.4	0.0	0.0	Empty talker neutral
	Verdi	*Il programma dei verdi: Una rivoluzione onesta e gentile.*			3.4	0.1	0.3	Empty talker decentralist
	Patto per l'Italia[h]	*Patto per l'Italia. Le idee, il progetto, il programma.*	46		2.5	0.4	1.1	Reluctant decentralist
	PPI	*Un programma per gli italiani.*			6.1	0.3	1.8	Empty talker decentralist

Not coded parties
Südtiroler Volkspartei (SVP), Lega d'Azione Meridionale, Vallée d'Aoste-Autonomie Progrès Fédéralisme

5

	Total seats:	630	99.2			
1996 Legislature XIII	Ulivo[j]	*Tesi per la definizione della piattaforma programmatica dell'Ulivo.*	285	5.1	0.6	3.2	Strong decentralist
	PDS	*Semplifichiamo la vita. Liberiamo le energie.*		2.5	1.0	2.5	Mild decentralist
	PPI	*Il programma per le elezioni del 21 aprile. L'adesione del PPI al programma dell'Ulivo.*		5.5	1.0	5.5	Strong decentralist
	RI	*Rinnovamento Italiano. Manifesto politico.*		9.3	1.0	9.3	Strong decentralist
	Verdi	*La Via Verde. Programmi d'azione e progetto dei verdi italiani.*		1.3	0.7	0.8	Mild decentralist
	Polo per le Libertà[i]	*100 impegni per cambiare l'Italia: programma del Polo per le Libertà.*	246	5.3	0.8	4.2	Strong decentralist
	AN	*Pensiamo l'Italia: il domani c'è già. Valori, idee e progetti per l'Alleanza Nazionale.*		4.0	0.01	0.0	Empty talker decentralist

(*continued*)

Table A.1 (continued)

Year legislature	Party acronym	Coded manifesto	Seats in the Chamber of Deputies (n)	Elected deputies of coded parties (%)	Salience	Directional certainty	Directional intensity	Typology
	CCD CDU	CCD-CDU.			0.2	1.0	0.2	Mild decentralist
	CCD	Punti di programma del Centro Cristiano Democratico.			39.3	0.6	22.6	Strong decentralist
	FI	Forza Italia. Contratto con gli Italiani: Ecco il nostro impegno di governo.			6.8	0.7	4.5	Strong decentralist
Not in coalition								
	LN	Programma elettorale della Padania. Elezioni politiche del 21 aprile 1996.	59		13.9	0.8	11.0	Strong decentralist
	RC	Ricominciare da sinistra per l'alternativa.	35		3.0	0.0	0.0	Reluctant neutral
	Not coded parties Democrazia e Libertà, Lega d'Azione Meridionale, Vallée d'Aoste-Autonomie Progrès Fédéralisme		6					
		Total seats:	630	99.5				

2001 Legislature XIV	Casa delle Libertà[k]	Piano di governo per un'intera Legislatura.	368	5.2	0.7	3.8	Strong decentralist
	CCD/UDC	Il manifesto del CCD.		0.0	.	.	Neglecting
	Lega/Polo	Documento Patto Lega-Polo.		16.4	0.9	14.5	Strong decentralist
	Ulivo[l]	Rinnoviamo l'Italia, insieme. Il programma dell'Ulivo per il governo 2001/2006.	250	2.4	0.9	2.1	Mild decentralist
	Not in coalition						
	RC	Un voto utile per il paese per costruire una sinistra di alternativa e una sinistra plurale.	11	1.6	−0.2	−0.3	Reluctant centralist
	Not coded parties Democrazia e Libertà, Lega d'Azione Meridionale, Vallée d'Aoste-Automonie Progrès Fédéralisme		3				
	Total seats:		632	99.5			

(continued)

Table A.1 (continued)

Year legislature	Party acronym	Coded manifesto	Seats in the Chamber of Deputies (n)	Elected deputies of coded parties (%)	Salience	Directional certainty	Directional intensity	Typology
2006 Legislature XV	Unione[m]	Per il bene dell'Italia. Programma di Governo 2006–2011.	348		4.7	0.5	2.3	Empty talker decentralist
	Casa delle Libertà[n]	Programma elettorale 2006.	281		3.6	0.8	3.0	Strong decentralist
	Not coded parties Associazioni Italiane in Sud America		1					
	Total seats:		630	99.8				
2008 Legislature XVI	Center-right coalition[o]		344					
	LN	Parlamento del Nord. Risoluzione federalismo.	(60)		41.0	0.8	34.0	Strong decentralist
	PdL[p]	7 Missioni per il futuro dell'Italia.	(272)		3.1	0.8	2.5	Mild decentralist
	Center-left coalition		247					
	IDV	11 punti per cambiare l'Italia.	(28)		0.0	.	.	Neglecting
	PD	Il programma di governo del PD. Elezioni 2008.	(211)		2.3	0.7	1.5	Mild decentralist
	Not in coalition							
	UDC	Programma elettorale.	36		3.6	−0.3	−0.9	Empty talker centralist
	Not coded parties Südtiroler Volkspartei (SVP)		3					
	Total seats:		630	99.5				

2013 Legislature XVII	Center-left coalition[q]	*Italia. Bene comune.*	345	3.1	0.9	2.7	Mild decentralist
	Center-right coalition (PDL)[r]	*Programma. Elezioni politiche 24 25 febbraio.*	125	5.7	1.6		Empty talker decentralist
	Center coalition (SC)[s]	*Cambiare l'Italia, Riformare l'Europa. Un'Agenda per un Impegno Comune. Primo Contributo ad una Riflessione Aperta.*	47	2.3	0.3	0.4	Reluctant decentralist
	Not in coalition						
	Movimento 5 Stelle	*Programma.*	109	1.5	−0.7	−1.0	Mild centralist
	Not coded parties						
	Movimento Associativo Italiani all'Estero, Vallée d'aoste, Unione Sudamericana Emigrati Italiani		4				
	Total seats:		**630**	**99.4**			

Note: Since 1994 parties have formed coalitions to contest elections.

Note: Since 2006 parties and coalitions have had to clearly state their party manifestos, which have thus become official documents (Legge December 21, 2005, n. 270).

Note: This study has sought to include the positions of most of the parties represented in Parliament in each Legislature. To clarify the extent of its coverage, Table A.1 shows the number of deputies elected from each political party whose electoral manifesto has been coded. This number was then divided by the total number of deputies elected in each Legislature and multiplied by 100, to obtain the percentage of total elected deputies belonging to parties whose manifestos have been coded. The resulting percentages range from 92% (1987 election) to 99%, meaning that this research accounts for the positions of almost the totality of the political forces represented in Parliament in each Legislature.

Table A.1 (continued)

Source of coded documents: The main source of these documents was the archive of the Center for the Study of Political Change (CIRCaP) of the University of Siena. Other documents were kindly provided by the Italian Policy Agendas Project (active partner of the Comparative Agendas Project) and by the Comparative Manifesto Project (CMP). A number of documents, especially the oldest ones, were personally assembled by the author from the archives of private foundations (Archivio Sturzo, Biblioteca Salvemini, Fondazione Nenni, Fondazione Ugo Spirito, and Fondazione Isec) and from private libraries and private collections.

[a] Deputies elected with the FDP alliance between PCI and PSI.
[b] Deputies elected with the *Blocco Nazionale* (PLI together with *Uomo Qualunque* and *Unione per la Ricostruzione Nazionale*).
[c] Deputies elected with the *Unità Socialista* (PSLI with *Unione dei Socialisti*).
[d] Deputies elected with the coalition between PRI and *Partito Radicale*.
[e] Deputies elected with the PSU alliance between PSI and PSDI.
[f] *Center-right coalition*.
[g] *Center-left coalition*.
[h] *Center coalition* (also includes *Patto Segni*).
[i] Center-left coalition; also includes *Südtiroler Volkspartei, Popolari per Prodi, L'Ulivo-Partito Sardo d'Azione, L'Ulivo-Lega Autonomia Veneta, Socialisti italiani, La Rete*, and other minor parties.
[j] Center-right coalition.
[k] Center-right coalition; also includes *Forza Italia, Alleanza Nazionale, Partito Socialista, Partito Repubblicano Italiano*.
[l] Center-left coalition; also includes *Democratici di Sinistra* (DS), *la Margherita, Südtiroler Volkspartei*.
[m] Center-left coalition (DS, *Margherita, Popolari*, UDEUR, RC, PCI, Verdi, *Italia dei Valori, Rosa nel Pugno*, SVP and others).
[n] Center-right coalition (FI, AN, UDC, LN, *Movimento per le Autonomie, Nuovo PSI*, and others).
[o] Also inclues *Movimento per l'Autonomia* (8 seats).
[p] This manifesto substantially coincides with that one of the coalition PdL–LN-MdP.
[q] Formed by PD, *Sinistra Ecologia e Libertà* (SEL), *Centro Democratico*, SVP.
[r] Formed by PdL, LN, *Fratelli d'Italia*.
[s] *Scelta Civica* (SC), *Unione di Centro*.

Table A.2 List of parties and acronyms

Party (full name)	Party acronym
Alleanza Nazionale	AN
Casa delle Libertà	CdL
Centro Cristiano Democratico	CCD
Centro Cristiano Democratico-Cristiani Democratici Uniti	CCD-CDU
Democrazia Cristiana	DC
Democrazia Proletaria	DEM.PROL.
Federazione dei verdi	Verdi
Forza Italia	FI
Fronte Democratico Popolare (alliance PCI and PSI)	FDP
Italia dei Valori	IDV
La Rete	LARETE-MOV.DEM
Lega Nord	LN
Lista Dini—Rinnovamento Italiano	RI
Lista Verde	Verdi
Movimento Cinque Stelle	M5S
Movimento Sociale Italiano/Movimento Sociale Italiano—Destra Nazionale	MSI/MSI-DN
Partito Comunista Italiano	PCI
Partito Democratico	PD
Partito Democratico della Sinistra	PDS
Partito Liberale Italiano	PLI
Partito Popolare Italiano	PPI
Partito Radicale Italiano	PRAD
Partito Repubblicano Italiano	PRI
Partito Socialista dei Lavoratori Italiani	PSLI
Partito Socialista Democratico Italiano	PSDI
Partito Socialista Italiano	PSI
Partito Socialista Unificato	PSU
Patto per l'Italia	Patto
Polo delle Libertà (coalition)	PdL
Popolo delle Libertà (party)	PDL
Rifondazione Comunista	RC
Ulivo	Ulivo
Unione	Unione
Unione di Centro	UDC

Index[1]

A

Accommodative strategy
  accommodative parties, 149
  accommodative strategy
    hypothesis, 115
  "accommodative strategy with
    differences," 115, 150
  See also Strategies of party
    competition
Administrative autonomy, 30, 37, 40,
    43, 45, 55, 63n65, 160
  juridical autonomy of the territorial
    authorities, 58n5
Administrative competencies, 153
  See also Policy areas related to
    decentralization
Adversarial strategy
  adversarial parties, 100, 153, 203, 206
  adversarial strategy hypothesis, 115
  See also Strategies of party competition
Agenda-setting, xiii, xxiii, 3, 20, 38,
    67–102, 145, 219, 222, 223
  mandate theory, 3, 71
Alleanza Nazionale (AN), 42, 48,
    84, 85, 91, 113, 125, 126,
    138, 139, 161, 162, 164,
    166, 179n43, 189, 203,
    206, 210, 211
Almirante, Giorgio, 158
Ambiguous strategies
  blurring strategy, 11, 111, 113,
    126–130, 132, 135, 141
  contradictory (or broad appeal)
    strategies, 11, 111–113, 115,
    126–130, 151, 222
Ambrosini, Gaspare, 35
Angius, Gavino, 163
Autonomist frame, 206
  See also Frames
Autonomist party, 3, 41, 44, 48,
    75, 90, 99, 100, 103, 189,
    200, 206, 219
  Lega Nord, 75, 219
  See also Entrepreneurial agent

---

[1] Note: Page numbers followed by 'n' refer to notes.

248　INDEX

B
Bassanini, Franco, 175n1
Bassanini Laws, 46, 89
　Bassanini reform, 43, 55, 152
　See also L. 59/1997; *Leggi Bassanini*
Berlusconi, Silvio, 42, 44, 47, 139
Bertolucci, Bernardo, 5
Bettiol, Giuseppe, 157
Bipolar system, 120, 161, 166, 174, 220
　See also Party systems
Blurring strategy, 11, 111, 129, 130, 132, 135, 141
　blurring strategy hypothesis, 116
　See also Ambiguous strategies; Strategies of party competition
Bobbio, Norberto, xiii
Bonatesta, Michele, 179n43
Bossi, Umberto, 42, 93, 139, 164, 190, 209, 210

C
Carboni, Angelo, 59n12
Cartia, Giovanni, 59n12
Casa delle Libertà (CdL), 42, 61n48, 86, 92, 105n7, 162, 164, 209
Case-study
　hypothesis-generating, 19
　research design, 18–20
　theory confirming/infirming, 19
Castelli, Roberto, 162
Cattaneo, Carlo, 29
Center-left government (1963)
　Democrazia Cristiana (DC), 134
　Partito Socialista Italiano (PSI), 134
Centro Cristiano Democratico (CCD), 77, 203
Centro Cristiano Democratico-Cristiani Democratici Uniti (CCD_CDU), 105n7
Chamber of the Regions, 84–86, 139, 154

　See also Senate of the Regions
Coding scheme (of TERRISS Dataset), 15
Colombo, Emilio, 134
Commissioner of the Government, 45
Communication, 15, 148, 149
　See also Policy areas related to decentralization
Comparative Manifesto Project (CMP), 11, 104n5
Consensual model, 121
Constituent Assembly, 35, 37, 38, 51, 58n6, 58n7, 58n8, 58n10, 58n11, 157
Constitutional legitimacy (question of), 46, 54
　article 127 Constitution, 46, 54
Constitutional reform (policy area), 143
　See also Policy areas related to decentralization
Constitutional reform(s), ix, 162, 179n46
　confirmatory referendum, 44
　constitutional referendum of 2001, 85, 139
　constitutional referendum of 2006, 86, 164
　constitutional referendum of 2016, 49; Referendum December 4, 2016, ix
　constitutional reform (of 2006), 46, 54
　constitutional reform (of 2016), 54, 87, 179n46 (*see also* Renzi-Boschi constitutional reform)
　constitutional reform (of Title V) of 2001, 44, 162 (*see also* L. Cost. 3/2001)
Constitution of Italy, 37, 45, 46, 179n41
　article 5, 35, 36, 58n8, 58n9, 58n11, 204

INDEX 249

article 114, 36, 46
article 115, 36, 53
article 116, 37, 50, 59n17
article 117, 37, 39, 45, 50, 53, 55, 62n52, 136, 162, 178n31, 179n41 (*see also* Constitutional reform(s), constitutional reform (of Title V) of 2001)
article 118, 45, 62n52 (*see also* Constitutional reform(s), constitutional reform (of Title V) of 2001)
article 119, 37, 45, 47, 53, 62n56 (*see also* Constitutional reform(s), constitutional reform (of Title V) of 2001)
article 121, 38, 44
article 122, 38, 61n39
article 123, 44, 55
article 124, 45, 53 (*see also* Constitutional reform(s), constitutional reform (of Title V) of 2001)
article 125, 45, 53 (*see also* Constitutional reform(s), constitutional reform (of Title V) of 2001)
article 127, 37, 53 (*see also* Constitutional reform(s), constitutional reform (of Title V) of 2001)
article 128, 46, 53 (*see also* Constitutional reform(s), constitutional reform (of Title V) of 2001)
article 131, 36
Title V, Part II, 36, 44, 61n47, 63n61
Content analysis, 8–10, 104n5, 146, 190, 191, 222
manual coding, 10
quasi-sentences, 11 (*see also* Comparative Manifesto Project (CMP))

Contradictory (or broad appeal) strategy, 11, 111–113, 126–130, 151, 222
ambiguous strategies, 112, 127, 128
contradictory strategy hypothesis, 115
See also Strategies of party competition
Conventio ad excludendum, 38, 94
Partito Comunista Italiano (PCI), 38, 94
Cossiga, Francesco, 71
Cottone, Benedetto, 161
Cultural differentiation *vs.* homogenization (dychotomy), 7
See also Territorial dimension
Culture, 7, 12, 54, 82, 152, 192, 202, 203, 206
See also Policy areas related to decentralization

D

Decentralist reforms, x, 2, 30, 42, 46–48, 52, 70–75, 78–89, 91, 103, 110, 111, 116–119, 121, 125, 129, 156, 161, 163, 166, 167, 169, 171, 179n46, 206, 207, 219, 220
Decentralization, 122, 212
Decentralization Index (DI), 54–56, 63n67, 76, 82, 87–89, 105n8
See also Decentralization in Italy
Decentralization in Italy, 28, 75, 104, 112, 188–190, 222
process of decentralization, xi–xiii, 12, 20, 28, 34–51, 54, 57, 67–103, 114, 140, 142, 145, 149, 154, 156, 185, 200, 206, 218–221
Decentralization *vs.* centralization (dychotomy), 7
See also Territorial dimension

Decentralized state, 28, 35, 142, 198–199
   See also Territorial organization (of the state)
De-concentration, 30
   See also Territorial organization (of the state)
Democracy frame, 191, 197, 198, 212
   See also Frames
Democrazia Cristiana (DC), 35, 38–40, 59n27, 61n40, 79–84, 98–102, 114, 120, 126, 127, 132–137, 150–152, 154, 155, 157–161, 174, 178n38, 179n39, 189, 193, 197–200, 203, 205, 207, 208
Democrazia Proletaria (DEM.PROL.), 81, 82, 126, 153
Determinants of party voting behavior, 122, 156, 166, 170
Devolution, 30, 46, 86, 139, 140, 153, 201
   See also Territorial organization (of the state)
Directional certainty, xxiii, 12, 13, 15, 17, 18, 22n10, 123–132, 135, 141, 142, 146, 147
   See also Measurement of party strategies
Directional intensity, xxiii, 100–102, 130–132, 171, 173
   See also Measurement of party strategies
Direction of the transfer of powers, 28
Dispersion of powers, 28
D. lgs. 56/2000, 43, 55
D. lgs. 68/2011, 48
   See also L. 42/2009
D. lgs. 88/2011, 48
   See also L. 42/2009
D. lgs. 446/1997, 43
   See also IRAP
Dorotei, 135

E
Economic issues and foreign and defense policy
   defense policy, 45, 154–155
   economic policy, 154–155
   fiscal policy, 13, 142, 154–155
   foreign policy, 31, 126, 129, 146, 149, 192
   See also Policy areas related to decentralization
Education, 11, 13, 18, 33, 46, 55, 62n51, 82, 97, 115, 142, 145, 146, 149, 151, 155
   See also Policy areas related to decentralization
Efficiency frame, 191, 193, 194, 196, 212
   See also Frames
Election of the regional councils, 159
   See also L. 108/1968
Electoral arena, 8
Electoral position, 110
Empty talkers centralist parties, 125, 129
   See also Party strategies on decentralization, typology of
Empty talkers decentralist parties, 126, 129
   See also Party strategies on decentralization, typology of
Empty talkers neutral parties, 126
   See also Party strategies on decentralization, typology of
Entrepreneurial agent, 75
   autonomist parties, 75, 90, 93
   entrepreneurial agent hypothesis, 90, 93, 101 (*see also* Proponent party)
   functional equivalent to autonomist parties, 94
   leftist parties, 90, 98, 101
   Lega Nord (LN) (*see Lega Nord* (LN))

INDEX   251

Partito Comunista Italiano (PCI) (*see Partito Comunista Italiano* (PCI))
Partito Socialista Italiano (PSI) (*see Partito Socialista Italiano* (PSI))
Entropy score
  attention diversity, 145
  Shannon's H entropy formula, 145
Environment policy, 209
  See also Policy areas related to decentralization
Equalization fund (*fondo perequativo*), 47
  See also L. 42/2009
Equilibrium (PE) theory, 69
Estimate of party attitudes, 1
European Union frame, *see* Frames
Europe of the Peoples, 210
Europe of the Regions, 137

F
Fanfani, Amintore, 134
Federal reform, 139, 140, 177–178n24
Federal senate, *see* Senate of the Regions
Federal state, *see* Federal systems
Federal systems
  coming together federations, 28, 31, 33
  defining features of federations, 43, 52
  hold together federations, 30–33, 52
  See also Territorial organization (of the state)
Federazione dei verdi (Verdi), 85
Filetti, Cristoforo, 161
Financial autonomy, 32, 37, 40, 41, 43, 45, 47, 53–55, 58n5, 80, 82, 83, 87, 137, 160

juridical autonomy of the territorial authorities, 58n5
Finocchiaro Aprile, Andrea, 58n9
Finocchiaro, Anna, 165
First Republic, 38, 41, 94, 120, 123–127, 130, 132–137, 155, 158, 161, 166, 168, 169, 171–174, 189, 193, 202, 206, 207
  party conflict on decentralization in the First Republic, 130
Fiscal autonomy, 55, 129, 143, 148, 155
  juridical autonomy of the territorial authorities, 58n5
Fiscal federalism reform, 47, 53, 86
  See also L. 42/2009
Fisichella, Domenico, 179n43
Follini, Marco, 179n44
Formigoni, Roberto, 61n49
Forza Italia (FI), 42, 55, 84, 85, 91, 139, 153, 162, 165, 189
Fragmented polarization, 121
  See also Party systems
Frames
  autonomist frame, 206
  coded frames, 16
  democracy frame, 191, 197, 198, 212
  efficiency frame, 191, 193, 194, 196, 212
  European Union frame, 206, 210–212
  liberalist frame, 191, 199
  list of frames, 13, 58n4, 190
  national unity frame, 202, 204, 206
  political foe frame, 206, 207, 209
  subsidiarity frame, 206
  territorial solidarity frame, 191, 199, 201
  See also Measurement of party strategies

Fronte Democratico Popolare (alliance PCI and PSI) (FDP), 79, 94, 130
Functional pressures, 13
   functional pressures frames, 13, 191–200 (*see also* Frames)
   triggers of decentralization, x, 13, 79, 89

G
Galan, Giancarlo, 61n48
Governing role of parties
   centralist governing party hypothesis, 119
   decentralist governing party hypothesis, 118
   opposition party preferences hypothesis, 119
   party preferences hypothesis, 117, 158
   party system hypothesis, 112, 121 (*see also* Robust logistic regression, determinants of party voting behavior)
Government Commissaries, 40, 53

H
Health
   identity policies, 152
   immigration, 152
   See also Policy areas related to decentralization

I
Identity frame, *see* Frames
Identity pressures, 13, 191, 201–206
   identity pressures frames, 201–204 (*see also* Frames)
   triggers of decentralization, 13, 89
Ingrao, Pietro, 159

IRAP, 43, 55
Issue competition, 68
Issue framing, 13, 20, 185–189
   issue reframing, 190
   See also Frames
Italia dei Valori (IDV), 124, 165, 169
Italy's unification, 29

L
L. 42/2009, 47, 48, 55, 86, 165, 166
   See also Fiscal federalism reform
L. 56/2014 (Legge Delrio), 63n64
L. 59/1997, 43, 85, 162
   See also Bassanini Law; *Leggi Bassanini*
L. 62/1953, 79, 156–158
   See also Legge Scelba
L. 108/1968, 39, 80, 87, 159
L. 127/1997, 43
L. 142/1990, 41
L. 249/1968, 39
L. 281/1970, 39, 40, 81, 87, 160, 161
L. 382/1975, 40, 81, 82, 161
L. 662/1996, 55
   See also IRAP
L. 775/1970, 39–40, 87, 160, 161
L. 1084/1970, 55, 87
Labor policy, 155
Laconi, Renzo, 35, 58n10, 178n37
Lakoff, George, 186–188, 213n1, 213n2
La Loggia, Enrico, 162
Land management and environment policies
   civil protection, 150
   transportation, 150
   urban planning, 150
   See also Policy areas related to decentralization

INDEX 253

Land Management and the Environment, 150–151
  See also Policy areas related to decentralization
La Rete (LARETE-MOV.DEM), 245
The Last Emperor (movie), *see* Bertolucci, Bernardo
Law and order, 45, 146, 148, 149, 152, 153
  See also Policy areas related to decentralization
L. Cost. 1/1999, 44, 55, 61n39
L. Cost. 1/2012, 49, 55, 56
L. Cost. 3/2001, 44, 59n16, 59n17, 59n18, 59n19, 59n20, 59n21, 59n22, 85
  See also Constitutional reform(s), constitutional reform (of Title V) of 2001
Lega Nord (LN), xivn1, 30, 41, 42, 44, 47, 48, 57n2, 75, 77, 84, 86, 91–94, 98–101, 104n4, 104n6, 105n7, 126, 129, 137–140, 152–154, 161–165, 173, 179n41, 186, 190, 191, 195, 198–203, 205, 206, 209–211, 213, 219, 221, 245
Legge Scelba, 55, 79, 156
  See also L. 62/1953
Legge Tatarella, 60n39
Leggi Bassanini, *see* Bassanini Law; L. 59/1997
Legislative arena, 8
Legislative autonomy, 30, 34, 37, 45, 46, 53, 55
  juridical autonomy of the territorial authorities, 58n5
Legislative change, 76
Legislative competencies, 30, 31, 53, 55, 85, 139, 140, 142, 146, 152, 153, 158
  See also Policy areas related to decentralization

Legislature I (1946–1953), 78
Legislature II (1953–1958), 79
Legislature IV (1963–1968), 39, 80
Legislature V (1968–1972), 39
Legislature VI (1972–1976), 40, 81
Legislature XIII (1996–2001), 43
Legislature XIV (2001–2006), 86
Legislature XV (2006-2008), 47
Legislature XVI (2008–2013), 47
Legitimacy control, 45
Letta, Enrico, 164
  government, 165
Liberalism frame, 198, 212
Liberalist frame, *see* Frames
Lijphart, Arend, 19
  See also Case-study
Limits to regional autonomy, 157
Lipset, Seymour, 4, 6, 90
Lista Dini-Rinnovamento Italiano (RI), 85, 245
Lista Verde (Verdi), 85, 245
Luzzatto, Giulio Mario, 158

M
Maastricht Treaty, 206, 211
Majoritarian systems, 121, 163, 171
  majoritarian model, 121
Malagodi, Giovanni, 159
Malagugini, Alberto, 160
Mandate theory, 71, 117, 119
  See also Agenda-setting
Maroni, Roberto, 61n48
Mattarella, Sergio, 120
  electoral law, 120
Mattarellum, *see* Mattarella
Measurement of party strategies
  directional certainty, 123
  directional intensity, 100
  frame, 8–10, 13–15
  position, 8–13, 123, 156
  salience, 8–11, 15, 17, 18, 75, 156
Meduri, Renato, 164, 179n43

Meguid, Bonnie, 4, 5, 13, 74, 75, 90, 104n3, 111
  See also Position, Salience, and Ownership (PSO) theory
Michelini, Arturo, 159
Mild centralist parties, 124, 228, 233, 243
  See also Party strategies on decentralization, typology of
Mild decentralist parties, 142, 166
  See also Party strategies on decentralization, typology of
Monti, Mario, 48
Moro, Aldo, 39, 60n28, 159, 178n38, 179n39
Movimento 5 Stelle (M5S), 86, 121, 125, 140, 152, 165, 167, 201, 245
Movimento Sociale Italiano/Movimento Sociale Italiano-Destra Nazionale (MSI/MSI-DN), 39, 42, 78–84, 98, 113, 124, 125, 129, 132, 134–138, 141, 153, 158–161, 169, 174, 177n17, 189, 194, 195, 197, 199, 204–206, 208, 245
Multipolar architecture of the state, 46
Multipolar party system, 120

N
National Assembly for Wales, 30
National conservative parties
  Movimento Sociale Italiano (MSI), 39, 42, 78–84, 98, 113, 124, 125, 129, 132, 134–138, 141, 153, 155, 158–161, 169, 174, 177n17, 189, 194, 195, 197, 199, 204, 205, 208, 210
  Partito Liberale Italiano (PLI), 39, 78–83, 120, 124, 125, 130, 132, 134–137, 141, 150–154, 158, 159, 161, 169, 174, 178n36, 189, 194, 197, 199, 208
National unity frame, 212
Neglecting parties, 123, 168
  See also Party strategies on decentralization, typology of
Nenni, Pietro, 35, 39, 58n11
Niche actors, 91
Niche parties, 90, 93, 104n3
Nobile, Umberto, 58n9
Northern question, 41, 190
Nuovo Centro Destra (NCD), 165

O
Opposition party, 119
Ordinary regions, 37–39, 44, 60n28, 68, 80, 83, 94, 143, 153, 161
Organization of the state, home affairs, and citizens' rights
  administrative competencies, 152
  identity policies, 152
  immigration, 152
  law and order, 153
  legislative competencies, 153
  See also Policy areas related to decentralization

P
Padania, 30, 57n2, 61n48, 190, 200, 203
Parliament of, 30
Parallel convergences, 159–161, 174
  See also Moro, Aldo
Paris, Danilo, 59n12
Parties as policy-seekers, 7, 73
Parties as vote-seekers, 7, 73
Parties' electoral stances on decentralization, 168

Partito Comunista Italiano (PCI), 35, 38, 39, 59n26, 79–83, 94, 95, 97–102, 105n9, 105n11, 114, 120, 126, 130, 133, 135–137, 151, 153, 157–160, 169, 171, 174, 178n37, 179n39, 189, 194, 196, 198, 205
Partito Democratico (PD), xivn1, 42, 61n40, 86, 87, 94, 140, 152, 164, 165, 169, 179n46
Partito Democratico della Sinistra (PDS), 42, 84–86, 94, 95, 97, 101, 102, 126, 137, 138, 189, 203, 205, 210
Partito Liberale Italiano (PLI), 39, 78–83, 120, 124, 125, 130, 132, 134–137, 141, 150–154, 158, 159, 161, 169, 174, 189, 194, 197, 199, 208
Partito Popolare Italiano (PPI), 84, 85, 114, 126
Partito Radicale Italiano (PRAD), 124
Partito Repubblicano Italiano (PRI), 39, 79–82, 120, 125–130, 132, 158–160, 194, 205, 210, 211
Partito Sardo d'Azione, 75, 226, 234, 235
 See also Autonomist party
Partito Socialista dei Lavoratori Italiani (PSLI), 79, 132, 158, 178n37
Partito Socialista Democratico Italiano (PSDI), 39, 81, 83, 98, 120, 126, 128, 155, 158, 159, 189, 194, 203, 205
Partito Socialista Italiano (PSI), 35, 39, 59n27, 79–83, 94, 96, 98–102, 105n10, 120, 126, 130, 132–136, 157–161, 168, 189, 197, 203, 207, 208
Partito Socialista Unificato (PSU), 81, 126, 150, 194

Party, 186
Party agendas, 11, 21, 71, 72, 104n2, 145
 See also Policy agenda
Party competition, 73
 agenda control (*see also* Party system agenda (PSA))
 consensual pattern of party competition, 3, 110, 111, 116
Party electoral strategies on decentralization
 accommodative strategy hypothesis, 115
 adversarial strategy hypothesis, 115
 blurring strategy hypothesis, 116
 contradictory strategy hypothesis, 115
 determinants of party electoral strategies on decentralization, 127
 party's stance on decentralization, 123
 plausibility and credibility (of party attitudes), 113, 174
 strategic consideration, 113, 124
Party manifestos, 9, 10, 15, 17, 22n7, 72, 76–78, 85, 110, 127, 131, 145, 163, 164, 186, 218, 219, 222
Party pledges, 156
Party politics, xii, 3, 7
Party politics of attention, 69, 109
Party strategies, xi, xiii, 1, 2, 5, 7–10, 21, 69, 103, 104, 112–114, 120, 122, 123, 130, 132–141, 149, 173, 175, 185, 186, 207, 212, 213, 218–223
Party strategies on decentralization, 112, 113, 175
 typology of, 123, 130, 226–243

Party system agenda (PSA), 69,
  72–76, 78–103, 104n4, 111,
  112, 137, 176n10, 185–186
Party systems, 120
  bipolar systems, 120, 161, 174
  multipolar systems, 120 (*see also*
    Fragmented polarization;
    "Polarized multi-party political
    systems")
  polarization of the party system, 6,
    151, 165
Party voting behavior on decentralist
  reforms
  centralist governing party
    hypothesis, 119
  decentralist governing party
    hypothesis, 118
  determinants of, 156
  opposition party preferences
    hypothesis, 119
  party preference hypothesis, 117
  party system hypothesis, 121
Patto Lega Polo, 91
Patto per l'Italia (Patto), 126
Perassi, Tommaso, 36
Pinto, Michele, 160
Polarized multi-party political
  systems, 120
Policy agenda, 5
Policy areas related to decentralization,
  190, 191
  coded policy areas, 14
Policy change, 56
  annual policy change on
    decentralization, 56 (*see also*
    Decentralization Index (DI))
  impact of party competition on
    policy change, 74
  "politics of attention" hypothesis,
    69, 219
Political agenda, 2, 20, 68, 90, 91,
  111, 143, 145
Politics of attention, 21, 69, 70,
  74, 219
  bounded rationality, 70
  party politics of attention, 69, 109
  See also Agenda-setting; Punctuated
    Equilibrium (PE) theory
Polo delle Libertà (coalition) (PdL),
  42, 85, 104n7
Popolo delle Libertà (party) (PDL), 42,
  126, 189
Position
  on decentralization (in Italy), 100,
    149, 150, 157, 167, 171, 174
  See also Measurement of party
    strategies
Position, Salience, and Ownership
  (PSO) theory, 90
  See also Meguid, Bonnie
Presidential decrees (D.P. R) no. 616,
  617, and 618 of 1977, 40
Presidential decrees of 1972 (D.P. R.
  1-11/1972), 149
Preti, Luigi, 59n12
Prodi, Romano, 43, 168
Productive activities
  agriculture, 149
  craftsmanship, 150
  energy, 125, 150
  tourism, 150
  trade, 150
  See also Policy areas related to
    decentralization
Proponent party, *see* Entrepreneurial
  agent
Punctuated Equilibrium (PE)
  theory, 57, 68

R
Red-belt
  Emilia Romagna, 38, 57n2, 94,
    105n9, 105n10
  Tuscany, 38, 94, 105n9, 105n10
  Umbria, 38, 94, 105n9
Referendum October 22, 2017
  (Lombardy and Veneto), ix

Referendum of Catalonia 2017, xi
Reform of Title V, 44–46, 50,
    63n61, 139
  See also Constitutional reform(s),
    constitutional reform (of Title
    V) of 2001; Constitutional
    reform(s), constitutional reform
    (of 2006); Constitutional
    reform(s), constitutional reform
    (of Title V) of 2016
Reform(s)
  consensual reforms, 117, 161,
    162, 220
  federal reform, 139, 140,
    177–178n24
  laws to change "rules of game," 2,
    109–122, 124
  majority reforms, 110, 116
  major reforms, 76, 78–81, 87, 89
  minor reforms, 60n39, 76, 87, 89
  partisan reforms, 121, 161, 174
  structural reforms, 103, 109, 139
Regulatory autonomy, 41
  juridical autonomy of the territorial
    authorities, 58n5
Reluctant centralist parties, 125
  See also Party strategies on
    decentralization, typology of
Reluctant decentralist parties, 126
  See also Party strategies on
    decentralization, typology of
Reluctant neutral parties, 126
  See also Party strategies on
    decentralization, typology of
Renzi-Boschi constitutional reform, 164
  See also Constitutional reform(s),
    constitutional reform of 2016
Renzi, Matteo, ix, 49, 63n62, 165,
    175n2
  Renzi government, 164
Ribaltone, 42
  Bossi, Umberto, 42
Rifondazione Comunista (RC), xivn1,
    12, 84, 85, 125, 126, 129, 130,
    139, 150, 152, 153, 162,
    163, 167, 168, 189, 198,
    201, 206, 210
Robust logistic regression
  determinants of party voting
    behavior, 122, 156, 166, 170
  predictive margins, 171
  See also Party voting behavior on
    decentralist reforms
Rokkan, Stein, 4, 6, 90
"*Roma ladrona*" ("robber Rome"),
    93, 164, 190
Ruggiero, Carlo, 59n12
Ruini, Meuccio, 58n8
Rumor, Mariano, 134
Russo Spena, Giovanni, 162

S
Salience
  of decentralization (in Italy), 76–78,
    82, 83, 87, 94, 97, 99, 219
  median salience, 77–81, 84, 86, 88,
    91, 92, 95, 96, 101, 102
  by party families, 5, 91, 99, 101
  threshold of relevance, 77
  See also Measurement of party
    strategies
Salvini, Matteo, 93
Sartori, Giovanni, 6, 120
Scelta Civica (SC), 195
Scottish Parliament, 30
Scottish referendum of 2014, xi
Second Republic, 42, 112, 120, 121,
    125, 126, 138–141, 151,
    153–155, 161–163, 165, 166,
    168–173, 189, 203, 209
  party conflict on decentralization in
    the Second Republic, 153, 203
Senate of the Regions, 49, 50, 125,
    137, 163, 211
Sicilian Independentist
  Movement, 58n9
Sinistra and Libertà (SEL), 164

Social policies and services to citizens
    education, 151
    health, 151, 152
    welfare, 151, 152
    See also Policy areas related to decentralization
Soro, Antonello, 165
Special Statute Regions, 36, 59n17
Sport, 15, 148, 149, 152
    See also Policy areas related to decentralization
State competencies, 5, 49, 53, 125, 149, 152, 153
    article 117 Constitution, 37, 45, 50, 62n52, 136, 162, 178n31, 179n41
State-Regions Conference, 41, 43, 60n36
Statutory autonomy, 37, 38, 44, 52, 55, 61n46, 158
    juridical autonomy of the territorial authorities, 58n5
Strategic considerations, 111–122, 124, 173, 174
Strategies of party competition
    accommodative strategy, 74, 111, 112, 115, 123, 126, 135, 137, 138, 141, 150, 151, 173, 174, 204
    adversarial strategy, 74, 111, 112, 115, 118, 124, 134, 135, 174
    blurring strategy, 11, 111, 129, 130, 132, 134, 135, 141
    contradictory (or broad appeal) strategy, 11, 111, 115, 127, 150
    neglecting strategy, 11, 74, 123, 136
    typology, 123
Strong centralist parties, 124
    See also Party strategies on decentralization, typology of
Strong decentralist parties, 43, 152
    See also Party strategies on decentralization, typology of
Structures of opportunity, 186
    structures of opportunity frames, 186 (*see also* Frames)
    triggers of decentralization, 34, 206
Subsidiarity frame, *see* Frames
Substantial change, 76
Südtiroler Volkspartei (SVP), 75, 226, 227, 229–235, 237, 239, 242
    See also Autonomist party
Surveys
    DOXA, 136, 176n11
    Ispo/Cra-Nielsen, 177n18
    ITANES, 139, 177n19
    LAPS, 140, 177n22
    public opinion, 71, 74, 103, 140, 141, 186, 187

T
Tabacci, Bruno, 179n44
Tangentopoli ("Bribesville"), 41, 195
Terracini, Umberto, 35
TERRISS Dataset, 15–18, 22n9, 22n11, 75, 77, 94, 100, 104n7, 123, 127, 170, 190
    reliability and validity, 17–18;
        correlative test of validity, 17;
        intercoder reliability test, 17;
        intraobserver reliability test, 17
Territorial authorities, 6, 7, 10, 29–31, 34, 58n5, 217
Territorial dimension, xii, 1, 3–11, 13, 16, 17, 19, 21, 22n1, 22n8, 70, 104n6, 110, 112, 113, 115, 116, 129, 187, 210, 217, 219, 220
Territorial distribution of authority, 6
Territorial issues
    cultural differentiation versus homogeneization, 217
    decentralization *vs.* centralization, 217
Territorial organization (of the state)

decentralized state, 28, 35, 142, 198–199
de-concentration, 28, 30
devolution, 28, 30, 201
evolution of Italian territorial administration, 221
federal state, 137, 138, 141, 154, 173
typology, 28, 32
unitary state, 27–29, 33, 51, 52
Territorial party politics, 7, 18, 90
literature, 5, 21
Territorial politics, ix, xi, 4, 6, 10, 13, 27, 190
Territorial solidarity frame, *see* Frames
Theoretical model
agenda-setting perspective, xii, 222, 223
patterns of consensus and conflict, 21
Tirelli, Francesco, 162
Togliatti, Palmiro, 35, 58n11
Transportation, 15, 33, 146, 149, 150, 196
See also Policy areas related to decentralization
Treaty of Maastricht, 41, 97
Triggers (of decentralization), xiii, 13, 33, 219
Turchi, Giulio, 59n26, 157

U
Ulivo, 43, 85, 97, 101, 104n7, 138, 139, 150, 151, 155, 163, 176n10, 196, 198, 201, 209, 211

Unione, 86, 98, 126, 150, 152, 199, 201, 210
Unione di Centro (UDC), 47, 86, 125, 139, 164, 166, 167, 179n44
Union Valdôtaine (UV), 75, 229, 231, 234, 235
See also Autonomist party
Unitary frame, 212
Unitary state, 27–29, 33, 51, 52
See also Territorial organization (of the state)
Use of frames
instrument of party competition, xiii, 13, 73, 114, 185–190, 204, 213, 218, 221
justification of attitudes, 188
tying position to party's worldview, 21, 185–190, 194, 197, 201, 206, 212, 221

V
Voting positions, 110

W
Welfare, 151
See also Policy areas related to decentralization
Worldviews (of parties), 21, 185–190, 194, 197, 201, 206, 212, 213n2, 221
of party families on decentralization, 188